Web Teaching Guide

Web Teaching Guide

A Practical Approach to
Creating Course Web Sites

SARAH HORTON

Yale University Press
New Haven & London

Published with assistance from the foundation established in memory of James Wesley Cooper of the Class of 1865, Yale College.

Designed and illustrated by Sarah Horton.
Photographs by Joseph Mehling.

Set in Monotype Bembo and Linotype-Hell AG Syntax by Sarah Horton.
Printed in the United States of America by Edwards Brothers.

See the illustration credits for URLs and copyright information for the Web site illustrations.

ISBN 0-300-08726-8 (cloth : alk. paper)
ISBN 0-300-08727-6 (paper : alk. paper)

Library of Congress Catalog Card Number: 00-105142

A catalogue record for this book is available from the British Library.

The paper in this book meets the guidelines for permanence and durability of the Committee on Production Guidelines for Book Longevity of the Council on Library Resources.

10 9 8 7 6 5 4 3 2 1

For Malcolm

Contents

Preface

Only connect.
– E. M. Forster, *Howard's End*

CONSIDER THE FOLLOWING scenario. You are teaching a course on American poets, and one segment of the course is devoted to Robert Frost. You own an out-of-print book with photographs of Frost that you would like your students to see. Your institution has a collection of audio recordings of Frost reciting his poems that you would like your students to hear. There is a short film in the media library shot when Frost was a visiting faculty member at your institution. And the library has two copies of the Frost collection and one copy on reserve. In short, you have a wealth of content on Frost, and access to these materials will help your students better understand his poetry.

In a traditional teaching model, this scenario plays out as follows. You pass the book around in class and perhaps make slides by photographing pages from the book and showing them during class. To view the film, you arrange a media setup for your class session and ask the media services department to hold a tape in their library on reserve for students to view there. Last, students visit the library reserve room and look at the book for limited times. Access to this book is restricted to the reserve desk's hours of operation, the number of copies placed on reserve, and whether the copies have been checked out by another student.

Now let's consider the same scenario using the Web. Under this model, you "digitize" the materials – get them onto the computer – and make them available to your students via a course Web site. First you scan the images from the book using your department's flatbed scanner. Better yet, you find the images in the catalog of an online, royalty-free image provider and purchase the rights to use them (because Frost's works are not in the public domain, all of the media in this scenario require the granting or purchasing of a license for use). Next you digitize the audio and video with the help of the media services department. Last, you scan in the poetry using the flatbed scanner. Once you have all the materials on the computer, you put them on your course Web site, where your students can easily access them. In the process, you discover that combining these different media sources in one medium – the Web – means that you can use them in new ways. You decide to provide the poetry text along with the audio of Frost's narration so that students can read and listen to the poems at the same time. You also provide images of Frost so that your students will connect the poetry to the voice and visage of the poet. Now that you've started to think about connections, you add links to Web sites with biographical information on Frost and his contemporaries. You adapt and reshape your approach to the Frost segment as you experiment with the Web and become familiar with its strengths.

Web teaching is all about making connections: connecting your students to one another and to resources around the world; combining different materials – music, motion, text, narration – into one presentation; collecting related information from multiple sources. When you incorporate the Web into your teaching, you also enable students to make their own connections by offering materials for download and use in their scholarship or by having them construct Web documents as part of their coursework. And this process of making *meaningful* connections is at the core of all learning.

What does this book cover?

In this book on Web teaching, I outline an approach to putting course content on the Web. I explain how to make your current course materials Web-ready. I also describe Web-enabled teaching tools that you may not currently use but that you might wish to incorporate into your teaching approach. I explain how to combine these materials and tools to create a useful and effective course Web site.

When I discuss "course" Web sites, I am not referring to those used for distance education, where teaching is carried out online instead of in the classroom. Course Web sites are designed to assist face-to-face teaching. They offer students materials that supplement classroom learning – such things as information about course logistics, online access to course materials, opportunities to explore topics covered in class, and forums for continuing class discussion. They also provide materials for students to download and use in their own scholarly efforts.

The development process I outline follows the following course:

- Planning the project with care
- Converting course materials and developing new content
- Developing the Web site

- Incorporating the site into your teaching method
- Evaluating the site's success

Creating a Web site is not a trivial task, and the potential value of a course site is significant enough to warrant doing it right. You should not undertake such an endeavor without a roadmap: you should have a clear idea of where you *can* go, how you will get there, and what to do once you've arrived. This book will give you a base map upon which to chart a Web teaching course.

Some commentators have complained that little truly innovative or pedagogically useful work has been done using the Web. In a provocative opinion piece for the *Chronicle of Higher Education,* Alistair Fraser stated that "virtually all of the instructional efforts on the Web are simply the delivery of shovelware," *shovelware* being content such as handouts and exams that are simply "shoveled" from print to the Web. It is true that providing access to existing materials *has* been the focus of most instructional Web endeavors, yet I disagree about the worth of such efforts. Yes, it would be beneficial if the Web were used for ambitious educational projects. But using the Web to deliver course content does mean that your students have timely and convenient access to course information. They can view and download materials that may otherwise not have been available to them or, if available, could be used on a limited basis, such as print materials on reserve or slide images shown in class. And although moving your course materials onto the Web may not shake the foundations of Learning, it is the first step to devising a Web teaching method.

With new technologies such as the Web, an analogy is often made to early films, which were simply recordings of staged productions. Once early filmmakers became familiar with movie technology, they began to realize that they could film real trees instead of cardboard stage cutouts, and then they began to consider filming motor sequences using real cars. Each "adopted" innovation – a category the Web appears to fit – undergoes a natural evolution as those who use it come to recognize its merits. Once your course materials are online, you probably won't push back your chair and call it a day. As you come to recognize the enormous potential of the Web, you will find yourself reorganizing, updating, and expanding your course site to take better advantage of its capabilities. And as you expand and refine your approach, you will be taking part in the evolution of the Web and its use as a tool for education.

Who is this book for?

Web Teaching Guide is for educators who are considering adding a Web component to their classroom teaching. It guides Web authors through the process of creating and using a course Web site. The process outlined here is thorough, so don't expect a "create a Web site in five minutes" approach. Also, the book covers well-established, sound technologies and concepts, so you won't learn how to create a "killer" course Web site. The focus of this book is on creating a site that is visually attractive, pedagogically useful, and easy to use and maintain.

Note that *Web Teaching Guide* is not a technical how-to guide. It is written for educators whose main interest in the Web is its pedagogical potential, not its technological underpinnings. As such, you will not find much detail about the technology that underlies the Web. You will not find details about Hypertext Markup Language (HTML), the computer language used to describe Web documents. You will not find specifics about the different tools and technologies that are used to create Web pages. In other words, this is probably not the only book you will need as you embark on this endeavor: you will need additional resources that will vary depending on what kind of site you decide to create and what tools you choose to create it. See the chapter references and the Bibliography for pointers to useful books and online resources, and visit the book Web site (www.webteaching guide.com) for links to the featured Web sites and resources. Also note that *Web Teaching Guide* is more of a practical guidebook than a treatise and only touches on the pedagogical effectiveness of instructional technology. For more about the theoretical aspects of technology in education, see the section entitled *Web Teaching* in the Bibliography.

If you are thinking about using the Web in your teaching and have little or no experience with Web authoring, this book is a perfect starting place. If you have had some basic experience with Web authoring and would like to refine your efforts, this book will provide the guidance you need to do things right. And anyone about to begin a new Web site project – whether they are experienced or inexperienced – will find value in the process, techniques, and approaches outlined in this book.

FIRST AND FOREMOST, I acknowledge my friend and coauthor of *Web Style Guide*, Patrick J. Lynch. I have lost count of the number of opportunities Pat has steered me toward over the years and the number of doors he has opened for me. What I have not lost sight of for even a moment is that, were it not for him, I would not have had the opportunity to write this book, nor would I have had the chance to work on the many interesting projects that he has brought to pass. So I thank Pat for his role in making my work interesting, challenging, and full of possibilities. I also thank him for the excellent focaccia and red wine and for being such a good friend.

I heartily thank my colleagues at Dartmouth College who gave me guidance on topics where my own experience and expertise is more limited: Richard Brown, Steve Campbell, Otmar Foelsche, Allegra Lubrano, James Matthews, R. Michael Murray, Mark O'Neil, Michael Sacca, John Wallace. I also thank Joseph Mehling, the official Dartmouth photographer, for giving me open access to his beautiful slide collection.

I am grateful to my good friends who generously gave their time to review the manuscript and provided many useful comments and suggestions: Malcolm Brown, Joan Campbell, Ned Holbrook.

I am deeply indebted to the Dartmouth faculty members who ask me for assistance in using the Web to teach. Most of what appears on these pages I learned from trying to help them realize their objectives. I especially thank those faculty whose sites appear as examples in this book: Joan Campbell, Elizabeth Chamberlain, Sheila Culbert, Eva Fodor, Margaret Graver, Sally Hair, Keala Jewell, Allen Koop, Jerome Rutter, Mary Turco, Lindsay Whaley, Mark Williams.

I thank the Web authors who allowed me to reproduce images of their sites throughout this book. I also thank the "Webbed" educators who took the time to meet with me and contribute their stories as case studies: Paul Christesen, James Davis, Dana Flaskerud, Cynthia Haynes, Frank Klucken, Jan Rune Holmevik, Megan Williams.

At Yale University Press, I thank Jean Thomson Black, Nancy Moore Brochin, Aldo Cupo, Laura Jones Dooley, Nancy Ovedovitz, Deborah Patton, and Manushag Powell for their excellence and hard work. I also thank the reviewers whose knowledgeable comments and observations helped make this book more accurate and complete.

I thank my friend Glenn Fleishman for being so generous with his valuable knowledge and guidance.

I thank my big and wonderful family for helping out with the logistics of daily life while I ran about chasing after details and pushing deadlines. I am particularly grateful to Malcolm Brown for his knowledge, good sense, and unfailing support. Last, I am grateful to my most precious boy, Nico, for his good company and boundless enthusiasm.

1 *Planning*

Bad enough! Again the same old story! When you've finished building your
house, you realize that in doing so you unexpectedly learned something that
you absolutely had to know – before you began to build.
– Friedrich Nietzsche, *Beyond Good and Evil*

THE FIRST STEP in developing a course Web site is to conduct a thorough means assessment. As with any large-scale, long-term endeavor, careful study of the possibilities can save time and prevent frustration. Begin by finding out what your institution offers for course Web site development: What software, facilities, funding, and development support are available? Also assess the personal impact of the project: How much time will you have to commit, and what gains can you expect to achieve? Understanding your means will help you define your objectives within the context of what is possible.

With a solid understanding of your resources, you can define your objectives for the Web site. Start by looking at other sites on the Web. With a sense of what others are trying to accomplish, you can devise your own goals and determine how extensively you will incorporate the Web into your curriculum.

Once you have assessed your means and formulated your goals, you're ready to devise an organizational structure for your Web site. Many of us have a tendency to jump into a project without much preparation. This approach might work, but more likely it won't: Have you ever been mixing up a batch of chocolate-chip cookies only to discover that someone has eaten the chocolate chips? Although planning a course Web site is less fun than creating one, nothing will influence its success more than sound objectives and solid organization.

ASSESS YOUR MEANS
Before you embark on a project to use computers in your teaching, make sure you clearly understand your means. Assess how much support you can expect to receive at your institution. Although there are educators who can accomplish such a project on their own, most of us need at least some assistance. Contact your computing services department and find out what support it offers for Web-based projects. Ask colleagues who have developed instructional materials to tell you about their process and experiences. And

think about how the project will affect you personally: your time, your position, your teaching style. Assess your situation before defining your strategy.

You may wonder why assessing your situation should be your first step. An alternative approach, one more typical in education, would be first to define the goals and purpose of your Web site and *then* to consider how to implement those goals. As an emerging technology, the Web has many possibilities for teaching. Yet how you use that technology to address your teaching needs is necessarily shaped by your circumstances. In higher education, as most everywhere, there are those who have, and those who have not. Consider this analogy: even though a Jaguar may be the best car for your purposes, your means may limit you to a Dodge. Assuming that you can have a Jaguar simply because there's one on the sales lot would be unrealistic.

The options described in this book are possibilities, but only *you* can place them in the context of your means – the time you can spend, the resources you have available, the support you can expect to receive. Once you've defined your circumstances you can assess your options, but not before you thoroughly understand your possibilities. You may end up with a Dodge after all, but at least it'll take you somewhere.

Tools

Selecting a software package is easy for some tasks. For example, standard tools have emerged as superior for editing a photograph or writing a book. By contrast, because the Web is relatively new, the choice is far from clear: there is no preeminent tool for Web site authoring. Complicating the decision is that you can approach a Web project in many ways. You can create your pages the old-fashioned way, writing your content and the HTML code that renders the page in the browser by hand using a basic text editor. You can use Web page design software, designing the pages and adding content, but letting the software generate the HTML. This second approach resembles working with page layout software, in which you position text and images and never need to look at the programming code that generates the printed page. Or, instead of creating your own Web pages, you can use a courseware system, which is a combination of tools designed specifically to deliver online instruction.

First find out what tools and options are available at your institution. Although it is important to choose software that suits you, choose whenever possible from those that your institution uses and will support for the foreseeable future. If you are collaborating on a project, try to select a tool that works for everyone involved.

COURSEWARE SYSTEMS

Computers have long been used to provide "systems" for accomplishing specific tasks or functions. An institution's central accounting system, for example, simplifies the tracking and maintenance of financial transactions. What makes an accounting system different from a spreadsheet program is that it performs a specific task – accounting – whereas a spreadsheet program, though it can be used as a *tool* for accounting, can also be used to keep track of birthdays or chart population growth or calculate an object's size and mass.

Until recently, most software written to facilitate the task of educating has been discipline-specific – for example, Mathematica for math and SPSS for statistics. There was no generalized "teaching" software, though many educators have written modules *for* teaching using such general-purpose tools as HyperCard and True Basic. With the advent of the Web and the increasing interest in online learning, education systems, or courseware, have emerged. Courseware provides a Web-based system for managing the transactions of teaching and learning. These systems support educators in the same way that accounting systems support budget planners and administrators, and they are becoming increasingly widespread in higher education.

Find out whether your institution uses a courseware system. Using courseware has many benefits, particularly if your goals are limited to the clerical aspects of administering a curriculum, such as grading, creating class lists, and distributing course information. These systems provide a suite of straightforward tools for administering a course, delivering instruction, and facilitating student interaction online.

Popular courseware tools	
Convene	www.convene.com
CourseInfo	www.blackboard.com
LearningSpace	www.lotus.com
TopClass	www.wbtsystems.com
WebCT	www.webct.com

When a courseware approach is applied institution-wide, sites have a consistent look and feel, and students become accustomed to a particular way of working with course materials online.

You may find, however, that courseware is not a good match for your online instructional goals. Because courseware aims to be an all-purpose tool, some educators may find it too inflexible for the idiosyncratic practice of teaching. If your needs fit nicely into the program's supported paradigm, then a course site created using courseware will demand less time, effort, and proficiency than one created from scratch. But do not adopt the system hoping to coax it into a form that will better meet your teaching needs. You will spend more time and suffer greater frustration than if you had built the site from scratch.

If a courseware system is available at your institution, ask colleagues who are using the system what their goals are for online instruction and whether the courseware tool provides the functionality they need. Review sites that have been created using the tool and see if they support the online classroom you envision. Schedule a demonstration of the product with the computing support staff. Be sure to keep your long-term goals in mind when reviewing the product: What should your course site look like in three years? Will the program accommodate your vision?

WEB AUTHORING TOOLS

If courseware is either unavailable or insufficient, explore the Web authoring software that your institution supplies and supports. There are two main types of software for creating Web sites: text editors and visual layout tools. With a text editor you write HTML in text mode and use a browser to preview the pages in a layout. A visual, or WYSIWYG (What You See Is What You Get), layout tool lets you design pages in layout mode. With this tool you position text and images on the page, and the software generates the codes needed to display the page in a Web browser.

Web pages are made up of text and special codes that are interpreted and "rendered" by the browser.

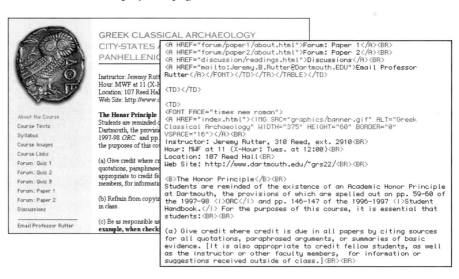

Review these different approaches and determine which best suits your working style. When choosing a tool, make support a high priority: don't use software that is not supported by your campus computing department.

Text editors

A Web page is simply text that is interpreted and displayed as a formatted page by the browser software. Developing a Web page requires no special software (a Web page can be written in SimpleText or Notepad), just a knowledge of the required HTML codes and correct syntax.

Most people, however, aren't fluent in HTML – a complex and evolving markup language – so they need a tool that will simplify Web page creation. For this, they turn to an HTML text editor: basic text software that has been customized for Web authoring. It still requires you to work in text mode, but it provides tools to facilitate markup and verify syntax; selecting a block of text and applying formatting, for ex-

Popular text editors		
BBEdit	Macintosh	www.barebones.com
HomeSite	Windows	www.allaire.com
HotDog	Windows	www.sausage.com
NoteTab Pro	Windows	www.notetab.com
TextPad	Windows	www.textpad.com
UltraEdit	Windows	www.ultraedit.com

ample, will insert the necessary tags. An HTML text editor is a good choice for people who are most comfortable working in text mode, understand the concept of "tagging" text, and want control over their HTML code.

Visual editors

Web page creation tools are going the way of other document creation tools. Graphic designers use desktop publishing software to design and lay out pages without even thinking about the computer codes that actually generate the document. As the tools for Web page design become more sophisticated, knowledge of HTML is becoming less essential to the process.

Visual Web page editors allow you to design and construct Web pages as you would documents using word processor or page layout software. To create bold type, for example, you select the text and apply bold formatting, which produces the following HTML:

```
<B>Sample bold text</B>
```

You need never even look at the <B> tags responsible for formatting the text as bold in the browser.

Visual editors have a fundamental drawback. Unlike other document description languages, such as PostScript, HTML was never intended to be used to create sophisticated layouts. HTML was designed to describe the structure of documents, with only incidental attention to their visual properties. Bending what is essentially a structural markup language to accommodate complex page layouts requires workarounds and makeshift solutions, and the results can be unpredictable. Given the limitations of HTML, visual Web editors are at a disadvantage in providing the same WYSIWYG interface as other document creation tools. As a result, what you see may not be what you get, particularly when pages have complex layouts. Although these tools purport to save time and effort, you may spend more time wrestling with the software than you would writing your own HTML.

That said, these programs are gaining popularity as the preferred method for creating Web pages. The WYSIWYG method of working with documents is far more accessible to most users. Also, the software is getting better — more stable, generating more robust HTML — which means that the results are more predictable. If you are not interested in writing code, a visual editor is probably the most sensible tool to choose.

Popular visual editors		
Composer	Macintosh/Windows	www.netscape.com
DreamWeaver	Macintosh/Windows	www.macromedia.com
FrontPage	Macintosh/Windows*	www.microsoft.com
Fusion	Macintosh/Windows*	www.netobjects.com
GoLive	Macintosh/Windows	www.adobe.com
PageMill	Macintosh/Windows	www.adobe.com
*Different revisions available for Macintosh and Windows		

CONVERSION UTILITIES

Computers have been common in education for long enough that much of what you use to teach may already be in a digital format. Now that so many people are using the Web to distribute information, most file formats have at least one method for conversion into a Web-readable format. For example, you may have course documents written in Microsoft Word that you want to publish on the Web. You could use one of the Web authoring tools described above to re-create the documents, or you could use a utility such as Word's "Save as HTML" option to convert the documents from Word format to HTML. If all goes well, the Web page document would look much as it looked when printed from Word.

Popular conversion utilities			Converts from
The Ant	Macintosh/Windows	www.telacommunications.com	Word
AscToHTM	Windows/VMS	www.jafsoft.com/asctohtm	Text (.txt) files
BeyondPress	Macintosh/Windows	www.extensis.com	QuarkXpress
Internet Assistant	Macintosh/Windows	www.microsoft.com	Word, PowerPoint, Excel
RTFtoHTML	Macintosh/Windows	www.sunpack.com/RTF	RTF (Rich Text Format) documents
Table2HTML	Windows	www.stefan-pettersson.nu	Tab or comma delimited table
WebConvert	Windows	www.webconvert.com	Microsoft Word, AmiPro, WordPerfect, ASCII
WebWorks Publisher	Windows	www.quadralay.com	FrameMaker
WordToWeb	Windows	www.solutionsoft.com	Word

If you are using the Web simply to distribute existing course materials, you may be well served by a conversion utility. Such a site would be a repository of course documents, so uniformity and integration of the documents would not be necessary.

For a course Web site, however, you cannot simply convert documents for Web use without attempting to tie the documents into a coherent presentation. To use existing materials as part of an instructional site, consider combining an authoring tool and a conversion utility, or using the conversion features that are built into your authoring tool. That way, you can convert existing course materials to HTML and then incorporate them into your overall site design.

TEMPLATES

Looking at a blank Web page and trying to determine what you want to achieve can be for some like staring at a blank canvas, paintbrush in hand, and having no idea how to get what's in your head onto the canvas. The Web is empowering because it provides autonomy, but it's also intimidating and even unrealistic: we are expected to be able to express our ideas visually and verbally and to be savvy enough in our use of technology to convey them using fairly sophisticated software and programming.

A template can be a good answer for people who are less comfortable with the design and layout aspects of Web site authoring. A template is a basic HTML file with the codes for page and typographic layout already in place. To use a template you need only to fill in the content, like a coloring book: with the outlines in place, you supply the color.

Using a template holds many advantages. If you are new to Web authoring, it is a good way to develop a useful and attractive site quickly without having to master the nuances of HTML. If after time the template does not suit you and you have a greater understanding of Web authoring, you can modify the template or create a new one. Templates also benefit the user by enforcing consistency. Putting your content into a template ensures that all the pages of your site will have a standard look and feel.

Courses

Most institutions offer courses on creating Web sites either for the entire community or specifically for faculty. As the Web becomes more established in the classroom, institutions are beginning to offer their faculty courses focused on using the Web to teach. Find out what courses your institution offers. Even a course in basic HTML is worth taking – it will give you a foundation upon which to begin building your site.

COURSE OFFERINGS

Just as there are many ways to create a Web site, so you are likely to encounter a variety of options when selecting a course. There may be an "Introduction of the Web" course, with little about creating sites but more about the Web, its components, and how to use it (search strategies, useful links). You may find an "Introduction to HTML" course, which explains HTML and teaches how to mark up Web documents. Or you may find software-specific courses for tools such as FrontPage or GoLive or for courseware systems like CourseInfo or WebCT.

If there is an introductory course that covers Web basics, take it. In the early days of the automobile, drivers were well advised to have some understanding of its inner workings in case things went wrong. The World Wide Web is a new contraption, and though you may never need to peek under the hood, it will pay to have some inkling of how it works should you find yourself stranded.

For tool-specific courses, your choice will depend on the tool you decide to use to create your site. But any course on using a site creation tool is worth taking, even if it's not your tool of choice. Though the method will be different, you will be able to apply the issues of design and structure to any software package.

Help

Some pioneering educators prefer to gather the necessary tools and knowledge and make their course sites on their own. The plausibility of this type of autonomy is one of the best aspects of the Web. In the bad old days, most faculty developing instructional software relied heavily on programmers to realize their instructional goals. All too often these projects stalled as programming support shifted to other projects or programmers were lured away by better-paying jobs outside education. The architecture of the Web is far more transparent than custom-programmed instructional modules. Many educators are fully capable of realizing their own vision with the Web as their development tool.

Yet there are many hats to wear when creating a Web site, and most of us don't have a large assortment to choose from. The librarian hat is for the first stage, where we determine what resources are available and where to find them. Then we don the educator hat to choose from the available resources those that best address the educational goals of the project. We wear the information and graphic design hats to structure and present the materials effectively. And finally, in the programmer hat we execute the vision conceived while wearing the educator and designer hats. Most of us lack experience in at least one of these roles, and seeking assistance in that area can make a world of difference in the realization of the project.

INSTITUTIONAL HELP

Most institutions have an academic computing unit devised to support the use of computing in educational ventures. Support for course Web sites may include facilities, software, instruction, programming, design, and content development. It may be enabling support – that is, support to get you started and set up before sending you off to fly on your own – or full course site development support, where a developer or team of developers works with you to create a site that meets your instructional needs. The team may include a programmer, graphic designer, instructional designer, and project manager.

It is worthwhile at this stage to investigate the assistance available at your institution. Try to get a sense of how much time you need versus how much help they can give. Review the array of options and determine which will complement your resources, skills, and knowledge, so that all aspects of the development process are covered.

STUDENT HELP

Faculty often hire Web-savvy students to develop their course sites. This may seem like a good option – the students are skilled in Web programming and often have an investment in and understanding of the course materials. Sometimes this approach works, particularly for sites that do not require fancy programming. But putting course site development in the hands of students can be risky. Students often know too much about technology for *your* own good. You may wind up with a super-spiffy course site that is too complicated for anyone but the (graduated) student to modify.

Student help can be a boon for faculty who are uncomfortable with the technology or those too busy to spend time developing and maintaining Web-based course materials. Keep in mind the risks, however: reliance on institutional computing support staff is better than reliance on transient students. Most institutions offer their faculty some level of computing support, so the chances are that you won't be abandoned. If you do use student help, keep a hand in what they're doing: spend time each term reviewing the site and outlining plans, and have your student webmasters thoroughly document their work and train replacements before moving on. Or opt for a hybrid approach: use student help, but have institutional support staff monitor students' work and documentation.

DO YOU WANT HELP?

One of the reasons the Web is popular is that it empowers. One person can author, edit, illustrate, design, publish, promote, and maintain his or her own work. Many people relish this autonomy: if something needs to be changed, they change it; if something breaks, they fix it. It is important at this planning stage to decide if the success of your site depends on self-sufficiency. Is one of your primary incentives for publishing a Web site the fact that you *can* have full control? If so, take steps at this early stage to minimize your reliance on others.

- Keep your site simple. Adding custom features like simulations or conference sign-up sheets may require a reliance on computing support, particularly if these features need modification to meet your needs.
- Make sure you're equipped. Help getting started is a good thing. Just make sure before you're cut loose that you have the equipment, software, and knowledge to continue on your own without relying heavily on support staff (or students) for assistance.

Facilities

Many institutions provide special computing facilities for faculty use. The aim of these project rooms is to give faculty access to software and hardware for specialized, limited-time use. A typical setup may include hardware and software for converting materials to digital format – for example, a workstation for transferring video from videotape to computer or a scanning station for converting slides or prints to computer images. The facility may be staffed with students or computing support personnel.

If you plan to use teaching materials on your course Web site, you may have use for such a facility. Converting standard teaching materials – texts, images, video – requires special hardware and software, and it makes little sense to purchase and maintain conversion systems for limited use if such a facility exists.

Funding

For large-scale Web-based instructional endeavors you may want to seek funding, either through your institution or through funding agencies. These days, talk of curricular development generally includes a technology component, and the current preferred medium for delivering instructional technology is the Web. Many institutions have either centers for curricular development or special monies for funding curricular innovation. Various agencies also support technology-based advances in teaching and learning.

The availability of funds can mean the difference between a basic informational course Web site and a full-blown educational resource. For faculty, the greatest demand of curricular development is time. A successful project needs intensive faculty involvement, and funding can enable this by offering a temporary break from teaching and administrative tasks.

Another great development hurdle is copyright permissions. The fair use doctrine that has facilitated instructional use of copyrighted content cannot easily be applied to Web-based materials (see Chapter 2: *Copyright and intellectual property*). Monies for curricular development could be used to acquire licenses for copyrighted materials. A grant could also be used to purchase hardware and software, pay for development and design support, and fund project assessment.

If you are planning a project that will have a wide impact at your institution, or in the world, consider seeking development funds. You stand a much greater chance of realizing your goals with monetary assistance, and others will benefit from your initiative.

Selected funding agencies		
Agency	**Grant**	**Contact**
Alfred P. Sloan Foundation	Learning Outside the Classroom	www.sloan.org/programs/ edu_careers.htm
Andrew W. Mellon Foundation	Initiative on the Cost Effective Uses of Technology in Teaching	www.mellon.org/cutt.html
Center for Academic Transformation Rensselaer Polytechnic Institute	The Pew Grant Program in Course Redesign	www.center.rpi.edu/pewgrant.html
Foundation for Independent Higher Education and AT&T	AT&T Learning Network Teaching and Technology Grants	www.fihe.org/fihe/whatsnew/ att00-01.htm
U.S. Department of Education	Learning Anytime Anywhere Partnerships	www.ed.gov/offices/OPE/FIPSE/ LAAP/

Personal means

You may have any number of reasons for undertaking the development of a Web-based teaching resource, from improving the classroom experience by enhancing your teaching-learning method to simplifying everyday administrative tasks. Whether high-minded or practical, it is important to be realistic about the impact fulfilling your goals will have on you personally.

WORKLOAD

How much time will it take to add a Web component to your teaching? And once the component is in place, how will its use affect your regular teaching workload? These are important questions to ask before beginning development, and the answers depend upon the nature of your endeavor. Consider the scope of your project: Are you using a course site to distribute information? Such a site takes time to develop, but once implemented it could decrease your regular workload. Are you using a course site for communication? Many faculty find that monitoring sites with discussion areas or other feedback mechanisms is like adding office hours because it makes them more "available" to their students.

Time is an important consideration, and it should not be taken lightly. Many ambitious projects fall by the wayside because the time demands are too great. At this stage in the development process, be realistic about the time required to realize your goals and the time you are willing and able to invest. Do not undertake a course Web site project with the sole intention of saving time or you will be disappointed. Neither should you undertake an ambitious project that augments your current workload without estimating the demands it will make on your time and gauging whether you can meet them. Given the number of variables involved – the scope of your site, the tools you use, your technology expertise, the amount of support available to you – it is not possible to provide an accurate measure you can use in estimating time demands. When budgeting time, consider your project's scope. If your goal is to create a full-blown Web-based classroom full of course content, instructional materials, and online communication, you should plan to spend at least as much time creating the site as you would preparing a new course. If your aim is to move existing course materials online, the time demands will be far less, though certainly still greater than doing things traditionally.

Another thing to keep in mind is that a Web site is never "finished" in the way that other publications are. In fact, keeping a Web site "fresh" is one of the responsibilities of being a Web author, and once a site is allowed to get stale (and Web sites have a short shelf-life) it loses its effect and its audience. Your course site is an ongoing project that will need updates and refinements for as long as it is in use. The decisions you make now about site structure and organization will need to be revisited again and again as your Web teaching method evolves, styles change, and new technologies become available. Decide whether you have the stamina to stick with the project for the long run.

PROMOTION

In the traditional model for higher education, rewards of promotion and tenure are generally influenced more by achievements in research and publishing than by teaching excellence. This appears to be changing as students assume the role of consumer and demand better services. An innovative curriculum with a strong technology component is seen as a selling point for many potential students. Yet although institutions may be shifting their attention to the classroom, shifting policy and resources is another matter. The traditional model is so firmly entrenched that it may be some time before classroom innovation is rewarded in the same way as print publications and advances in research are esteemed. As things now stand, developing a course Web site may not gain you much institutional recognition.

The rewards for using the Web to teach are many: new challenges, better teaching and learning, increased interaction. For many educators, however, it may not be realistic to hope to gain some tangible institutional reward for course Web site efforts.

It is impossible to adopt a new medium like the Web without undergoing a transformation. Using the Web in teaching, when done right, is not a case of old message, new medium. If you opt to use the Web as a tool for teaching – and you really *use* it – your teaching method will change. And change is best when you're ready for it.

When you approach your project, be ready to accommodate change. Trying to pound your time-tested methods into a new medium is analogous to bashing a square peg into a round hole: you will expend energy and experience frustration, and you will never get the two to fit. The Web was built for change, and your approach to using it should be equally flexible. As you use the medium, adapt your message: exclude materials not well served by the Web, experiment with new teaching methods enabled by the Web, apply the Web to aspects of your teaching poorly served by traditional methods. Think about ways to incorporate the strengths of the medium by investigating new tools for teaching and learning, such as real-world simulations, computer-based collaboration, and automatic feedback. Understand that when you make a commitment to using the Web to teach, you are making a commitment to change, and make the most of it.

Summary

This first step has been an institutional review to assess your means and set reasonable expectations. At the end of this step you should have made the following decisions: which tool you will use to develop your site; which preparatory courses you will take; what level of help you can expect to receive, as well as how much and what type of help you will need; and what funding, if any, you plan to seek. Last, you should have taken a realistic look at how this effort would affect your time, position, and teaching methods and either have decided to forge ahead or are getting ready to close this book.

Before you begin your planning process (or close the book), consider the following:

- Are your goals realistic given your means?
- Are you equipped to undertake the project? Do you have the necessary time, skills, and resources?
- Do you feel well supported in your endeavor? Do you have adequate institutional backing?

DEFINE YOUR OBJECTIVES

Now it's time to examine your motivation for creating a course Web site and to develop and refine your ideas within the context of what's possible in your situation. The Web can enhance learning or ease the burden of administering a course in many respects. Take time now to define your purpose for creating a course site – what challenges you are hoping to meet, what tasks you are hoping to simplify – and how you intend to combine the Web and the classroom.

Goals and objectives

You may have embarked on this project because a colleague is having success with his or her course site and you hope to achieve similar results. Or maybe your institution is requiring that all courses have Web sites or your students are demanding Web access to course materials. Or perhaps you see the Web as a solution to a teaching challenge you've been wrestling with for years. Whatever the motive, now is the time to clarify your goals and objectives for using the Web in your curriculum.

LOOK AROUND

One of the best ways to define your Web teaching approach is to look at other teaching sites. Although some course Web sites are not open to the public, many are, which means you can peek into online classrooms and see how others are using the Web to teach. Your impressions of other teaching sites will help you form your own approach.

Explore the Web at other institutions to locate course sites in your discipline, or any instructional sites that seem to share your goals. Use your own critical thinking to evaluate the sites: identify where they succeed and where they fail. Look for new ideas or approaches you may be able to incorporate into your own online method. Bookmark those sites that you find particularly effective. Remember to evaluate what the site offers, not its aesthetics. Last, consult colleagues at your institution who have experience using the Web to teach. Ask them to demonstrate their Web-based materials and explain their approach. Such demonstrations are likely to stimulate your ideas.

ASK QUESTIONS

Many questions need to be addressed before you develop your own site. The answers will guide your development efforts.

Audience profile

- What hardware and network connections are your students working with?
- What software are they using?
- What is their comfort level with technology?
- Do they expect Web access to course materials?

Usage profile

- How much time do you want students to spend with the site?
- Will the site be an addition to the regular course load? Or will the materials replace some from the traditional curriculum?
- Will the site be operative during the full term of the course?
- Will you use the site during class sessions?

Teaching goals

- What do you hope to accomplish that cannot be addressed using other tools or methods?
- What do you want your Web site to look like in two years? In four years?
- What have others done with the Web that might enhance your teaching?
- How will you use the technology to best effect?

Scope

A basic question is whether the Web site you create will be integral to the course. Many course Web sites serve an administrative function, offering students online access to materials such as a course syllabus or scheduling information. Although access has its merits, such a Web site is an adjunct – it supports the learning process. On the other end of the spectrum is a course that is conducted online, with perhaps occasional face-to-face class meetings. A Web site used in this way is clearly essential to the learning process.

Given that most students are overcommitted, a site that is used as an adjunct will probably not get your students' attention in any significant way. This does not mean that such a site is not worth doing – it requires little investment, eliminates the "I lost my syllabus" excuse, and may save time and trees – but do not expect it to transform your curriculum. If you want to use the Web to change how you teach, and how students learn, make your course site integral to your curriculum. Populate it with materials students normally cannot access – don't offer what they already have or have too much of (like reading), offer something new that will help them learn.

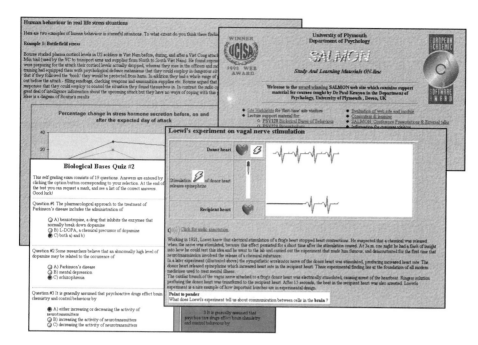

SALMON (Study And Learning Materials ON-line) provides students with an extensive collection of learning materials, quizzes, and animations to support a curriculum in psychology.

ADMINISTRATIVE

Web sites can handle many of the administrative tasks of teaching a course, particularly a site created using a courseware tool (see *Courseware systems,* above). Students can use the course site to get information about scheduling or office hours, or to submit their assignments or check their grades. Instructors can use the site to maintain class lists and grade books, post announcements, and distribute handouts.

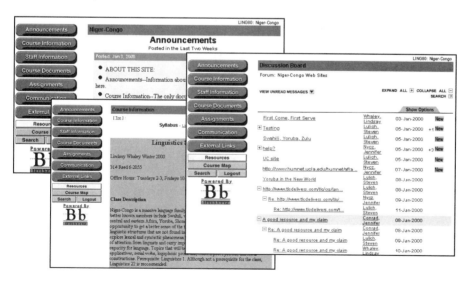

This course Web site, designed using CourseInfo courseware, provides standard course information and an online forum for submitting course assignments.

A course site can offer students aids to understanding, such as links to related sites or an online area to discuss class topics. Depending on how these aids are proffered, this use of the Web may or may not get your students' attention. A course Web site can suffer neglect if it contains only supportive materials that are not integrated into the course. A site that supports the curriculum works best when it is made part of the classroom experience: for example, assign the links to related sites as required reading, or bring topics to class from the students' online discussion.

This economics course Web site is an extensive compilation of online resources to supplement the curriculum. Among its many offerings are online quizzes with scoring and feedback, lecture slides, and an annotated list of related sites.

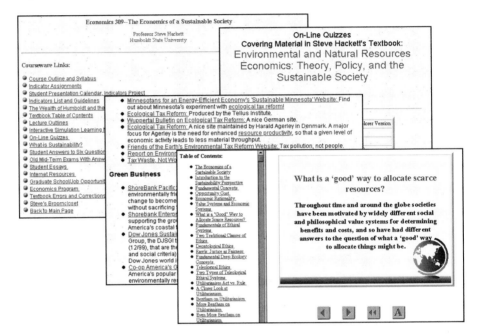

CLASS RESOURCE

A more essential use of the Web would be to offer materials you use in your teaching on your course site. This use is particularly compelling for materials to which students have limited access. Students often view videos and images during class time and then later must rely on their memory to compose an essay or other assignment on some aspect of what they saw. Allowing students to revisit the video or images on a course site enhances their access to the material and makes their task easier and their realizations more profound. This use of the Web is still supportive, but its impact is great.

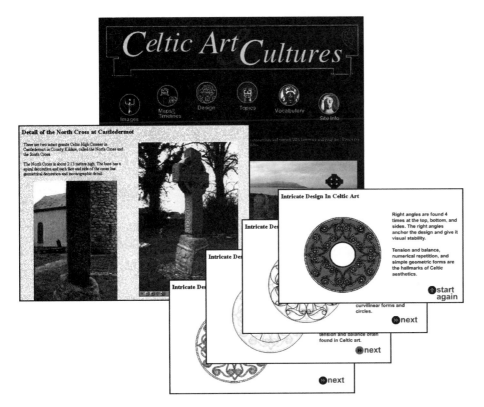

The Celtic Art & Cultures multimedia database is a collection of maps, images, animations, and interactive sequences used as a resource for an art history course. The instructor selects content from the site for use in lectures, and students use the site to develop topics and to find media content for their projects.

INSTRUCTIONAL

Distance learning is perhaps the most integral use of the Web in education. Distance learning is online learning that takes the place of classroom instruction. In distance learning, the Web is the delivery mechanism for *instruction,* along with course materials, learning resources, and course administration. The focus of this book is on sites used in support of classroom teaching. Yet there is no reason that such a site cannot be integral to the course. Offer students opportunities to learn on your Web site, for example, with narratives that support or extend what you have covered in class. Use the site in lecture and class discussion, either by bringing up topics from online discussion or by displaying and working with the site during class. Include tools and aids that allow students to explore concepts covered in class. A course site that offers instruction will take more time, invention, and resources, but it has the potential to greatly enhance your students' learning.

The Biology Project site contains modules on many topics, along with problem sets, tutorials, and other online learning activities.

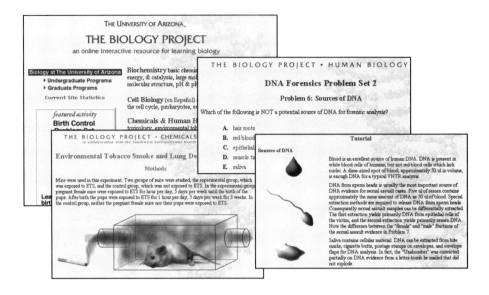

Short-term instruction

Thus far this discussion of course Web sites has focused on sites that support classroom activities for the full term of a course. You may, however, have use for the Web for only a part of your curriculum. For example, you might "activate" a Web site for a section of your course that addresses the literary analysis of images. The site could contain the images along with relevant supporting materials, and for this section the site would be integral to the course.

Through a series of explanations, questions, and experiments, the Circles of Light online lab teaches how rainbows are formed.

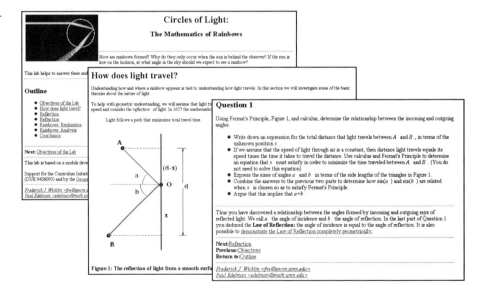

Summary

At the end of this step you should have situated your Web site in your overall pedagogical approach. You should have defined your purpose for creating a course Web site, determined to what extent you plan to use the Web in your teaching, and, through inquiry, refined your ideas.

A good exercise at this stage is to write a proposal that includes a statement of your goals, a basic project description, and an implementation plan for your course Web site.

Sample project proposal

Goals

When I teach Web Design I use the Web extensively in class. My primary reason for creating a course Web site is to give students easy access to the Web sites shown and discussed during class. I also hope to establish an online forum for discussion and peer review. I also see the site as a means for offloading some of the basic administrative aspects of teaching the course. In addition, I hope that monitoring student contributions to the online discussion area will allow me to resolve basic questions online instead of during class time.

Project description

The Web Design course Web site will support in-class activities by giving students opportunities for further exploration, discussion, and exchange outside class. The site will also serve an administrative function by giving students access to course documents and other course materials. The site will include the following sections:

- Course documents: There will be printable pages for all course handouts and access to any illustrations and slides used in class.
- Links: All Web sites used in class will be listed and annotated on the site.
- Critiques: For each Web site critique assignment, students will post links and commentary on the course site.
- Discussion: The discussion area will focus on a new topic every week, and students will be required to post at least two comments to each discussion.
- Portfolio: Student Web projects will be posted to the course site for peer review.

Implementation plan

I will complete my course Web site in three months' time following the schedule below:

1. Discuss authoring options with instructional computing support staff. Also find out what interactive tools are available for Web site discussion and peer review. Ask if they offer any courses that might be suitable for my needs and skill level.
2. Get a Web account for the course site.
3. Expand the site outline to include all possible content, and define navigation links.
4. Gather site content together, and create any new materials. Request permission to use any copyrighted materials.
5. Create the site, including pages for materials that will be filled in at a later date.

Get feedback on the proposal from colleagues who have experience creating course sites, and anyone who might be involved in the project, such as support staff or teaching assistants. When reviewing your proposal, consider these questions:

• Is the focus of your project well defined?
• Does a course Web site fit comfortably within your overall teaching approach?
• Do you have a clear sense of how you intend to use the site?
• Seeing your plan sketched out, would you say that your expectations are realistic?
• Show the proposal to your computing support staff: Do *they* think that your expectations are realistic?

PLAN YOUR SITE

The success of your Web site depends as much on how well you organize your content as on the content you offer. A jumbled, incoherent presentation of materials is not likely to be popular with students, no matter how valuable the content. And Web sites, because they are by nature works in progress, soon become unmanageable when created ad lib. Without a clear outline of your content from the start, you may find yourself with an unruly collection of pages you cannot update and maintain. A careful review and classification of your content can be painstaking work, but the rewards are better site usability and ease of maintenance.

Content inventory

The first step in designing your site is to create a list of items you want to include as content on the site. A content "item" should be the most detailed category of information that needs to be accessed individually. For example, "Composers' Biographies" is not a content item, but "Mozart's Biography" is. At this stage in the process do not limit your thinking to what is possible. Think big, and think long-term. Use this step to list any Web-based teaching materials you think might aid you in your teaching.

Now you'll need to establish priorities and realistic expectations. Next to each content item rank its priority: Does this content need to be there from the start, or can it be added later? Also rate the item for feasibility: for example, a video segment from a VHS tape of the movie *Amadeus* will have a low feasibility ranking because of copyright restrictions. Last, rate the item's availability: the above example would also rank low for availability because the content would have to be digitized and processed before it could be made available on the Web.

Sample content list

Item	Description	Priority	Feasibility	Availability	Comments
Course information	General course information, including hours and meeting location, information about the instructor and office hours, grading policies, etc.	1	1	1	Text currently in Word
Course schedule	A weekly outline of the class topics and activities	1	1	1	Text currently in Word
Assignments at-a-glance	A calendar showing when assignments are due	3	3	3	Not sure if program is available for this feature: check with computing support
Required reading	A list of required readings for the course and due dates	1	1	1	Text currently in Word
Lecture notes	PowerPoint presentations	2	1	2	Not sure how to do this on the Web
Illustrations	Scans of print materials used as examples during class sessions	3	3	3	Many of these items are under copyright: Would course site use be permitted under fair use? How do I get them on the site?
Links	An annotated list of links to all sites used during class discussion	1	1	1	
Critiques	Description of Web site critique assignments and an area where students can post links and their written critique	1	3	3	Is there a way to post links and comments? Need to check with computing. Also, can students post things besides text, such as images or video?
Discussion	Class discussion area	1	2	2	What Web-based discussion options are available?
Portfolio	Links to student projects	1	1	1	Students will have their projects in their personal accounts

Having completed this step, you may want to revise your content list for use in the next stages of the development process. Remove items that, after consideration, seem untenable, and leave all content items you are committed to including, either now or in the future.

Jim Davis: Harvard University

Being accessible is clearly central to the teaching philosophy of Harvard Senior Lecturer in chemistry and official Car Talk chemist Jim Davis. When I arrived for our interview, he was on the phone with a student, patiently explaining some interaction of molecules and atoms. Throughout the interview, he acknowledged passersby through a window that opens from his office onto the busy main corridor of the Science Center. So I was not in the least surprised to learn that his main use of his course Web site is to give his students even *more* access.

We talked mainly about Jim's use of the Web for his freshman chemistry course. This large class – with about 350 students and 20 teaching fellows – meets for lecture three times a week. One way that Jim increases his accessibility is by digitizing his lectures and making them available on his course Web site. "I guess I was the first person at Harvard to digitize lectures because I'm here in the Science Center, a few doors down from the Instructional Computing Group. They asked me if they could do some of my lectures for a trial run in summer school two or three years ago. We did that and it was no bother to me, and they seemed to learn quite a bit about what they needed to do. Then we did it for a whole course two years ago, and then they did it for another course in the spring. When the trial run concluded, the students were extremely unhappy that they no longer had access to the digitized lectures. So, that was an indication that they found the digitized lectures to be very useful. Now the digitization is a regular feature of the course."

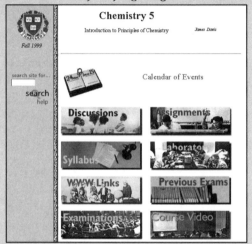

Along with digitized lectures, Jim puts other course materials on the Web, such as problem sets and solutions and a link to an archive of old exams. Jim also provides a discussion forum for students to post questions for other students, teaching fellows, or Jim himself to answer: "I've encouraged students to use the Web site for questions instead of email, because chances are the other three hundred people might like to know the answer, too." In fact, when Jim receives an interesting question via email, he puts the question and its answer on the Web site, with the questioner's name deleted.

Jim also uses the Web to economize on lab time. Lab sessions typically begin with a "chalk talk" by a teaching fellow that provides an overview of the experiment. This approach has two disadvantages: first, it eats up valuable lab time, and second, some teaching fellows are more adept than others at giving these presentations. Working with Gregg Tucci, the assistant lab coordinator, Jim devised a better approach; they recorded Gregg giving the pre-lab talk and made a digitized version available on the course Web site. Now students watch the pre-lab lecture online, "and when they get in the lab, they hit the ground running."

The Chemistry 5 Web site was created using a courseware package created by Harvard's Instructional Computing Group. Jim has had little to do with the actual creation of the site. "I don't speak HTML," he says. The site is a collaborative effort between Jim and graduate students who not only understand the technology but, as Jim's teaching fellows, are intimately acquainted with his teaching approach. "I think there are relatively few faculty of middle age and beyond who make their own Web sites, but we all have students who can create them for us." Indeed, Jim claims that "part of the expectation of the job of being the head teaching fellow in a large course is that you will be the 'webmeister.'"

Jim is modest about his use of the Web. "I haven't done anything revolutionary with the Web. I've been teaching nearly forty years, and I've worked out things that work for me. I haven't tried to do anything very different with the Web. I've used the Web to help me do what I've always done more efficiently." Jim does, however, see ways that teaching with technology can improve on the traditional lecture format. "One of the curious things is that we don't know – at least, I don't know – how to determine whether people really *do* understand things in large classes. What we have is an article of faith that if they can work the problems, then we can assume that they understand what they're doing. However, educational research seems to have shown that often students can do the problem without the slightest idea of what they are doing." Jim plans to use more conceptual learning in his approach next year, more problem-solving strategies where students "try to figure out what is going to happen through a process of reasoning." One way to do this is on the Web by presenting "thought questions": questions that involve no calculation but require an understanding of the materials. (Eric Mazur of Harvard's physics department is an expert on this approach: for more information, visit mazur-www.harvard.edu.)

Jim also plans to incorporate computer-based simulations into his Web teaching, primarily to make up for limited resources. At Harvard, there is only enough lab space to offer labs for freshman chemistry every other week. Jim and Gregg Tucci are working on finding a way to handle this deficiency online. "Our idea, since we are not likely to be building any new freshman chem labs in the immediate future, is to set up a situation where it becomes routine that we do a 'wet' lab experiment one week and a computer-

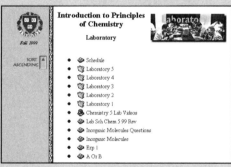

based 'dry' lab the next week." They will also be able to simulate experiments that are not feasible in standard lab facilities. "You can simulate experiments that are too complicated or dangerous to run in the lab. For example, synthesizing ammonia from nitrogen and hydrogen is usually run at a couple of hundred atmospheres of pressure. You can't do that in a freshman chem lab. But you can simulate that experiment, and the reaction has all been digitized so that you run it under various conditions and a computer can tell you what your outcome is – what the yield is."

Before ending the interview, I couldn't help but ask the usual question about how putting lectures online affects attendance at the lectures. Jim patiently explained, "We don't get 100 percent attendance anyway, but I haven't noticed that it's any worse since we started digitizing than before. It does mean that students can re-watch the lectures if they weren't clear about something, or they can watch them for the first time if they slept through them, or…for whatever reason." Getting students into the lecture hall is not a priority for this educator. Giving them opportunities to learn is. ■

Site architecture

The aim of this next step is to organize your content list into an organizational architecture that will comfortably house your content. This site organization will also form the basis for your site's navigation system.

At the base of a site architecture is an organizational scheme – a way of creating groups of content by identifying common characteristics. We use organization schemes in all facets of everyday life. For example, when locating a book in the bookstore, first we determine what logical category the book falls under (topical scheme), then we locate the title alphabetically within the section (sequential scheme).

The main difference between organization schemes is the type of activities they support. An activity like browsing is best supported by a generalized scheme such as subject groupings, whereas targeted searching is best served by an exact scheme such as an alphabetical listing. Think of the different ways you might navigate a bookstore, either searching a shelf for a specific book or browsing a section and finding something new and unexpected. Because we often don't know precisely what we're looking for, having a category to browse narrows the field. And while browsing we may find something that serves equally well, if not better, than what we were originally looking for. In contrast, when we *are* searching for a specific item, a sequential organization is most effective: for example, books within a category are normally alphabetized by title or author so that customers can easily find them.

The Celebration of Women Writers site lists authors by name, century, and country.

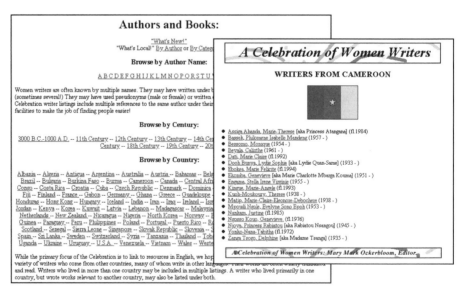

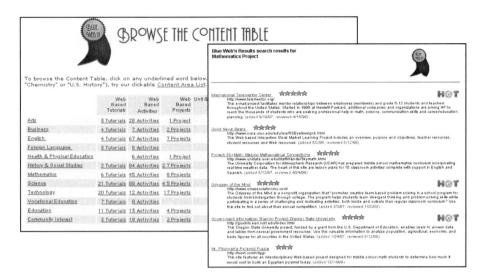

The contents page on the Blue Web'n site is organized by topic and type of materials, and each subsection is organized by rating.

A course Web site will likely need to support both browsing and searching. A browsing environment supports the kind of associative and user-defined learning that the computer enables. In browsing, students are presented with an array of options, organized in a systematic fashion, and chart a course through the information, making serendipitous discoveries along the way. But students also need to be able to locate specific course materials quickly: a student should not have to scan through multiple pages to find out when the course next meets. One reason why the Web is so effective is that it can support a range of activities.

CLASSIFYING CONTENT

The first step in creating a site architecture is to create a classification system that effectively describes the items on your content list. To classify your content, you will review your content list and come up with main categories that cover all the items listed. Then you will list each content item under its appropriate category label.

The categories you select should have schematic consistency. A well-defined site architecture allows users to quickly construct a mental model of the site content and effectively locate their objective within it. For example, if you organize your site by topic, users can look at your site navigation links and say, "Ah, this site is organized by topic; let me see which topic best describes my objective." Stick with a single organization scheme. If you mix schemes – for example, if you list tasks with topics – users must scan *all* your links to find the one that best relates to their objectives.

With a clearly defined organization scheme, users can quickly determine how the site is organized. Otherwise, they must read each menu item to find what they are looking for.

Web Design 101	Web Design 101	Web Design 101
Lecture notes	Classroom	Handouts
Course information	Course information	Lectures
Online readings	Assignments	Presentations
Post a comment	Lecture notes	Discussions
Contact the instructor	Student center	Readings
Student center	Presentations	
Student presentations	Discussions	
Presentation calendar	Library	
What is Web design?	Articles	
Web design resources	Links	
Jumbled links	Location metaphors	Functional groupings

You will most likely find, however, that the content for your course Web site requires multiple schemes. There may be areas that make sense by topic ("Musical Forms," "Composers," "Instruments"), by sequence ("Assignment 1," "Assignment 2"), and by task ("Submit an Essay," "Post a Comment"). Multiple schemes can coexist, as long as they are not jumbled together. Recognize the different attributes of your teaching materials and keep the schemes separate and intact throughout the design process.

Labeling is another important consideration when classifying content. A robust organizational structure and well-defined navigation system will not serve unless you communicate it to users in a language they understand. Labeling is particularly challenging on the Web because the labels you devise for your content are multipurpose: they are descriptors of your content as well as navigational pointers. Ill-conceived labels can mystify users, forcing them to read or click on to find out what's actually being offered.

When choosing labels for your content items, describe your content in terms your users will understand. If your students are beginners, use general terms, not labels that are meaningful only to experts in your field ("Theme," not "Motive"). Also use labels that *really* describe your content — don't use empty terms like "Stuff" or "Miscellaneous." Last, be consistent in your grammatical treatment of labels. If you are using single-word nouns for subject labels like "Musicians," "Composers," and "Instruments," don't mix in a verb like "Listen" or a phrase like "Understanding Musical Forms." Your labels should reflect your organization scheme: if your categories are subject-based, so too should be your labeling system.

The following are some methods to help you classify your content.

Card sorting

Make a pile of index cards, each listing a content item you intend to include on your site: for example, "Madrigals," "Sonatas," "Dulcimer," "Mozart," "Monteverdi." Ask several people, perhaps three to five, to go through the stack of cards and make piles of the items they think belong together. Once they have gone through the stack, ask them to identify higher-level similarities: have them pull the piles together to form larger groups, and then name each pile. This exercise should yield logical groupings for the content items and establish main categories to describe them.

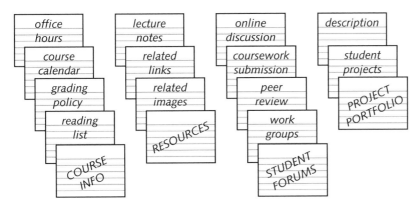

A card-sorting activity is a good way to create logical groupings of information and define categories that describe the groups.

Outlining

For a less involved method of classifying your content, use the outline function in your word processor to arrange the items on your content list into logical groups. Move the items around, using the different heading levels to define the relationships among main categories and content items.

Sample site outline

COURSE INFORMATION	STUDENT FORUMS	PROJECT PORTFOLIO
General information	Discussion	Description
Class schedule	Topic 1	Project 1
Assignments	Topic 2	Project 2
	Topic 3	Project 3
RESOURCES	Topic 4	
Related links	Critique	
Related images	Post critique	
Lecture notes	Review critiques	
Lecture 1	Student 1	
Lecture 2	Student 2	
Lecture 3	Student 3	
	Student 4	

Once you have established a classification system, use it to index all the items on your content list: for example, group all instrument descriptions under the "Instruments" classification. Don't worry about redundancy: go ahead and list "Mozart's Biography" under "Composer's Biographies" and "Required Readings" if that makes the most sense.

SITE STRUCTURE

A site structure shapes the mental model users form of your content – what there is to be found and how to find it – and it is also the foundation for your site's navigation interface (see *Navigation,* below). An organizational structure allows users to retain a sense of context as they move through your information, so that they are constantly aware of where they are, where they've been, and where they can still go. To devise a sound site structure, you need a clear understanding of your information and its interrelationships.

A number of organizational structures are possible, and each supports different activities. You may find that you need multiple organization structures to accommodate the information in your site. As with hybrid organization schemes, multiple structures can be effective as long as you keep them separate and complete.

A site organization can consist of multiple organization schemes as long as each scheme is intact and complete and the different types of navigation are visually separated.

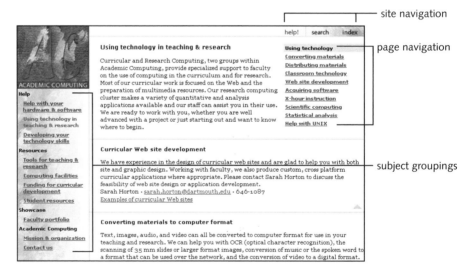

Linear

A linear organization is one in which the content of the site is presented in a sequence. Use a linear structure if your Web content is best accommodated by an organizational scheme such as a chronological or alphabetical listing or if you want users to move through your content sequentially.

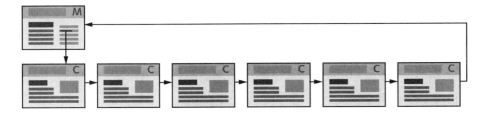

A Web site based on a sequential organization scheme supports a linear progression through the pages.

Teaching sites can be well served by a linear structure when the content needs to be learned in sequence in order to be understood. In this case, the page navigation supports only the linear path through the content.

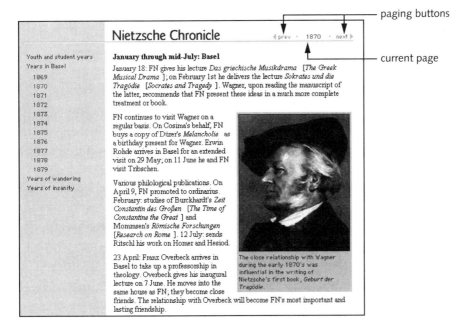

paging buttons

current page

Paging buttons encourage users to follow a linear path through this chronicle of the life of Friedrich Nietzsche.

Hierarchical

A hierarchical structure is one in which the content of the site is grouped into main categories and subsections. We are all familiar with hierarchies – the books we read and the organizations we work for are all based on hierarchical structures – and so a Web site organized hierarchically is easy for users to understand and navigate. Indeed, Web sites are typically groupings of pages organized around a central, or "home," page. Another benefit of hierarchies is that they force authors to think analytically about their content; hierarchies are most effective when based on well-organized materials.

This resource site for educators has a well-designed navigation system based on a hierarchical structure. The main categories are defined on the home page and appear in the page header graphic. Within each category, the section navigation options display in the left column under the section title.

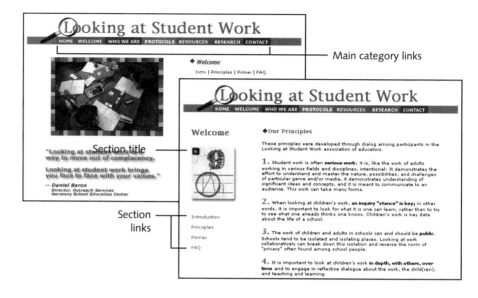

Main category links

Section links

As you develop a hierarchy for your Web site, there are a few things to consider. Web sites often fail because content is buried deep in the site. If you force users to click through multiple menu pages to get to the real content of your site, they will become frustrated and may give up.

The downfall of some hierarchies is that the content is many layers deep in the structure, which means that users must click through several menu pages to reach information.

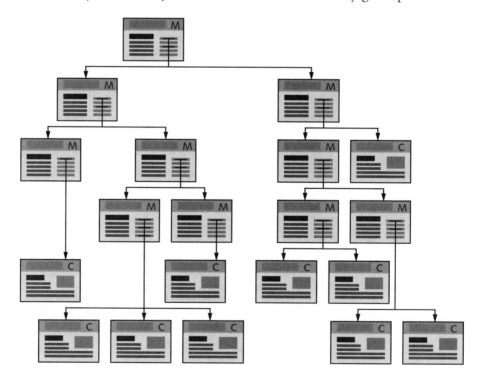

Conversely, you can overwhelm users with choices if you make all your content accessible directly from your home page. A shallow hierarchy can result in a complex menu page that offers a list of unrelated links:

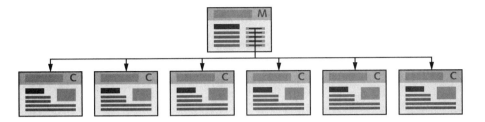

If the information hierarchy is too shallow, users are overwhelmed by too many unrelated choices on the main page.

A good Web site hierarchy presents eight or fewer main level options and incorporates the content only a level or two away from the main page.

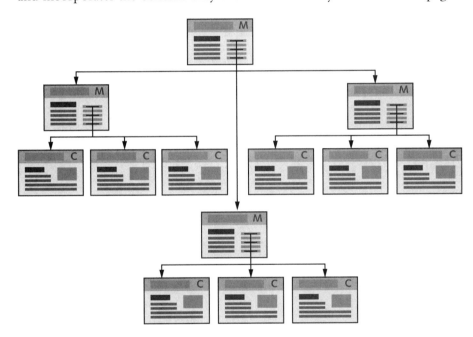

A good hierarchical structure for the Web is one in which information is categorized and content is only a few pages away from the main home page.

After considering the different organizational structures, review your outline to determine which form would best house your content. Consider how users should interact with your information: Should they access pages individually or in sequence? If you use a hierarchical approach, how many layers will be required to represent every content item? Map out a structure for your site.

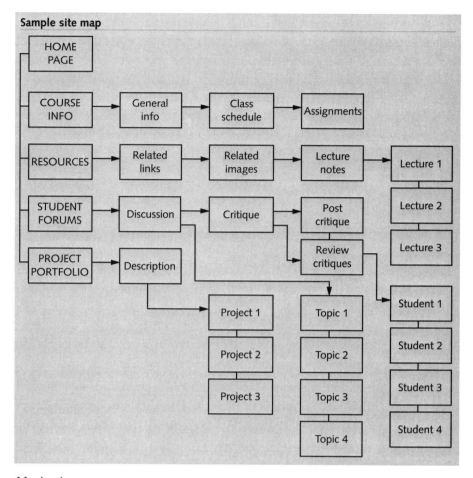

Sample site map

Navigation

Navigation systems are not just for navigation: they also give users information about content and context. A well-designed system that reflects the site structure gives users an overview of the site's content. Navigation labels can provide context, serving a "you are here" function by showing users where they are in the site. Last, navigation links allow users to move flexibly through a body of information.

Site navigation is intrinsically tied to information structure. Navigation links that are added ad hoc will disorient users, whereas a navigation system that rests on a solid site structure will enable users to move through a site with ease. There are a few things to consider, however, when designing a navigation system. Although options are useful, too many can overwhelm users. Don't be so generous with navigation links that you obscure the site's structure. Offer only the most relevant links, and keep them to a minimum.

Also bear in mind that links, by nature, are an invitation to go elsewhere. Think about the content of your site: Is there a narrative, or are the materials essentially independent chunks of information? Extensive linking will likely disrupt the narrative flow, but too few navigation options could frustrate users who are looking for specific information.

In designing a navigation system, try to predict how users will want to access the materials on your course Web site. Consider, too, how *you* want users to access the materials. Review the different types of links detailed below to decide which links will compose your site navigation system.

SITE LINKS

Site links are the links that appear on every page of a site, allowing users access to other site areas without having to return to the home page or to navigate using the browser's Back button.

In determining which links should be sitewide, think about the likely usage patterns of your users. Will they probably visit your site for one purpose, for example, to check what homework assignment is due? Or will they move between pages located under different subject headings, for example, to check the homework assignment, post a comment to the discussion area, and then review the day's lecture notes? If you predict that users will be one-stop browsers, then your sitewide navigation can be minimal, perhaps no more than a link to the home page. If, however, you predict that users will need to perform unrelated tasks when visiting your site, you should plan to provide links to the other main subject areas on every page. Extensive site links allow users to move laterally through your site structure without forcing them back to the home page to access other areas.

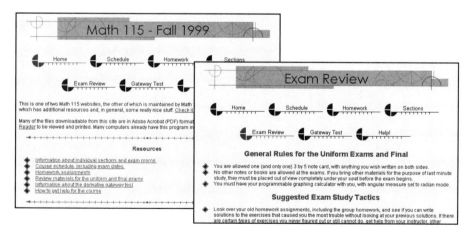

The site navigation options for this mathematics course site are clearly displayed in the banner graphic at the top of each page. The graphic also provides context cues by incorporating the page title and by changing the color of the link to the current page.

Local links are page-specific links that relate to the content of a page. An example of local navigation would be a contents page–style group of links pointing to different sections of the page. This system provides an overview of the page contents and gives users direct access to page-level information. Page links also include pointers to other pages in the site that relate specifically to the content of the page.

If your content is made up of chunks of information that need to be accessed directly, adding extensive page-level navigation will give users better access and mobility. If, however, your content should be absorbed sequentially, minimize your page-level links. Include links to related pages where relevant, but place them at the foot of the page.

The pages in this Shakespeare site contain contents page links that point to the main sections on the page and a list of sites that relate to the page. In addition to providing quick access, this page-level navigation device gives an overview of page contents.

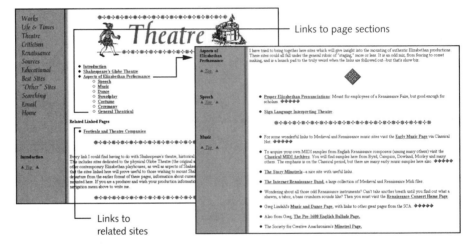

Links to page sections

Links to related sites

SITE GUIDES

So far the navigation links discussed have been content-specific. In this section we will discuss additional navigation tools that will help guide users to their destination. If you employ one or more of these devices, you will want to include a link (or, in some cases, the function itself) as part of your sitewide navigation.

Search

Students will sometimes need to seek information that is too specific to be listed on the home page menu. Scanning the menu and following links is time-consuming and may not yield the desired results. Keyword searching can complement a well-structured organization by offering direct access to information not represented on the site menus.

The search functionality can be provided either by a search page or by a basic search feature on every page in the site. A search page allows users to perform advanced searches, such as searching a specific area of the site or combining keywords to limit the search. A page-level search function provides basic searching and is usually a simple field on each site page.

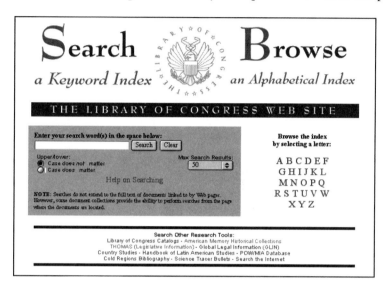

The Library of Congress site provides a page that offers both searching and browsing functions.

Fast Find

A Fast Find feature (sometimes called Shortcuts) is a quick way of directing users to specific areas of the site. The Fast Find menu might include links to pages you want to highlight or links to frequently sought information that is too granular, or specific, to be listed on the site menus.

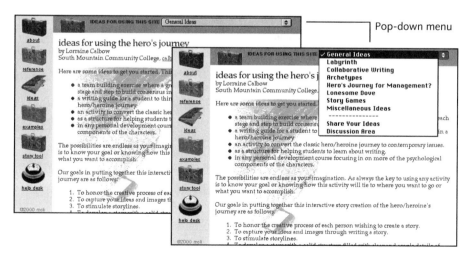

Pop-down menu

The pop-down menus on the Hero's Journey site provide quick access to subtopics within each main section.

Fast Find can be represented as a pop-down menu on every page in the site. It is most relevant, however, on the home page as a way for users to bypass the menus and go directly to their destination.

Contents and index pages

A contents page normally presents the top few levels of the site's information hierarchy as navigation links. This structured presentation of a site content has a twofold purpose: it gives users an overview of the available content and provides access to specific information.

The graphical contents page on the main page of the F. Scott Fitzgerald Centenary site provides an overview of, and access to, the main sections of the site.

Just as a contents page supports browsing, a site index provides direct access to content for users who know just what they're looking for. A site index is a collection of relevant keywords, listed alphabetically, that are linked to either pages, paragraphs, or phrases, depending upon the specificity of the index.

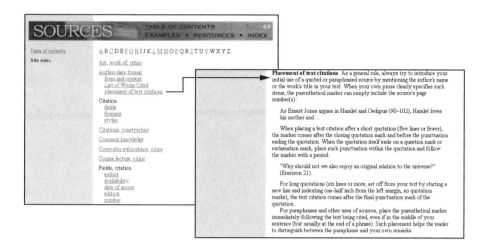

The Sources site index is arranged alphabetically by keyword and provides users who know what they are looking for direct access to specifics about citing sources. In this example, the phrase "placement of text citations" takes the user to a section on that topic on the page that covers citation formats.

Paging links

If your site structure is based on a linear model, you may want to include paging links as part of your navigation system. Paging links invite users to move through pages in an ordered sequence by providing access to the next and previous pages, normally as links in the page header, footer, or both. Paging links work well for multiple pages on a single subject, such as composers' biographies or descriptions of instruments.

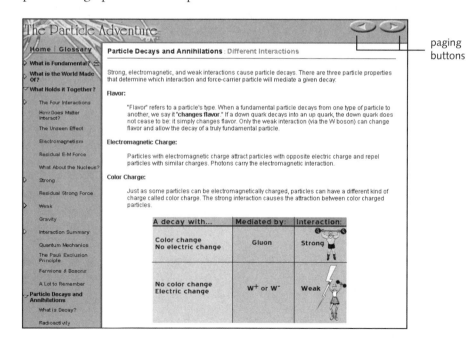

paging buttons

The navigational interface for the Particle Adventure includes paging buttons that guide users sequentially through the tutorial.

Review your site map to identify links for your global and local navigation. Determine which site guides you will offer, such as a contents page or search feature. Use your site map to sketch out the paths between the sections of the site.

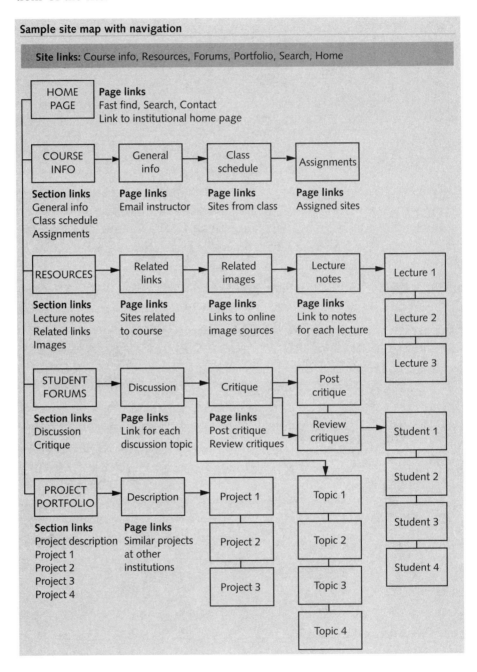

Sample site map with navigation

Site links: Course info, Resources, Forums, Portfolio, Search, Home

HOME PAGE

Page links
Fast find, Search, Contact
Link to institutional home page

COURSE INFO → General info → Class schedule → Assignments

Section links
General info
Class schedule
Assignments

Page links
Email instructor

Page links
Sites from class

Page links
Assigned sites

RESOURCES → Related links → Related images → Lecture notes → Lecture 1, Lecture 2, Lecture 3

Section links
Lecture notes
Related links
Images

Page links
Sites related to course

Page links
Links to online image sources

Page links
Link to notes for each lecture

STUDENT FORUMS → Discussion → Critique → Post critique, Review critiques → Student 1, Student 2, Student 3, Student 4

Section links
Discussion
Critique

Page links
Link for each discussion topic

Page links
Post critique
Review critiques

PROJECT PORTFOLIO → Description → Project 1, Project 2, Project 3 → Topic 1, Topic 2, Topic 3, Topic 4

Section links
Project description
Project 1
Project 2
Project 3
Project 4

Page links
Similar projects at other institutions

Summary

At the end of this last planning stage, you should have a site map that represents your site content. The content represented came from an inventory of teaching materials, which you organized into a classification system. Then you mapped out an organizational structure for the content based on its characteristics, and finally you devised a navigation system to give users mobility within the site structure.

Ask a few students to look at your site map to evaluate its effectiveness in helping users find information. Sit your testers down with your site map and ask them questions that relate to the content of your site, for example, "When was Mozart born?" or "What readings are assigned for tomorrow?" Ask them to describe the path they would take to locate the answers. Also evaluate your labeling system by asking the students to explain what *they* think your link labels describe. See if you can spot potential problems with the organization of your site, and revise the map accordingly.

Also, in reviewing the site map, ask yourself the following:

- What is *your* sense of the site structure? Does it seem manageable?
- Is your organization consistent? What about your labels?
- Do you have items that do not fit comfortably into your classification system?

If you feel that your grasp of the project is shaky, you should return to the beginning of the *Plan your site* section and refine your site structure. Starting with ill-defined concepts or an unstable structure will mean trouble later on. If you feel comfortable with your site map as it stands, you are ready to begin developing content.

References

Boettcher, Judith, and Rita-Marie Conrad. 1999. *Faculty guide for moving teaching and learning to the Web.* Mission Viejo, Calif.: League for Innovation in the Community College.

Frayer, Dorothy A. 1999. Creating a campus culture to support a teaching and learning revolution. *Cause/Effect* 22:2. http://www.educause.edu/ir/library/html/cem9923.html (5 April 2000).

Lynch, Patrick J., and Sarah Horton. 1999. *Web style guide: Basic design principles for creating Web sites.* New Haven and London: Yale University Press. [See also http://info.med.yale.edu/caim/manual]

McCormack, Colin, and David Jones. 1998. *Building a Web-based education system*. New York: Wiley Computer.

Nielsen, Jakob. 1995. *Alertbox: Jakob Nielsen's column on Web usability.* http://www.useit.com/alertbox.

Rosenfeld, Louis, and Peter Morville. 1998. *Information architecture for the World Wide Web.* Sebastopol, Calif.: O'Reilly.

Spool, Jared M., et al. 1999. *Web site usability: A designer's guide.* San Francisco: Morgan Kaufmann.

2 Developing content

"What is the use of a book," thought Alice, "without pictures or conversations?"
– Lewis Carroll, *Alice's Adventures in Wonderland*

THE NEXT STEP in developing your course Web site is to gather the materials on your content list. Some items may already be on the computer, whereas others may need to be converted to digital format from other media. Still other materials will need to be created from scratch. Once you have gathered all the materials onto your computer, you will be ready to begin creating your site.

Developing materials for the Web means finding ways to provide valuable content within the constraints of a networked environment. Much of what you will do as a course Web site author will be to try to make your teaching materials suitable for networked delivery. For this reason, much of this chapter is devoted to describing the characteristics of Web-based content and providing strategies for delivering substantive content using this ubiquitous but in many ways limited medium.

As you gather and create content for your site, you must keep in mind issues of ownership: both ownership of content created by others that you wish to use and ownership of the content you create. For educators using copyrighted materials in a Web-based classroom, there is even more confusion than in a traditional classroom about what use is and is not considered "fair." Another concern is ownership of the teaching materials you publish on your institution's Web site and how you can protect those materials from infringement. To address these concerns within the context of developing content, this chapter concludes with a discussion of copyright and intellectual property rights as applied to educational Web sites.

TEXT

Developing content for a Web site will probably mean writing new materials. The writing you have already done for your courses – for handouts and other instructional materials – may not work well on the Web. Writing Web documents is different from writing for print, and if you simply move your print documents onto Web pages, you are not using the medium to its best advantage. If you are including textual information on your course Web site, you should rewrite or adapt your materials to the style of the genre.

Web readers tend to *scan* text online and *read* text offline. They typically do not read a page from start to finish on the computer screen. Instead, they scan a site looking for relevant items and then print pages that contain the information they seek. You need to apply a style and method to your Web documents that accommodate this type of reading.

Writing style

Among the Web's many peculiarities is its writing genre. Most Web documents follow a style that you may not normally use in your writing. One of an author's tasks, however, is to write in the language and style of the reader. You cannot afford to bury your message so deep that the typical Web reader scanning your pages will either skip over it or not even bother to find it. The following approach will help ensure that Web readers will find your information:

- Summarize first. Put the main points of your document in the first paragraph, so that readers scanning your pages will not miss your point.
- Be concise. Use lists rather than paragraphs, but only when your prose lends itself to such treatment. Readers can pick out information more easily from a list than from within a paragraph.
- Write for scanning. Most Web readers scan pages for relevant materials rather than reading through a document word by word. Guide the reader by highlighting the salient points in your document using headings, lists, and typographical emphasis.

These stylistic devices are meant to accommodate the reading habits of online readers. Be careful, though, that you do not undermine your message simply to be accommodating. Readers will happily print lengthy Web documents if they are comprehensive and provide needed detail. For materials that do not lend themselves to the clipped style of online documents, do not compromise your content to fit the genre. Assume that most readers will print your materials, and make printing easy (see Chapter 3: *Layout grid*). Your readers are more likely to thank you for providing depth than to grouse about page length.

CHUNKING

Another peculiarity of the Web is that readers generally do not read pages in sequence. Novels are intended to be read sequentially, so readers know that they can't pick up a work of fiction at chapter 3 and expect it to make sense. Likewise, novelists can be fairly confident when writing page 32 that their readers will have just read page 31 and will likely continue to page 33, which means that they do not have to keep setting the stage for the reader throughout the story. Web readers, by contrast, are unpredictable. There is no way to tell where they've been or where they'll go after visiting your page. Even if you try to provide context using links to tie related pages together, you cannot force a Web reader to follow those links. As a result, your approach must be encyclopedic, giving the reader a fairly comprehensive presentation of the topic on every page.

Much of what is on the Web is reference information, and providing this type of information in precise segments, or "chunks," allows readers to quickly locate the materials they seek. A well-constructed chunk provides readers with a comprehensive account, as well as links to related or supporting pages for further study.

When deciding what defines a chunk of information, consider the following:

Access. Your content list should already be composed of information chunks, because the definition of a content item is any piece of information that needs to be accessed individually. Consider how users will interact with your materials: What items will they want to access directly? Define your information chunks to accommodate the expected usage patterns of your users.

Page length. Chunking provides a way to limit the length of your Web pages: Web readers generally prefer shorter pages. Don't arbitrarily divide a document, however, and don't divide a document that is likely to be printed anyway (see next entry).

Printing. Don't break your narrative into small segments if you expect that most users will want to print the information. Documents are easier to print from a single Web page. Or, if usage is difficult to predict, offer both a Web version and a link to an easy-to-print page or printing alternative, such as a downloadable PDF (Portable Document Format) file.

On the *Chronicle of Higher Education* site, selecting an article's "easy-to-print" link takes you to a clean page with no navigation column, links, or advertisements.

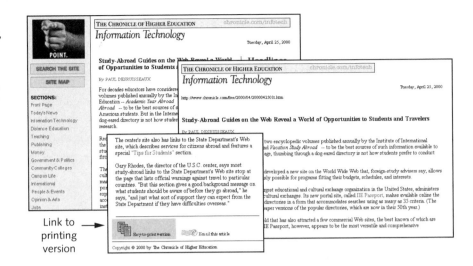

Link to printing version

There are also hazards to watch for when chunking information:

Fragmentation. Be careful not to over-subdivide your information. If you break up your information into many small chunks, your readers will be overwhelmed and frustrated by too many choices. You will also find it hard to create a coherent narrative if the information chunks are too specific to make sense out of context.

Redundancy. If you provide a comprehensive narrative for each information segment, you are going to be redundant. Don't resort to an incomplete presentation of your materials or to excessive use of links (see next entry) in order to avoid repeating yourself. It's okay – even necessary – to be redundant when writing for the Web.

Excessive linking. Web authors often try to avoid redundancy by using links. Instead of providing a full account on one page, they sprinkle the page with links to other pages, either within their site or elsewhere. These linked pages are employed to supply the reader with the context needed to understand the materials. A well-constructed information chunk, however, provides a *complete* account of the subject, with an appropriate amount of background, and links to pages providing *supporting* information. Readers should not have to follow links to gain an understanding of the information; the links are for those who wish to pursue the topic, or some aspect of the topic, further.

PAGE LENGTH

One reason that Web authors chunk information is to limit page length. It is generally believed that longer pages are unsuited to the Web, based on the notion that the physical act of scrolling is a deterrent for some users. Scrolling may have implications for a casual audience: for "surfers" skimming along the surface of the Web, scrolling goes against the grain. In this discussion of course Web sites, however, your audience is made up of committed users, and scrolling is probably not a big concern. If you have information that students need, they will scroll to get it.

The primary measure of page length should be content. Create logical divisions and subdivisions based on the *structure* of your information. Do not arbitrarily divide your information to conform to some alleged measure of acceptable page length.

PRINTING VERSUS READING ONLINE

Most people prefer to read lengthy or complicated texts offline. If your presentation includes extensive texts, dividing them into chunks only makes it harder for users to print your information. If you know that your content is likely to be printed, either present it as a single Web page or divide it into subdivisions but provide a link to a printing version.

If your content is more like a reference work than a novel (that is, more segmental than linear), users are likely to read it online, and providing direct access should be the highest priority. In this case, break your information into chunks and write for scanning to accommodate online readers.

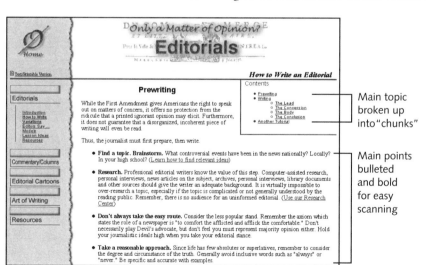

When writing for the Web, break your text into sections so users have direct access to specific information and use typographical emphasis to highlight the salient points on the page.

Main topic broken up into "chunks"

Main points bulleted and bold for easy scanning

Links

Although the ability to link documents is one of the advantages of putting information on the Web, the misuse of links is perhaps the most common failure of Web authors. Used effectively, links can supplement a narrative by providing background information, reinforcing concepts, and adding detail. Used poorly, links disrupt narrative flow in several ways:

Visual distraction. Colored and underlined text within body text pulls the eye by disrupting the uniformity of the text block. If you place a link within a paragraph, the user's eye will be drawn to the link. Many users will click on that link directly without ever reading the text that forms its context.

Disruption of narrative. Links lead to stories half-told. If halfway though your account you offer a link to another site, users may follow the link (and another link and another) and never return to your site.

Lack of context. When readers follow a link, they move from the contextual framework of your site into unfamiliar territory. Users also may not be able to ascertain the connection between the materials on your site and the linked site. This plunge from the known to the mysterious can frustrate and bewilder users.

When creating content for your Web pages, do not mistake a collection of links for content. Links are useful, but only within the context of a narrative. Use links to support your presentation – to provide information that is not critical to your argument but may be of use. And remember that links break – Web pages change, move, or are removed – so the coherence of your presentation should not rely on content from linked sites.

Summary

This section addressed editorial aspects of creating Web documents. The online reader is best accommodated by a writing style that resembles journalism more than scholarly writing: highlight the main points at the start of the page, and keep the overall tone clipped and concise.

Many Web sites are created with textual materials that originated as printed documents, with little or no adaptation to the new medium. This is a bit like taking up jogging but not bothering to buy new running shoes:

you *can* run in ordinary sneakers, but you won't run as fast or as far (and you could hurt yourself). Make the extra effort to style your textual materials to fit the genre.

Consider the following when gathering text for your course Web site:

- Which documents do you expect will be read online, and which printed? For online reading, will you write new materials or rework existing documents?
- How will you segment your content to provide the best access for your readers? Do your materials work as small chunks of detail or as larger, more general segments?
- How will you use links? Will they support your materials? Will you rely on content from other sites?

ONLINE RESOURCES

The Web is a resource so vast that finding what you're looking for can seem akin to looking for a needle in a haystack. And the Web continues to grow daily, not only in volume, but in diversity. The Web is not "for" any one thing anymore: you can use it for purposes as diverse as sending a greeting card to submitting a hospital preadmission questionnaire. Part of developing content for your site is locating Web resources that are relevant to your course and gathering the information you'll need to make them available from your course Web site.

Web sites

Many instructors assign Web sites as either primary texts or supplementary readings. The most convenient way to point students at online resources is to create a Web page with links to the sites. In fact, many course sites start out as lists of pointers to other online resources.

Using Web sites in the curriculum raises a number of concerns. One worry is that you will adopt a Web site as a primary reading only to discover that the site has moved or changed. Another concern is the accuracy and authenticity of Web-based content. But with the glut of information on the Web, perhaps the biggest concern is how an instructor can separate the wheat from the chaff and find good, accurate, dependable sites for use in the classroom.

As the Web continues to burgeon with each passing day, it becomes harder and harder to find the "right" Web sites. A basic Web search can yield millions of matching Web pages. Looking for relevant content in a long list of links can feel a bit like shopping at a flea market: you may find what you're looking for, but not without picking through a lot of junk. When following up on search results, you may find that many links are broken (point to nonexistent pages) or unrelated (a search for "renaissance music" returns links to pages about the rock band Renaissance) and that most of the links that are related are insubstantial, poorly executed, or otherwise unreliable. But the "right" sites *are* out there. You just need to know where, and how, to find them.

Search engines

The premise of a search engine is similar to that of a library catalog: to list the pages on the Web so that users can find them. The principal difference is that in a library, cataloging is done by humans, whereas on the Web most search engine catalogs are created by software robots that roam the Internet looking for new or updated pages. The trouble with robots is that they cannot make fine distinctions between, for example, Jefferson, the president, and Jefferson, Texas. Another significant difference is that libraries tend to have most of their holdings cataloged, whereas no search engine has indexed more than a quarter of the Web. In spite of these limitations, search engines still provide the most extensive catalog of Web holdings.

Popular search engines		
AltaVista	www.altavista.com	One of the largest catalogs Good support for phrase searching Can search for only images, video, products, discussions, etc.
Google	www.google.com	Ranks pages according to popularity ("votes" are links from other sites) Automatically does "match all" Fast
Northern Light	www.northernlight.com	Puts search results into folders for easier browsing "Special Collection" links to full-text articles available for a fee
MetaCrawler	www.metacrawler.com	Meta search engine sends your search query to multiple search engines

Subject directories

Using a subject directory is more like consulting a librarian than using the library catalog. With a general notion about the topic you are researching, a librarian can suggest possible options or send you to the appropriate area in the library to browse the shelves. Subject directories are compiled by Web librarians who collect, review, and index Web sites into categories. A subject directory is most useful when you want a broad survey of a subject, for example, celestial navigation or transcendentalism. Because humans, not robots, compile subject directories, they tend to have a much smaller catalog than a search engine, with information that is not as current.

Popular subject directories		
Yahoo!	www.yahoo.com	Largest and most comprehensive subject directory
Magellan Internet Guide	magellan.excite.com	Lists "recommended" sites
Argus Clearinghouse	www.clearinghouse.net	Database of links to specialized subject directories
		Guides collected and rated by experts
About.com	www.about.com	Topic-specific guides maintained by About.com experts
Specialized searching		
Artcyclopedia	www.artcyclopedia.com	Index of museum sites and image archives
Ask Magpie	www.magpiemagazines.com	Index of magazines worldwide
		Provides link to magazine Web site (when available)
INFOMINE	infomine.ucr.edu	Index of Web-based scholarly resources
SearchEdu.edu	www.searchedu.com	Searches for sites only at educational institutions

Searching smart

Every search engine has a variety of methods for refining searches. Although many methods are used broadly, search engines are not standardized, so a command that works with one may not work in the same way with another. You may find that some of the commands listed below don't work exactly as shown with your favorite search engine. Don't despair: check the search engine's help pages. Just because the command doesn't work as shown does not mean that the method isn't available – it may just be implemented differently.

When you type a string of words into a search field, most search engines look for pages that match *any* of your search terms. For example, if you enter "renaissance music" into a search field, the result will contain sites that contain the words "renaissance" *or* "music." Of the millions of sites listed as the result of this query, only a small number will relate to music from the Renaissance period.

You can use simple operators to formulate more precise search queries. Use the "+" operator to find pages that have *all* the words you type in your search. The following search locates pages that mention "renaissance" and "music."

+renaissance +music

Use the "−" operator to exclude particular subjects. The following search locates pages that mention "renaissance" and "music" but excludes pages from that set that mention "baroque."

+renaissance +music −baroque

These methods locate words, not concepts. You may get a result that contains the words "music" and "renaissance" somewhere on the page but is actually *about* the Harlem Renaissance.

To narrow in on a topic, try a phrase search using quotation marks. When you enclose your search words in quotation marks, pages that have all the words in the order specified are returned. A phrase search on "renaissance music" is more likely than a search with operators to locate pages about Renaissance music. You can combine operators with phrase searching for greater precision. The following search will locate pages that deal specifically with music from the Renaissance period by matching the *phrase* "renaissance music" and excluding those pages that mention "medieval" or "baroque."

"renaissance music" −medieval −baroque

Because a document title is normally a good descriptor of page content, you can sometimes home in on a subject using a title search, which searches for words or phrases that appear in the document title. The search "title:renaissance music" returns pages that have either renaissance or music in the <TITLE> tag. You can also combine phrase searching with title searching. The following search returns pages with the phrase "renaissance music" in the title.

title:"renaissance music"

Another useful method for refining your results is to search for pages within specific domains. For example, you can search for pages at educational institutions by limiting your search to domains that end in ".edu."

"renaissance music" +host:edu

You can also limit your search to specific sites. The following search query looks for pages on Renaissance music only on the Medieval.org Web site.

host: medieval.org "renaissance music"

EVALUATING WEB CONTENT

Too often it is hard to determine who authored a Web site, never mind his or her credentials. But with the free-for-all that is the Web – with sites authored by everyone from grade-school children to movie fans to political organizations to extremist groups to Nobel laureates – and with no governing body to ensure quality or accuracy, users need to turn their critical evaluation skills to Web site content.

One of the hardest aspects of evaluating Web sites is the lack of standardization. In print, we can normally find information about the provenance of a document – the author's name, information about the publication, usually something about the author's qualifications. On the Web, nothing is required. There is no standard way to indicate a document's origins, so the information is often omitted. Also, many of the visual cues we get from printed materials are not on the Web. The typography and quality of the printing and paper for a scholarly journal, for example, instills more confidence than that of the daily rag. By contrast, Web documents of the utmost reliability may be poorly designed and executed. Without proven evaluative systems, you will need to devise your own methods for selecting quality Web sites.

Here are some things to look for when evaluating Web sites:

Origins. Where is the site from? Is it from a source you trust, such as the *New York Times?* Is it from an educational or government organization (that is, sites that end in .edu or .gov, such as www.nasa.gov or www.yale.edu)? Or is it impossible to tell from the page where it comes from and who the author is? If there is no indication on the site of authorship or affiliation but you feel that the materials are credible and useful, you may wish to do a bit of sleuthing to determine its origins, such as searching the domain name registry to find out who owns the site's domain.

Freshness. How recently were the materials published? Well-designed sites include a publication date (the date the materials were first written), as well as a last-updated date. Web pages have a short shelf life. Beware of pages that have been untouched for more than a few months.

Bias. Many informational Web pages are sponsored by organizations that are trying to sell something. For example, you may find a page about migraine headaches on a pharmaceutical company's Web site. This association does not necessarily render the materials useless, but it is wise to regard them with some skepticism. Also be wary of sites from not-for-profit organizations (for example, www.freecannabis.org): because their mission is to promote a point of view, the information they offer may not be objective.

Popularity. One way to get endorsement for a Web site is to see who else likes it. You can use link searching to check a site's popularity by seeing who links to it from their pages. For example, in AltaVista, typing "link:www.dartmouth.edu/~compose" will show the sites that link to Dartmouth College's Composition Center home page. If only a few sites link to the materials, and they are mainly personal pages, you might consider looking for an alternate source. If, however, you get many search results and you recognize some listings (perhaps the English department site at your institution), then you have some assurance that the materials are of high quality.

USING WEB CONTENT

The greatest mishap you may encounter when using materials from the Web is that the site might not be there when you need it. For example, you may have assigned your students to read online documents supporting a copyright case, but when the assignment comes due, the site where the documents reside is down for maintenance. Unfortunately, broken links are all too common on the Web: in a typical online session, you are likely to encounter at least one broken link. This fly-by-night aspect of Web sites can be unsettling, particularly when one is designing a course around materials from the Web.

Here are a few steps you can take to keep from being left in the lurch:

Choose wisely. It is best to choose sites from established organizations, like sites from government or educational institutions (see *Evaluating Web content,* above).

Contact the author. Send a message to the site author explaining that you intend to use the site as a primary text in your class. Ask whether the author has any major plans for the site – any extensive site redesign or relocation – that might affect its availability during the time you'll need it.

Download the site. Perhaps the best way to ensure a site's availability is to download and install it on your own Web server. Some authors offer their Web sites for mirroring, which means you can download the site and install it locally on your institution's Web server for more convenient access. Then you point to the local site when you create a link to the materials on your course site.

It is possible to download a site directly from the Web browser without following a formal procedure: Microsoft's Internet Explorer, for example, has a "Save As…Web Archive" feature that allows you to save a site with accompanying images and media to your hard drive. But you should not mirror any site on your own server without first seeking permission from the site author. If you download a site without permission, you are violating copyright (see *Copyright and intellectual property,* below).

Have an alternate. Whenever possible, have a backup source for Web-based materials. In the copyright example above, an alternative could be a print source for the documents or printing the Web pages and asking the library to hold them on reserve. This strategy is useful both in case the site is ever unavailable and for students who cannot access the materials online.

Databases

A search engine is essentially a database with a Web "front end," as is an online "people finder" or "airfare finder" or any collection of similar information that users can search and review using their Web browser. More and more materials are being offered via database with a Web interface, including library catalogs, online journals, databases, and texts. Any volume of content with shared characteristics – such as author, title, date of publication, or subject – is suited to a database approach.

In gathering content for your course Web site, think about including links to materials from online databases. In many cases, you can save a link that points to specific database materials for use on your Web page (see *Saved searches,* below). For example, if you are assigning a reading that is on reserve in the library, you can include a link to the book's online library catalog entry on your Web site. Or if you want your students to read an article from an electronic journal that your institution subscribes to, include a link directly to the article on your course site. Another approach would be to search an online database to compile a data set for your course, for example, data from one of the online genome databases. You can send your students directly to a page that displays your search results, where they can review and download the data for use in their coursework.

SAVED SEARCHES

You can sometimes save a link to a database-generated page for use as a link on your own site. The benefit of this approach is that you can point your students directly at the materials you want them to review without their having to search for them on the site. This process can be as easy as copying the URL (Uniform Resource Locator), the complete Web address that appears in the location bar in the browser after successfully completing a search.

Saving a search is not always that straightforward, however. Say, for example, that you assign an article available through an institutional online journal subscription. The path to the article may be a bit convoluted, so you would like to provide a link that takes students directly to the assigned article. Because this type of service normally requires a login, simply saving and using your URL will not work: it contains session identification information that will not work for other users.

The easiest way to see whether you can save a search is to copy the URL from the location bar, quit the browser to clear any persistent session infor-

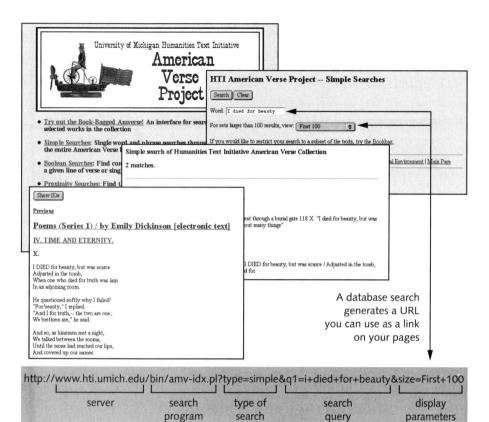

You can create links to content from online databases by executing a search and then copying the URL from the location bar in the browser for use as the link reference.

A database search generates a URL you can use as a link on your pages

http://www.hti.umich.edu/bin/amv-idx.pl?type=simple&q1=i+died+for+beauty&size=First+100

| server | search program | type of search | search query | display parameters |

mation, reopen the browser, paste the URL back into the location bar, and see what happens. If the link is "generic," the search embedded in the link will be executed and you will receive a page with the search results. If the link is tied to a specific session, you will receive some sort of error message, probably mentioning that it is not a valid session.

Many online subscription services provide the option for creating "custom" links, with the institutional login and search query embedded in the link. Ask your reference librarians about the electronic holdings available at your institution and whether it is possible to create custom links directly to the materials.

Downloadables

We use the Web to *do* things — order concert tickets, chat with colleagues, watch the latest movie trailers. We use the Web to *find* things out — what the current weather is in Bangkok, what the symptoms are for diabetes. We also use the Web to *get* stuff — to download software, images, or documents.

In this last case, the Web functions as a virtual warehouse where you can locate and acquire materials online.

One possible function for a course Web site is to distribute course materials. With this option, you need not translate documents from their original format into HTML in order to display them on the Web. Instead, you upload the documents onto the Web server in their native format – say, as Word or Excel files. Then you put links on your site that point to the files that you uploaded. When a user clicks a link, the file downloads onto their machine.

The course handouts on this Chemistry course site are available for download in PDF or Postscript format.

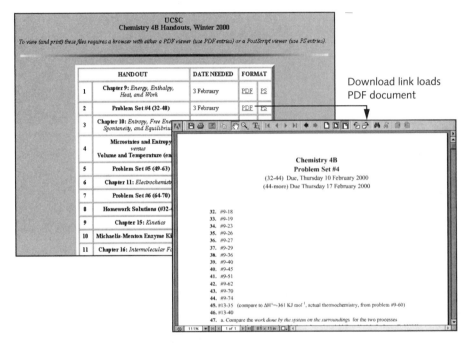

Download link loads PDF document

Say, for example, that you want to give your students dependable access to course handouts such as the syllabus and reading list. That way, if they lose a handout, they don't need to contact you for another copy. In this case, you are not interested in *publishing* information about your course on the Web. Your goal is to provide easy access, so you put the documents somewhere public – on the Web server – and create a Web page with links that point to the documents.

A more ambitious use of this method would be to offer students access to downloadable materials for use in other applications. For example, you might have a data set that you would like your students to use for data analysis. You can save the data in a portable format, such as a tab-delimited text file, upload the file onto the Web server, and offer a download link to the file on your course Web site. With this method, students can easily download, import, and work with the data in their spreadsheet or statistical analysis package.

Other applications of this approach include:

PowerPoint presentations. Many instructors use Microsoft's presentation package, PowerPoint, to create slide sets for use as backdrops for lectures. The slides contain the salient points of the lecture and any supporting artwork, images, video, and audio. Providing Web access to these "lecture notes" makes it easy for students to review the points made during a lecture.

To make your slides available for download from your course Web site, save the presentation as a "PowerPoint Show" and upload the file to the Web server. PowerPoint is part of the popular Office suite of productivity software, so many students will be able to view the slides with no additional installations. Those who do not have PowerPoint can view the presentation using the free PowerPoint Viewer.

To publish a PowerPoint presentation directly on your course site, use PowerPoint's "Save as HTML" feature. This option creates individual HTML and image files for each slide as well as a navigation interface for the presentation.

PDF documents. You can make print documents available on your Web site by converting them to Portable Document Format. As its name suggests, PDF is a format used to port documents from one system to another while maintaining document integrity. Say, for example, that you wish to make a chapter from a textbook available to your students on your course Web site. The chapter was created using a page layout program such as QuarkXpress or FrameMaker. If you upload the document onto the Web server as is, students could download the materials but would need to have QuarkXpress or FrameMaker to see the chapter. They would also need to download any associated image files and document fonts.

If instead you convert the chapter to PDF, all document fonts and images are embedded in the PDF file as part of the conversion. Simply upload the PDF version of the chapter to the Web server and provide a link to the file on your course Web site. Your students can now either download the file and view it using the free Adobe Acrobat Reader or, if they have the PDF Web plug-in installed, can view the document in the Web browser.

You can create PDF documents using PDFWriter, a utility that comes free with Adobe software. Some programs allow you to save directly to PDF. If you plan to create PDFs from complex documents – those with many images or multiple page sizes – you should consider purchasing Adobe Acrobat. This full-blown suite of tools for creating PDFs provides more compression options and can reproduce documents most accurately.

Summary

One of the main attractions of the Web is simple convenience. You can offer your students convenient one-stop shopping by gathering an assortment of course materials in a single location: your course Web site. In this section we covered some of the types of materials you can offer from your Web site – from your own course handouts and notes that you upload to the server to other Web-based resources.

Questions to consider at this stage include:

- Have you had success in finding relevant Web content? If not, are you using the right tool? Are you using smart searching strategies to limit your search results?
- Are the Web sites you plan to use in your curriculum reliable and accurate? Have you contacted the site authors? Do you have alternatives should the sites become unavailable?
- Are there other online resources, such as texts or data banks, that you could use?
- Do you have course materials in digital format – PowerPoint slides, handouts, images – that you could distribute to your students from your Web site?

INTERACTIVITY

The interactive potential of the computer is one of the principal reasons it is used as a medium for instruction. In computer-based instruction, learners actively participate in the learning process: they are presented with an array of choices from which to construct their own path to knowledge and understanding. The Web is by its very nature interactive: Web users actively construct a path by choosing which links to follow. In this section we will discuss more advanced forms of Web-based interactivity, including quizzing, online communication, and simulations.

Note that some of the interactivity options described here work best in a restricted environment, in particular, discussions and on-line peer review. Students may feel more at ease taking part in online conversation and exchange if they know that their contributions can be viewed only by the instructor and fellow classmates. It is fairly easy to limit access to a single Web

Popular interactivity software	
Discussion software	
Discuss	www.discusware.com
Web Crossing	webcrossing.com
WebBoard	webboard.oreilly.com
WWWThreads	www.wwwthreads.com
Chat software	
Chat Blazer	www.chatblazer.com
ParaChat	www.parachat.com
Motet	www.motet.com
Quizzing software	
Test Pilot	www.clearlearning.com
Question Mark Software	www.questionmark.com
Quiz Factory 2	www.learningware.com

page or an entire site, so keep this option in mind when reviewing these interactivity features. For details on implementing access restriction, see Chapter 4: *Limiting access.*

Discussion

Online discussion allows students to interact with classmates outside class. An online discussion is not fixed in time or space: students can log on at any time from any Internet-enabled computer to seek clarification for issues they encounter in their coursework, to discuss topics raised in class, or to initiate new discussions on related topics. A successful online discussion has the same synergistic effect of group or in-class discussion, in which students build on one another's perspectives to gain a deeper understanding of the materials.

An online class discussion area can be beneficial in a number of areas:

Class preparation. You can use a course discussion area to prepare for class and adapt class time to address the needs of the students. Monitoring the class discussion will help you identify topics that need clarification or that have captured the interest of your students, and you can use the insights you gain to structure class time. Also, if you use the Web discussion area to address some of the more straightforward student questions, you can make better use of class time.

Shy students. Students who are reticent in class may find an online discussion area the perfect place to discuss class topics. Participating in an online discussion is less threatening than speaking in front of peers. And in an online discussion, students can compose, edit, and refine their ideas before expressing them to the group. If you set up a discussion area for your course, you may find that some of your quiet students actually have a lot to say!

Sensitive issues. Discussion areas work well for courses that cover topics that may be too sensitive, controversial, or personal for some students to discuss face-to-face. Students contributing to online conversation may feel less exposed than in a classroom setting, particularly if you allow them to write using pseudonyms.

There are also drawbacks to using online discussion:

Too much participation. An active discussion area can add hours of reading to the regular course load, or distract students from other equally or more important coursework. A discussion area can also become unwieldy for the instructor: weeding through submissions and responding where needed can quickly become impractical.

When thinking about whether to include a discussion area on your Web site, decide how much time you can (and want to) spend monitoring submissions. Consider assigning the task to a teaching or research assistant, but be sure to have him or her bring to your notice any items that might require your attention. You can also take a hands-off approach: create the discussion area for your students and make no attempt to monitor the activity. Although this approach does not take advantage of some of the benefits of a discussion site, it is still an advantage for your students. You might find that students are more apt to contribute if they know you're not listening.

Not enough participation. If you are contemplating online discussion for a course that does not normally have much in-class discussion, consider whether it is worth the effort. If the subject doesn't normally provoke much discussion in the classroom, you may find that the online discussion is limited to questions about assignments or scheduling. Be realistic about your expectations: don't go to the effort of setting up a forum thinking that your students will converse online if you are teaching a subject that elicits little in-class exchange (see Chapter 4: *Encouraging participation*).

Much online interaction relies on programs called CGIS (Common Gateway Interfaces), which negotiate a dialogue between the user and the Web server. The dialogue goes something like this: the user types information into a form on a Web page and submits the information to the Web server. The server accepts the information and processes it in some predefined fashion – adds it to a database, emails it to someone, appends it to a Web page. The server often sends a confirmation to the user, perhaps an acknowledgment of receipt or a page that displays the submission.

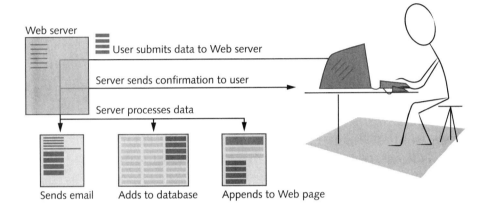

Web server

User submits data to Web server

Server sends confirmation to user

Server processes data

Sends email   Adds to database   Appends to Web page

In a typical online CGI transaction, the user submits information from a Web page to the Web server. The server processes data and sends a confirmation to the user.

There are plenty of commercial and homemade options available for online communication, so you don't have to write your own CGIS in order to have a discussion area on your course Web page. Check with computing support staff to see what is available at your institution. Programs that provide some form of Web-based communication may already be installed on the Web server. If you are using a courseware tool to create your site, interactive features such as online discussion or chat are likely to be built into the software.

TYPES OF DISCUSSION

There are two main types of discussion modules, the "chat room" and the discussion area, and the main distinction between the two is time. Participants in a chat room post and are responded to in real time. If you are not in the "room" while the dialogue is taking place, you're not part of the discussion. The chat model provides *synchronous* communication; it is like a phone conversation or a face-to-face dialogue. People who post to discussion areas, by contrast, are *asynchronous* participants in online conversation:

to contribute to a discussion you needn't be online when a comment is submitted, and a posting can be responded to days later.

In an educational endeavor like a course Web site, a discussion area is likely to be more useful than a chat room. The type of student dialogue sought by educators is better suited to the discussion format than the less-structured and somewhat ephemeral chat.

Single-topic discussion

In a single-topic discussion all contributions are listed in sequence on the Web page in order of submission. The discussion may be guided, for example, covering class readings, lectures, or films. A single-topic discussion is a group conversation: one person speaks at a time, and you enter the discussion where it left off.

In this discussion of class lectures and readings, participants use a form to compose their message, and their submission is appended at the bottom of the page.

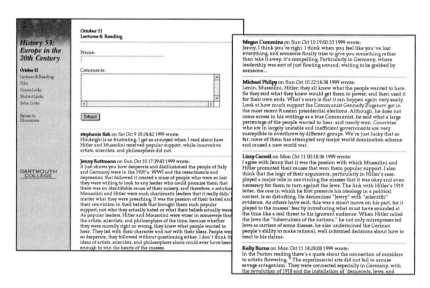

Threaded discussion

In a threaded discussion users have the option of responding to one another directly. Although there may be a general topic, as in the discussion example above, subtopics emerge as students respond to specific postings. These secondary postings are the "threads" that spin off from the main discussion: a student responds directly to a comment made about the main topic, and another student responds to the response, and so a thread is formed. A threaded discussion is a group conversation with simultaneous side conversations. There is little sense of sequence in a threaded discussion; you can easily chime in at any point in the conversation.

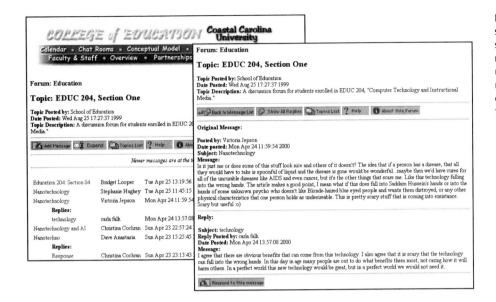

In a threaded discussion, users can respond directly to a message, and other users can respond to a response, and thus a discussion "thread" is formed.

Chat room

Online conversations take place in real time in chat rooms. When a user posts a message to a chat room, every other user who is viewing the chat room Web page sees the message and can respond immediately. Participating in a chat room is like participating in a face-to-face group discussion: you need to pay attention and speak up if you want to contribute.

As its name implies, an exchange in a chat room can be less substantial than that in an online discussion area. In fact, for educational purposes a chat room provides few of the benefits of online communication. Because the conversation takes place in real time there is little time to craft a response. Chats are unstructured so it is difficult for students to follow the thread of discussion, and instructors will likely find trolling the chat archive for cogent contributions arduous and possibly fruitless. Setting up a course chat room is not a *bad* idea, but its pedagogical value is likely to be less than that of an asynchronous discussion area.

And yet, chat is an excellent tool for building community online. This can be particularly important in distance education, where students cannot speak face-to-face because much (or all) of the course is online. A chat mechanism can facilitate one-to-one online communication, as well as online conferencing to support collaborative activities. Ambitious examples of such synchronous interaction include the virtual environments known as MUDS and MOOS (Multi-User Dimensions and MUD Object-Oriented).

The virtual environment of the MOO allows users to move around a virtual location and talk with whomever happens to be in the room.

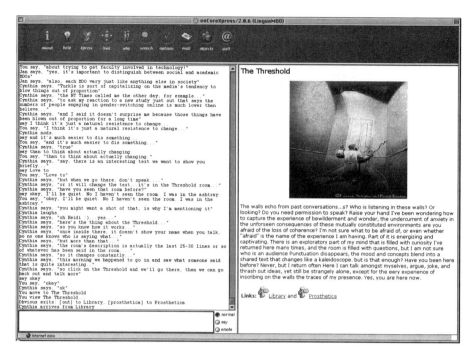

Coursework submission

A Web site can be a collection point for coursework: either a private point for the instructor only or a public location for peer review. In a typical implementation of this feature, a student writes an essay using a word processor, copies and pastes the finished work onto a form on the course Web site, and presses Submit. The essay is sent to the Web server, where it is made available on the course Web site for review by the instructor and other class members.

Using the Web for coursework collection has a number of benefits:

- Convenience. Collecting all coursework in one online location is more convenient than collecting printed coursework, and you can't spill coffee on a file that's on the Web server. If you are comfortable reading online, it is not necessary to have printed copies of the student work at all.
- Control. The posting mechanism can time-stamp submissions so that you can track when your students submit their work.
- Quality. The quality of your students' work may improve when it is published in a public forum.
- Flexibility. Your Web-savvy students may include links to supporting materials – Web sites, images, video – in their coursework.

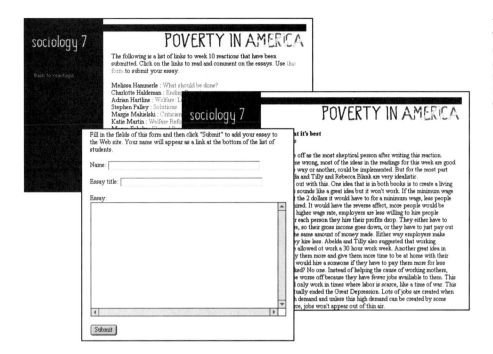

This sociology course Web site provides a coursework submission area where students submit their essays and review and comment on one another's work.

You can also use your Web site to create an online gallery of student multimedia work. Be sure to get permission from your students if you plan to publish their work on your course site, and review your institution's copyright policy for Web-published materials (see *Publishing student work,* below).

PEER REVIEW

If you use your course Web site to collect student work, you have already established the framework for online peer review. Publishing students' work on your course site means that students in the class can visit the site to review their peers' work. You may even consider an online review option, in which students post comments to the site about one another's work (and post comments on the comments).

Online peer review may even work better than the face-to-face equivalent, because many students feel more comfortable critiquing online, where they can compose their comments privately with care. However, this feature may be underused unless you make it compulsory, for example, by assigning each student an essay to review. Students are not likely to add reading to their coursework unless it is assigned.

Collecting and posting student work online means students can easily review one another's work. On this American Civil War course Web site, classmates can post comments about each other's work, and the comments display at the bottom of the page.

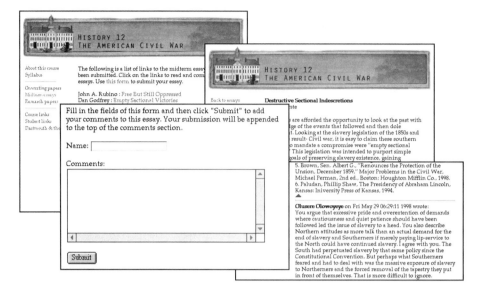

Online quizzing

It is relatively easy to construct a Web page questionnaire using standard HTML commands. The biggest challenge is what to do with the responses. You could have responses sent to your email account, post the questions and responses to a Web page, or gather responses into a database, but any of these options requires special processing using, for example, a CGI script. If all you want is basic data collection, check with the computing support staff for available options. Most Web servers have a standard library of CGIs installed, in which case you will only need to know how to point to the script on the server.

Collecting data on the Web is a relatively straightforward process. For this course site, students are asked to write about a painting and submit their work using a form on the site, and the submission is mailed to the instructor.

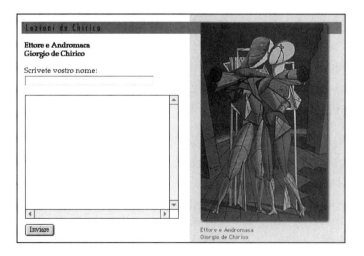

The real power of computer-based quizzing goes far beyond collecting responses; it lies in the computer's ability to provide feedback based on user actions. Our computers give us feedback all the time. If we click the wrong button, it beeps. When we click the right button, it highlights and something happens, and while the computer is processing the request, the cursor changes to let us know it's working on it. This feedback guides our interaction by pointing out our errors and confirming our successes.

The best online quiz modules do not simply collect responses but provide feedback throughout the quizzing process, so that students learn while they are assessed. Through feedback, the computer can point out errors and provide explanations as well as reward successes. In a well-implemented quiz, student performance improves as they make their way through the questions, because they learn as they go. And depending on your approach – whether the primary purpose of the quiz is knowledge assessment or learning – you can allow students to repeat the quiz as often as they wish.

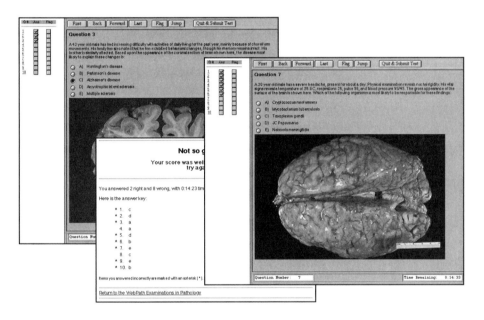

The WebPath quizzing modules require users to answer questions about a collection of pathology images. The quizzes are timed, and once you have completed the module you can check your answers and, if necessary, retake the quiz.

A quiz with feedback is much harder to implement and is likely to require custom programming, though many courseware packages, including WebCT and CourseInfo, do offer a quiz option. Check with your computing personnel about available options for Web-based quizzing. Regard-less of the method, perhaps the hardest aspect of feedback is keeping the set of questions and answers narrow enough so that a computer can tell which answers are right. For example, quizzes that use multiple choice work best, whereas a quiz in which users type responses is far more complicated because of the potential for misspellings or multiple correct answers. If you plan to use an online quiz and would like to provide feedback, you will need to keep the quiz format simple.

Frequently asked questions (FAQ)

Most instructors answer the same questions every time they teach a course. Many have devised methods to preempt these questions, perhaps in the form of a handout distributed at the beginning of term. Instructors using a course Web site can answer common questions on a course FAQ page.

An FAQ is a compilation of frequently asked questions with their answers. FAQs are often searchable to help users to find answers to specific queries. As an accessible and dependable resource for users with questions, they reduce the demands on the answer source – in this case, the instructor. Although creating an FAQ requires an initial time expense, deflecting common questions may reduce the everyday demands on your time and free you for more challenging tasks.

The General Chemistry *Online!* site provides, among many other things, an FAQ with answers to common chemistry questions.

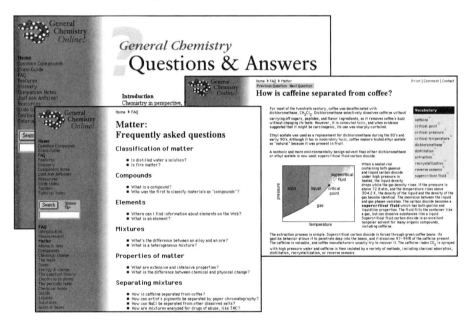

A good way to develop the content for an FAQ is to review student correspondence and collect a list of common questions. Then write answers to the questions, again using your correspondence as a source. The final FAQ will depend on how many questions it will contain, how you are creating your site, and the available institutional support. A simple FAQ could be a page on your course site listing the questions with their answers. A complex FAQ would work best as a database-driven collection that users can search for answers as well as ask additional questions.

Getting students to use the course FAQ may require a little prodding. When students ask a question that you know is answered online, point them to the course FAQ page without answering their question directly. See if you can habituate them to look at the Web site before contacting you. The site is far more likely to be available when they need to have their question answered.

Simulations

One of the great strengths of the computer is that it can be used to simulate real-world situations without affecting the real world. Computer-based simulations allow us to pilot WWII bombers, dramatically alter ecosystems, and blow up dragons without ever breaking into a sweat. In an educational setting, simulations are an excellent teaching tool: they allow students to explore different scenarios and observe and analyze the outcomes. For example, students conducting an experiment using a chemistry lab simulation *can* mix bleach and ammonia without succumbing to toxic fumes.

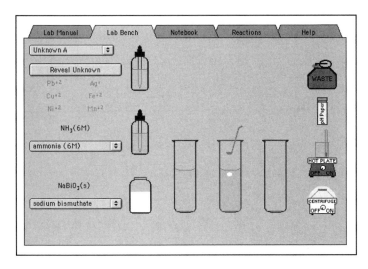

This chemistry simulation allows students to combine, heat, test, and even discard chemicals at a virtual lab bench. Their interactions at the bench are recorded by the applet, and students can make additional notations in their lab notebook.

For many reasons, simulations have been slow to reach the Web. Although most educators have the technical mastery needed to create and maintain Web pages using HTML, simulations require a good amount of interactivity, and HTML is *not* a tool for programming interactivity. Most simulations are written in the Java programming language or with such multimedia authoring tools as QuickTime and Flash. These methods are not accessible to most nonprogrammers, so the gap between subject knowledge and technical mastery is too wide for most educators to construct simulations.

In many cases, however, instructors have worked with programmers to create custom instructional modules for use on the Web. Survey your field to see if colleagues at other institutions have developed resources that might work on your Web site. Such programs are usually available at no charge or for a nominal fee.

Summary

There are many ways to add interactive features to your course site. You should now have an idea of which methods might apply to your site goals. Adding interactivity of any type is not simply a matter of saying, "I'll take one of those," except perhaps if you are using a courseware tool to create your site. You will likely need help from computing support staff to implement interactivity on your course Web site. In fact, your first step should be to check with them to find out what types of interactivity are installed and in use at your institution.

Consider the following when contemplating using interactive features on your course Web site:

- Would your students benefit from an online forum for discussing class-related topics? Does the subject you're teaching normally provoke much in-class dialogue? Or might the subject be better debated in the relative shelter of online discussion?
- Are you prepared to monitor an online discussion? Do you have the time? Or will you adopt a hands-off approach?
- Do you see any benefit to publishing student work on your course site? If you do post student work, will your students read it?
- Do you teach the course regularly? If so, are there commonly asked questions that you could compile into a course FAQ?
- Do you know of any simulations that have been developed in your field? Can you arrange to use them on your site?

MULTIMEDIA

One of the most important advantages of Web-based instruction is the ability to employ multiple media types to present ideas and concepts. With Web multimedia, you can combine text, images, sound, and moving images on a single page. For example, a Web site for a language course could offer a visual orientation using maps and photographs, listening practice using audio narratives by native speakers, and authentic texts for reading comprehension. All of these elements can be integrated for greater effect: for example, the audio component could actually be a recitation of the text, so students can read and listen at the same time. The text could be presented with supporting visual materials, such as photographs. Video segments could further support the aural and visual framework. Presenting students with multiple media options addresses learning at several levels and allows them to choose their own approach to comprehending the materials.

You probably already use multimedia materials in your classroom teaching: slide trays of 35mm slides, videotapes, television and radio broadcasts. Simply making these materials *available* on a Web site is of great value to your students. Say, for example, that you have been displaying slides during lectures for your neurobiology class. In most cases, students have either no or only limited access to the images outside class, which means that they must do their analysis and coursework from memory, relying on scribbled notes and sketches. If you put the images online, students could not only view the images but also download and use them in their work.

If you are using your course Web site for instruction, you will want to think of ways in which combined media could enhance your presentation. Is there any benefit to offering the same materials in different ways, such as presenting a lab procedure with text as well as an illustrative video? Can you provide multimedia materials that relate to the topic of your course?

This section covers the process of identifying and digitizing multimedia content. In the next chapter, *Creating the site,* we will explore how to edit and customize materials for use on your course Web site. But before we go into specific media types, here are general notes about multimedia.

ANALOG AND DIGITAL

In the analog world, image, sound, and motion are captured by all manner of devices – cameras, microphones, recorders, audio- and videotape, film, chemicals, paper. Using such content on the Web requires an encoding process to convert the analog materials to digital bits and bytes. As more and more devices capture information digitally, this conversion process becomes less necessary: all that is needed is a method to transfer the content from the capture device to the computer.

Some analysts predict that in time all content will be in digital format, but that time is a long way off. When authoring content for the digital medium, at some point you will probably need to convert analog materials to computer format.

COMPRESSION

Compression is an essential feature of all Web multimedia for a very practical reason – size. One uncompressed image file is normally several megabytes in size, and a one-minute uncompressed audio file would occupy about 9 megabytes. Uncompressed desktop video needs about 27 megabytes of data per second of video. There is simply no way to send this much data across even the biggest and fastest network without applying compression.

Compression algorithms, or methods, vary. One method identifies and removes redundancies to reduce file size: for example, for movie data that does not change from frame to frame, the algorithm stores and repeats a single instance for as long as necessary rather than recording data for each frame. Another method selectively removes data based on importance: for example, in an image file, the algorithm identifies the most-used colors and removes the remainder. Most compression algorithms are "lossy" because the removal of data degrades the image or sound quality. Compression can also introduce such "artifacts" as blocky image quality or noisy sound.

Compression algorithms have become so sophisticated that compressed and uncompressed materials are sometimes indistinguishable: some audio compression options, for example, produce near CD-quality sound. As a Web page author, however, you need to note that compression is fundamental to the task of preparing multimedia materials for the Web.

DOWNLOADING MULTIMEDIA

If you come across a potentially useful image on the Web, downloading that image onto your computer is a simple mouse-click away. The same holds true for other types of multimedia content. But this method of acquiring content for your course site has several shortcomings. First, unauthorized use of downloaded materials often violates copyright (see *Copyright and intellectual property,* below). Even if you do request permission from the author

The Computer and the Campus
An Interview with John Kemeny

Produced by EDUCOM and Dartmouth College

Requires QuickTime 4 or higher
Get QuickTime 4

Copyright 1998-2000, Dartmout
Page maintained by Academic C
Video copyright 1991, E
Used with p

Open this Link
Save As Source...
Save As QuickTime Movie...
Plug-in Settings...
About QuickTime Plug-in...

Even though it is easy to download and reuse images and other multimedia content, it's not always a good idea. Web multimedia files are low-quality since they have to be compressed. Also, downloading and using someone else's work is probably a copyright violation.

of the site, it may be difficult to determine whether he or she actually holds reproduction rights to the materials in question. Second, Web multimedia content is inherently low-quality: multimedia files small enough for Internet delivery have been compressed or otherwise reduced, compromising the materials. Downloading, for example, a Web image is likely to produce inferior results in your image composition, particularly if you need to modify the image.

Materials downloaded from Web pages are really "for consumption only." With all the compression and downsampling, or quality reduction, that must be done to make multimedia files small enough for network delivery, the files do not hold up as source material for other multimedia projects. Downloaded multimedia can be used if the materials do not need to be heavily modified for use on your pages *and* if you secure permission from the copyright holder.

Images

A picture truly is often worth a thousand words. When trying to explain something to students, how often do you reach for a paper and pencil or go to the blackboard? Often a quick sketch or outline can be just the thing to get the point across. When thinking about content for your course site, consider whether visuals would enhance your narrative: Do you find yourself wishing for a virtual pad and pencil? Could you better represent the concepts if you had supporting illustrations? Do you have photographs to accompany descriptive texts? Or are images the focus of your site?

ABOUT WEB IMAGES

The best part of Web imaging is that, in contrast with print publishing, there is no economic penalty for using images – in full color, no less – and the number of images you publish is limited only by your time and server space. And color reproduced on the computer screen is true color, whereas color in print is simulated, typically through a four-color process. Color images on the monitor are more vibrant because the color shines out from the screen, whereas color on the printed page receives its intensity from re-flected light (see Chapter 3: *Web color*). On the down side, because every monitor is different, images that look great on your monitor may look dark or washed out on another.

The biggest drawback of screen images is resolution: both the spatial di-mensions of the screen and the low resolution of computer monitors. Computer monitors are oriented horizontally, with a 4:3 ratio (640 × 480, 800 × 600, 1024 × 768). This fixed proportion can be extremely limiting if you think of the screen as a canvas: imagine Henri Matisse having only one size canvas to work on, and then only in landscape orientation.

The horizontal aspect of the screen presents design challenges, par-ticularly when display-ing vertical images.

In addition, images must share the screen with such other page elements as text and navigation links.

Main site content occupies only about two-thirds of the screen

In addition to displaying within the limited size and aspect of the standard computer monitor, content images must share the screen with site graphics and navigation links.

Added to spatial restrictions is the fact that the resolution of the computer monitor is coarse in comparison with printed materials (see Chapter 3: *Resolution on the Web*). Put simply, this means that there are fewer sample points available to represent an image on screen than in print.

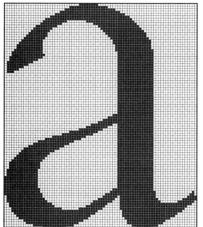

The pixel grid of the computer screen is much coarser than the halftone grid of printed images, which means there are fewer samples available to represent an image.

Enlarged type at screen resolution   Type at print resolution

As a result, images that require sharp detail in order to be understood, such as a lever on a piece of equipment or the fine outlines of a sketch, don't fare well onscreen.

Given these drawbacks, designing meaningful images for the screen can be a challenge. If you scale an image to fit the screen, you may not be able to show enough detail for the image to be useful. If you leave your image large so that the details are clear, you force users to scroll to see it all. As you gather images for your Web site, keep these limitations in mind. Choose images that fit comfortably within your page design and that do not rely on fine details to be understood. And don't get discouraged: although it may seem limited in many ways, the Web is still a great way to get images into the hands (or onto the screens) of your students.

IMAGE SOURCES

Images for your site may already be in digital format – online, on CDs, or as digital photos – or they may be in an analog format, such as a book or videotape, and need to be converted. Several methods for acquiring images for use on your site follow. Chapter 3: *Creating the site,* will show you how to work with the images once they're on the computer.

Shooting original photographs

Shooting your own photographs is an ideal way to get visual content for your course Web site. That way, you own rights to the images and can customize them to fit your pedagogical needs.

If you are taking photographs for use on your course Web site, shoot with the screen in mind. Take close shots, omitting unnecessary background detail. If your subject is too detailed – the ceiling of the Sistine Chapel, for example – consider shooting a series of close shots rather than trying to represent the subject with a single image. And shoot horizontal shots whenever possible to make best use of the 4:3 proportions of the computer display.

35mm camera. When you shoot images using a film camera, you will need to convert the images to digital files for Web use. It's a good idea to determine what method you will use before you take photographs for Web use (see *Scanning* and *Photo CD,* below). Whenever possible, scan from slides or film negatives: it's easier and yields better quality images than scanning from prints.

Digital camera. A digital camera has many benefits for Web site projects. Images can be transferred directly from camera to computer: no film, no developing costs, no delays. However, only high-end digital cameras take images whose quality rivals that of images shot on film. The low resolution and compression used by the low-priced cameras produce inferior images, and any manipulation you do – adjusting color, scaling, sharpening – will emphasize the flaws.

On the other hand, the computer screen is a low-resolution medium, so the imperfections in a low-quality digital image may be less obvious on a Web page than in a printed document, particularly if you limit your modifications to the image. If you plan to shoot your own images for Web use, consider using a digital camera. For many projects, the convenience of having images in digital format outweighs any compromises in image quality.

Use the highest quality settings available on your camera. Even if the files are large, you will have more data to work with and fewer compression artifacts to work around. And keep in mind the points outlined in *About Web images,* above: shoot closeups against a simple background whenever possible.

Scanning

One way to get images for Web use is to scan them using an image scanner. The scanning process converts an image's color samples to pixels, creating a computer reproduction that you can manipulate and save for use on your Web page. You can scan images from such sources as books, slides, postcards, and other printed media. You can even scan objects as long as they fit on the glass top of the scanner, for example, pottery shards or fabric swatches.

When scanning photographs or artwork for your Web pages, set the dimensions to roughly the size you will want on your Web page. Scan the image at medium resolution, about 133–150 pixels per inch (ppi), especially if you plan to modify the image. Though the final resolution on your Web page will be 72 ppi, you should scan at a higher resolution and then reduce the resolution *after* working with the image. Save the scans in an uncompressed format such as Photoshop or using non-lossy compression such as TIFF (Tagged Image File Format), and *always* keep your original scans (for more on images, see Chapter 3: *Working with images*).

Photo CD

If you have many images for your Web site and some money to spend, consider making a Photo CD. Photo CD is an imaging service developed by

Kodak. To use the service, you send your negatives, slides, or unprocessed film to a Photo CD service provider (check the Kodak Web site to locate a service bureau near you). The service bureau performs high-quality scanning and transfers the scans directly to compact disc, then returns your original images along with the CD containing three resolutions of each image and a printed guide with thumbnails, or small versions, of the images on the disc.

Photo CD is a feasible alternative to do-it-yourself scanning, particularly for projects that involve many images. The cost is reasonable – ($1–5 per image), the quality is better than that of a homemade scan, and the convenience is unquestionable. Photo CD is particularly useful when creating virtual reality sequences such as QuickTime VR panoramas or object models (see *Virtual reality,* below).

Note that many film processing companies can produce computer files of your images when developing film. This consumer-level service provides less quality and fewer options than Photo CD, but it also costs much less. The company will post your images on the Web for you to view and download or send you the files on disk along with your prints.

Images for purchase
Several companies sell royalty-free images or image licenses, either as a collection on CD or on a per-image basis via the Web. For most Web authors, the online purchase option is the more practical of the two. When purchasing a CD, you purchase a collection of images – say, "business and industry" or "health care" – of which only a handful of images may be germane to your subject. Online purchase enables you to purchase *only* the images you wish to use, and you can select, purchase, and begin using an image within minutes.

To purchase an image online, you search the collection for images that match your search criteria: for example, you may want images of the Parthenon, so you enter "parthenon" as your search term. You browse thumbnails of the images that match your search, mark those you wish to purchase, enter billing information, and then download the images. Many sites allow you to download low-resolution complimentary images to try out before making your purchase. The cost per image can run from a couple of dollars to several hundred, but most services offer low-resolution images licensed for Web use for about $20–40 per image.

Images from video

Video scanning is a method for capturing still frames from video for use as still images. This setup requires a video player – VHS deck, video camera, digital video camera – hooked to a computer with some sort of facility for video capture (for more on video capture hardware, see *Video,* below). In the capture process, video from the player is fed by cable to the computer's video input. You can then use software to capture individual video frames.

Images from video are of lower quality than those from a still camera. Video resolution is inherently low, and video also has a characteristic called interlacing that, though practical for video, does not work well for still images. With interlacing, the television picture is updated 60 times a second, but only every other horizontal line of the image is displayed at each update. Together these alternating frames make 30 whole frames per second. Although interlacing speeds up the display of TV video, the consequence for still images is that, because a still frame is really two blended fields, the "interlacing artifacts" that we scarcely notice on TV are glaring in a still video image.

Enlarged detail of interlacing

Interlacing artifacts can be a problem when capturing still images from video. The alternating fields are most noticeable when there is motion in the video, as here with John Kemeny's gesturing hand.

Although video scanning has its challenges, video remains a rich source for still imagery. To get the best images possible, always use the highest resolution and quality available on your hardware. A messy video grab will sometimes improve if you scale the image (make the image smaller) using image editing software such as Photoshop. You can also use Photoshop to sharpen the image (remove blur) and correct interlacing artifacts using the de-interlace filter (see Chapter 3: *Working with images*).

Jan Rune Holmevik and Cynthia Haynes: Lingua MOO

My interview with the creators of Lingua MOO took place online "in the MOO." We had virtual coffee together and chatted for about an hour and a half. While discussing their work, Jan Rune Holmevik and Cynthia Haynes showed me the books they'd written and the Web sites they've developed, and they took me on a guided tour of the MOO "facility." Jan was in Norway, Cynthia in Texas, and I in Hanover, New Hampshire. At the end of our interview, Jan emailed me the transcript of our interview, some of which is excerpted below.

A MOO is one of the many forms of communication possible on the Web. According to Jan, a MOO is "a synchronous online multiuser space. It was originally developed for online gaming and socializing purposes, but since about 1993–95 it's been used more and more for academic learning purposes." A MOO environment is different from an asynchronous online discussion because it takes place in real time. A MOO is unlike a chat because, in addition to real-time dialog, a MOO is immersive: users move around a virtual space and can build rooms and create objects. Says Jan, "A chat is functional and flat in comparison." (For a screen image from LingaMOO, see *Chat room,* above.)

> Sarah asks, "But why do you use a MOO? How do you use it in your teaching? What is a typical class session like?"
> Cynthia says, "I use MOO as a supplement to traditional teaching, and a typical class session varies, but usually in the beginning I have students discuss something as a group or in small groups. This gets them used to the environment and sets up the conditions of possibility for substantially 'different' ways of interacting. Then I get them used to viewing the MOO as their primary work environment."
> Sarah asks, "Can you say more about 'different'?"
> Cynthia says, "Different in the sense of how this space encourages more reticent students to speak up, in the sense of how this space breaks down racial and gender cues (or can). Then the class discusses how the MOO changes how we think of each other, and how 'identity' figures into how we interact."
> Jan says, "It's important to keep in mind that this is not a Web site, it's a lived space with a window to the Web."
> Cynthia nods at Jan.
> Cynthia says, "Students are encouraged to set up a space here, to build their own world and to see this as a lived space where they become part of a community."

Cynthia is assistant professor of literary studies and director of rhetoric and writing at the University of Texas at Dallas. She uses the MOO and the Web in such courses as Rhetoric, Textuality, and Technology, and Electronic Expression: Writing, Reading, and Virtuality. At the University of Bergen in Norway, Jan uses the MOO for his Digital Culture and Object-Oriented Programming courses. They started building Lingua MOO in 1995 as a pilot program for a freshman rhetoric class and now both use the MOO and the Web extensively in their teaching.

> Sarah says, "Would you give me a 'for instance' for classroom use? I am having trouble imagining how you would incorporate this into a classroom session."
> Cynthia says, "Let's say you have assigned your students some readings on sexual harassment. You want to record their discussion of the readings and have them read *that* as a follow-up, to see *how* they interacted and what they had to say."

Jan says, "Let me add to that example. In the MOO you could also easily have your students enact their discussion through role-playing and thereby engage in a deeper experience of the texts they are reading."
Sarah asks, "How would you do that?"
Jan says, "Well…by setting up a situation and have male students play females and vice versa: give them some starters and see what happens. The beauty of it all is that the students will be writing a whole lot and expressing themselves through writing without even thinking about it."

For Cynthia's rhetoric and composition courses, using the MOO has changed the way she looks at the process of writing – specifically, at how she evaluates student work.

Sarah says, "Do you notice improvement in writing?"
Cynthia says, "It depends on what you mean by writing :)….I think this kind of writing is something teachers may have trouble seeing as productive discourse, but if students can *see* how much they write, and if it *counts* as writing, which I think it should, then we begin to value other genres of writing and interactivity equally. Plus we encourage teachers to build into their assessment of the student the notion of 'activity' as much as the 'writing products' we are used to grading."

Jan has much of his class activity take place in the MOO. For example, he invited Victor Vitanza, author of *CyberReader*, to meet with his Digital Culture students in the MOO. He also uses the MOO for meetings with students. "Since they are in Norway and I live in Texas part of the year, this has worked out really well."
Because of its multidimensionality, the MOO has great advantages for online collaborative work. During our interview, for example, Cynthia and Jan "showed" me things by causing them to appear on my screen. We looked mostly at the Web sites we were discussing, but for collaborative group work, students could share and discuss such things as texts, images, and multimedia.

Sarah asks, "Why did you start with MOO? What did you see in this particular technology?"
Jan says, "interactivity"
Jan says, "it's a social learning space"
Cynthia says, "a community"
Jan says, "collaborative"
Cynthia says, "fun"
Cynthia says, "in real-time"
Jan says, "yep :)"
Sarah exclaims, "Okay, okay!"
Cynthia giggles.
Jan grins.

It *was* fun. And it is clearly a terrific tool for collaboration at a distance. In the MOO, I had a chance to meet Jan and Cynthia and see their work, and I had a transcript of our conversation to refer to later. Also, I was surprised to find that I had gained as much a sense of these people who were thousands of miles away as I would have had we been sipping coffee at the café down the street. ■

Audio

Sound is in many ways more effective than video at imparting information. Take away the audio from a video presentation, and its utility is greatly reduced. But take away the video and leave the audio, and often you can get the gist of the presentation. This is perhaps why silent movies were abandoned when soundtracks were introduced but radio remains popular.

An audio-only solution is particularly attractive when bandwidth, or network capacity, is an issue, for example, in the case that the majority of your students connect to the Web using slow modems. Audio files can be compressed far more than video while still maintaining quality. Another consideration is that audio processing is less demanding than video, so it is easier to acquire good-quality Web audio quickly. This is a plus, for example, if you want to get a recording of an invited speaker on your Web site soon after the lecture or perhaps even to broadcast the event live.

ABOUT WEB AUDIO

The characteristics of Web audio are largely defined by its delivery mechanism. As with images, audio files need to be small enough to travel across the Internet to users connecting to the Web with low-end modems. To make the files small, the quality of the audio must be degraded. Ominous though this sounds, the good news is that it really *is* possible to deliver audio materials of sufficient quality on the Web.

Here are some methods that are used to reduce file size for Web audio:

Sample rate. A sample is a measurement of the audio signal, and the sample rate, measured in kilohertz (kHz), or sample frequency, is the number of samples per second. CD-quality audio has a sample rate of 44.100 kHz. One way to reduce file size is to reduce the sample rate of the audio; much Web audio, for example, is sampled at 22.050 kHz.

Sample size. Audio sample size, or bit depth, is the number of bits used to record a sample. High-quality audio is sampled at 16 bits. Reducing from 16-bit to 8-bit reduces file size, but also seriously reduces the audio's dynamic range. Eight-bit audio is sometimes adequate for voice only, but music needs the full 16-bit sample size.

Channels. A stereo signal contains two audio channels: left and right. Although most audio formats can contain multiple channels, combining channels into a single, or mono, signal reduces file size, and because most people listen to Web audio on low-end computer speakers, the additional channels will scarcely be missed.

Compression. Applying compression can allow you to maintain higher audio settings. For example, with QDesign compression and QuickTime audio, you can deliver CD-quality audio (44.100 kHz, 16-bit, stereo) on the Web.

AUDIO SOURCES

As with images, some sources for Web audio are already in digital format and are ready for use on your Web site, whereas others are in analog format and require encoding to transfer the materials from the analog source to the computer. Still others may have been recorded on a digital device and only need to be transferred to the computer. You may even want to use audio materials that do not exist in *any* recorded format, in which case you'll need to record the materials, either using a purely digital process or some combination of analog and digital.

Recording original audio

Although not always feasible, the best possible option for acquiring audio content for your site is to record original material. Recording and encoding audio for the Web is not a walk in the park, however, so you might want to hire a professional. A full-fledged recording facility can offer the location, equipment, and know-how needed to produce professional-quality audio, though usually at a considerable price. If your institution has a media services department, find out about their services and charges. Some institutions offer free audio-visual services for course-related projects.

If you prefer (or are limited to) the do-it-yourself method, you *can* record audio with as little as the microphone that came with your computer, though the resulting quality will be as low as your expenditure. And the compromises you have to make to get audio files small enough for networked delivery will emphasize any flaws in your recording. If you plan to record your own audio, consider the following:

Location. Noise may be the most significant factor in audio capture: any background noise – a whining hard drive, passing footsteps, the hum of the ventilation system – is recorded along with your audio. Choose a recording location with minimal environmental noise.

Equipment. Of all the needed equipment, most important is a good micro-phone that fits the setting. For example, you should use a lavaliere micro-phone (the kind you hook on) to record a guest speaker. If you plan on recording directly to computer, consider purchasing a desktop audio mixer to optimize the audio before it goes into the computer. As with any con-version process, you are better off optimizing the materials at capture time than trying to fix flawed materials on the computer.

How you record the audio depends on your recording device. With many computers you can record directly to the computer by connecting a microphone (or audio mixer) to the computer's audio inputs and using software to record the signal. Another method is to use a digital video cam-era to record the audio and then transfer the digital signal to the computer (see *Video,* below). If you are recording the audio using a device such as an audiocassette or DAT (Digital Audio Tape) recorder, you will need to en-code the audio to transfer it to the computer (see *Encoding audio,* below).

Encoding audio

The method you use for encoding audio depends on how it's stored. To convert audio CD tracks to digital files on your computer, all you need is a CD drive and software such as Macromedia's SoundEdit 16 or Syntrillium's CoolEdit Pro. To convert materials on tape, you'll need to connect a player (audiocassette or DAT player, VHS deck) to the audio input jacks on your computer, and software such as Adobe Premiere. Depending on your setup, you might use a fast data transfer protocol, such as FireWire or i.LINK, and a digital device like a digital video camera to transfer the materials to the computer. For more on encoding options, see *Encoding video,* below.

When encoding audio, capture using the audio's original quality settings, normally 44 kHz, 16-bit, stereo. Check and adjust volume levels at capture time so that you don't record your audio at too low an amplitude.

Video

Of all the available media, video is the hardest to deliver on the Web. Given the challenges of delivering single images on the Web, imagine delivering video content, which is in essence multiple still images, at about 15 images *per second.* Sending uncompressed, full-screen video, at about 30 images (frames) per second, would saturate the network with as much as 27 megabytes of data per second. The challenge, then, of delivering Web-based video is the magnitude of data required to represent the content.

Until fairly recently, Web video generally meant postage stamp–sized clips lasting about 30 seconds, and the subjects were nothing too elaborate. This is because, when people first started to put video on the Web, the best available tools were those used for CD-ROM, which can support higher data transfer rates than any network. Applying these options to Web video created small, jerky movies that did not look very good, and trying to produce substantive video content under such conditions was not feasible.

Now that most content development is targeted at the Web, software developers have created new compression technologies and tools specifically for Web delivery. As a result, you can now produce substantive video materials for use on the Web.

ABOUT WEB VIDEO

The quality compromises required to deliver Web video are far greater than those with Web audio. In fact, delivering video content over the Web is sometimes simply not worth doing. If, for example, you have a video detailing a lab procedure that contains shots with fine details – say, a discussion of the measurement marks on a beaker – Web video cannot adequately display those details. Motion, too, is inferior with Web video, so you may not be satisfied using the Web to deliver content that has to do with motion, such as video illustrating dance movements or brush strokes.

The following methods are used to reduce file size for Web video:

Resolution. The resolution of video is the size of the image, and full-screen video dimensions are 640 × 480 pixels. To reduce file size, Web video is scaled down to quarter-screen (320 × 240) or smaller.

Frame rate. Movies are made up of frames, or single still images. The frame "rate" is the number of frames used to represent one second of movie, or frames per second (fps). Reducing the frame rate is a good way to reduce file size. Standard NTSC (National Television Standards Committee) video has a frame rate of 29.97 fps; Web video is normally 15 fps or fewer. Reducing the frame rate can create "jerky" video, particularly in segments containing a lot of motion.

Compression. Video compression algorithms use both temporal and spatial compression schemes to eliminate redundant information, thereby reducing the amount of data required (see *Compression,* above). Applying audio compression further reduces file size.

Duration. Obviously, a 30-second video clip is going to be smaller than an hour-long segment. This is an important consideration, especially when the video must be downloaded and stored somewhere on the user's computer: even a highly compressed hour-long movie will occupy *many* megabytes of storage. For segments longer than about 5 minutes you should use streaming delivery, which sends the video to the user in real time and does not store more than about 30 seconds of movie data on the computer at a time (see Chapter 3: *Multimedia*).

VIDEO SOURCES

Recording and encoding video is getting easier as digital video cameras become affordable, video capture hardware comes standard in new computer systems, and storage devices get faster and cheaper. Quality video capture used to require a major purchase of professional-level hardware and software. Now the essentials for capturing desktop video are standard on most entry-level computers.

By far the easiest method for creating video for Web use is to record the video using a digital video camera. With the materials stored in digital format, the video can be copied from camera to computer much as files are copied from one disk to another. If you need to convert video from analog format, such as a VHS tape, the material will require encoding.

Shooting original video

For Web use, you should shoot video that will compress well and be meaningful at the small size required for networked delivery. The first step, then, is to get access to a good camera. To compress well, the video image should contain minimal detail. Cheap cameras produce grainy video, and this unnecessary video "noise" significantly degrades compression. If you do not own your own camera, check with your media services department. It may have video cameras to loan (or may shoot your video for you). If you are planning on purchasing a video camera, consider buying a digital video (DV) camera, which captures a fairly high-quality signal that can be transferred directly to computer (see *Encoding video,* below).

Here are some recommendations for shooting Web video:

Use a tripod. For video to compress well, it should have minimal differences between frames. This is because inter-frame, or temporal, compression examines consecutive frames and stores only the differences. The fewer the differences between frames, the better the compression. Handheld shooting can cause excessive camera movement, creating needless differences between frames. Whenever possible, shoot video using a tripod, and make any camera movements as smooth as possible.

Shoot against a simple background. This is important for two reasons. First, Web video sizes must be small, usually 320 × 240 or smaller. An image that size with a lot of detail will be difficult to interpret. Also, video compression does intra-frame, or spatial, analysis by looking for similarities within each video frame and removing redundant information. Less detail means that more redundant data can be removed, which means better image compression. An interview shot in front of a crowd of people will not compress well because of motion in the background. In this case, throwing the background out of focus while shooting will simplify the image.

Don't zoom. Because you'll need to limit the frame rate to no more than 15 frames per second in order to keep file sizes down, you should avoid unnecessary motion such as zooming. To cut to a close shot, don't record while using the camera's zoom control. Instead, stop recording, change the composition of your shot, and resume shooting.

Encoding video
Once you have identified and created video source materials, you need to get them onto your computer so you can prepare them for use on your course Web site. This digital encoding process varies depending on the source medium.

Digital encoding. The easiest way to encode video content is to record the video on a digital video camera and then transfer it to computer using a high-speed connection such as FireWire and software to manage the capture. Even if you have an analog source, such as a VHS tape, you can connect a VCR to the DV camera, record the materials from the VHS tape to the camera, and then transfer the DV files via FireWire to your computer.

Many new computers have built-in FireWire capabilities (also known as IEEE 1394 or i.LINK).

Analog to digital. If your source material is analog, you will need to use either the analog-to-digital encoding scenario detailed above or connect the appropriate playback device (for example, a VCR or Hi8 deck) to your computer audio and video inputs and capture the signal using a capture card. Some computers, such as AV Macintoshes, have built-in hardware for digitizing analog audio and video. If you are planning on doing a lot of digital video, however, you should consider purchasing a high-quality video capture card. Another component for successful video capture is a hard drive fast enough to store the incoming video signal. Last, you will need software to set parameters and perform the video capture.

Your video source will need to be reduced to produce files small enough to be delivered over the Web. For this reason, it makes sense at each step of the process to work at the highest quality your circumstances will permit. Here are measures you can take at capture time that will make the transition from source to Web video more successful:

Quality. Most software offers different quality settings for video capture. These settings determine how much the video is compressed during capture. Choose the highest quality settings that your computer can capture without dropping frames. Also, when encoding video from an analog source, such as a VHS tape, use the master tape and not a copy. Every time a video copy is made, there is generation loss (a copy of a copy is three generations from the original) as each generation introduces more video noise. The more noise there is in the video signal, the more the image quality will degrade in compression.

Resolution. Capture the video at the highest resolution your computer can manage. Whenever possible, capture full-screen video (640 × 480 for a standard NTSC signal), though this may not be possible if your computer's processor and hard drive cannot process and store data fast enough. Even though your final movie will be smaller – quarter-screen (320 × 240) or smaller – you will have much more flexibility when processing the video: for example, you will be able to crop and scale the video without degrading the image quality. In fact, scaling video from a full-screen source will likely *improve* the image quality.

Although it is not truly video, virtual reality, or VR, is included here under video as part of the family of moving visuals. VR presentations provide a realistic computer-based experience of a place or object by providing images and controls that allow users to move about or otherwise manipulate their environment.

There are many methods for creating VRs. The most common is to take a sequence of photographs and use software to find the image overlap and "stitch" the images into a single continuous image. In a panoramic VR, you rotate the camera around a central point and photograph the surroundings. In an object movie, you focus the camera on the object's center and take photographs at regular positions around the object.

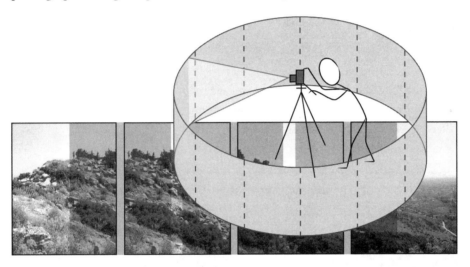

To make a panorama movie from photographs, you attach a 35mm or digital camera to a special camera mount and take photographs at regular intervals around a central, or "nodal," point. The still images are then "stitched" together using software that compares the photographs and identifies where they overlap, then merges the images into a single panoramic image.

The educational applications for VR are many, including:

Virtual walkthroughs. A strength of VR technology is that you can arrange different media – panoramas, movies, sound, still images, object movies – into one presentation. A carefully arranged VR presentation of imagery and sound can allow your students to "visit" an otherwise inaccessible location, for example, an archaeological site in another country that they cannot visit in person.

The QuickTime VR panoramas on the Classic Panos site allow students to "visit" archaeological sites in Greece and Turkey. A site plan accompanies the VR so that students can keep their bearings while moving around the site.

Object manipulation. VR object movies allow your students access to objects that are otherwise unavailable, such as museum objects that cannot be handled. A "virtual" object can be held, rotated, and viewed from many perspectives without fear of damaging the object.

This object VR movie allows site visitors to "walk around" and get eight different views of this statue entitled *Mother with Dead Son.*

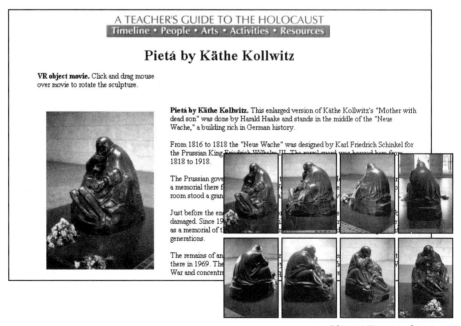

Object VR movie frames

Creating VRs is not as difficult as it would seem. The biggest challenge is getting good images to work from, not actually creating the VR movie. When developing content for your course Web site, consider VR, particularly if you have course content that should be "experienced" by your students but for whatever reason is inaccessible.

Summary

In this section we reviewed the most common media types and discussed possible applications for multimedia on a course Web site. Most Web sites have images for one purpose or another, whether they are content images or images for site graphics. Other potential forms of multimedia are audio and video content.

Questions you should ask yourself about multimedia include:

- What equipment do you have for creating multimedia? Is there a computer facility on campus? Does your media services department offer digital multimedia services? Does your department have equipment?
- What audiovisual materials do you use in the classroom that you could put on your course site? Could you record new materials and distribute them via the Web?
- Does the quality of Web-based multimedia satisfy your pedagogical needs? Given the compromises in quality required to deliver multimedia, will your materials be adequately represented on the Web?

COPYRIGHT AND INTELLECTUAL PROPERTY

Although the Web may feel like a new medium with different rules, in fact the rules are much the same. Authors of Web content have the same rights as those of other materials, and anyone who violates those rights is subject to penalty. What makes the Web different is that, in this networked environment designed for information exchange, violating copyright is so very easy: text can be selected and copied, images downloaded by way of a simple mouse-click.

But the fact that the technology makes copying and distributing works easy does not make it a right. Unless stated otherwise, those rights belong to the creator. And although in some instances the public interest outweighs the creator's rights, as in fair use, the current criteria and tests that define the classroom use of copyrighted materials as "fair" are difficult to apply to a course Web site. Unless the parameters of fair use are broadened

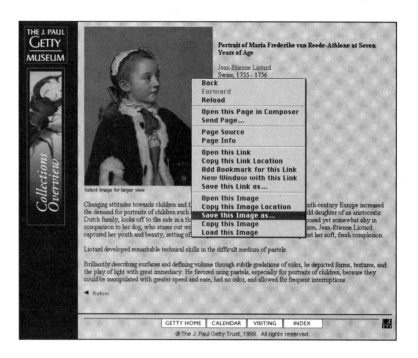

to sanction the educational use of copyrighted materials on the Web, it is best to consider your course Web site a publication and seek permission as you would in any other publishing medium.

As a Web site author, you also need to be concerned with establishing and protecting ownership of your online materials. Who owns rights to the Web-based course materials you produce, you or your institution? What controls should you implement on your site to protect your materials from infringement? And last, if you plan to publish students' work on your site, do you need to obtain their permission? You'll need answers to these questions in the early stages of your project, as they will inform your choices along the way.

Using content

There is a common misconception that if something is on the Web, then it's up for grabs. This idea originates from a combination of the technology that facilitates copying and the idea that if someone put the information on the Web, then he or she must not mind if it's appropriated. Copyright is granted to the creator of a work the moment it is "fixed in a tangible medium." Though the computer bits and bytes that compose a Web page hardly seem tangible, copyright is granted to Web authors upon creation of a page. A page needn't have a copyright notice in order to be protected by copyright law. The inclusion of a copyright notice and registration with the United States Copyright Office increases the legal ramifications should a copyright violation occur, but the rights granted under copyright law apply to a work the moment it is created, notice or no notice (see *Notice and registration,* below). This means that in most cases, when you copy and reuse materials downloaded from the Web, you infringe on the rights of the page author. It is true that often people put materials on the Web without restriction, but unless it is explicitly stated otherwise, you must assume that the materials are protected. Likewise, unauthorized use of copyrighted materials from other media, such as images from a book or video segments from a film, on your Web page is likely to be an infringement.

Educators are starting to chafe under the limits imposed by the current copyright policy. When teaching took place primarily in a controlled environment in the classroom, instructors could use copyrighted materials and meet (at least somewhat) the criteria defined in the fair use doctrine (see *Fair use,* below). When using copyrighted materials in online teaching, the environment is harder to control: use of the materials is harder to measure and control, and the visibility is far greater than in a classroom setting (that is, it's easier to get caught). Also, given people's ability to integrate content from different media into a single presentation and deliver it over the global network, educators who are using the Web want *more* access to materials, not a more restricted environment. Just as the advent of the photocopier forced changes to copyright policy, the growing use of the Internet and the Web requires that policymakers revisit copyright and fair use and revise the policy to enable teaching on the Web.

FAIR USE

Just as the rights of the creator of a work are protected by copyright, the rights of free speech and public interest are protected by the fair use doctrine, and these public rights outweigh those of the creator. The fair use doctrine is intended to serve the public good by promoting such activities as education, criticism, research, and scholarship. But even under fair use, the rights of the creator are protected by the narrowly defined criteria and tests outlined in the fair use doctrine. The definition protects the creator by ensuring that the quantity of the work used is negligible, and thus of little adverse effect to the market for the work, and that, whenever possible, permission of the creator is sought.

Four factors define fair use:

Purpose. Materials used on an academic Web site are more likely to meet this criterion than materials used on a commercial site, because the use is instructional and not for profit.

Nature of the work. Use of works that were developed for research or scholarly use is more likely to meet this criterion than works created for commercial purposes. The measure of this criterion has much to do with the expectations of the author: a professional photographer expects remuneration for use of his or her work, whereas scholars expect their work to be used for educational purposes.

Amount and substantiality. This criterion refers to both the amount – length, duration – and the qualitative measure of the materials used in relation to the whole. Even when the portion is brief – for example, the four-note theme from Beethoven's Fifth Symphony – if it is the basis of the work, then its use is not considered fair.

Market effect. In order to meet this criterion, the use has to have little or no effect on the creator's ability to make money from the work. For example, posting entire chapters of a text on the Web is not fair because it may reduce the author's potential market.

In addition, there are three "tests" to help define educational fair use:

Brevity. Specific amounts or relative portions of a work can be used for education purposes without seeking permission from the copyright holder.

Spontaneity. In some instances, the decision to use a copyrighted work may come too late to get permission before using the materials. The spontaneity test is difficult to pass for Web-based content. Although timely posting of materials may be necessary to maximize their use, if the materials remain online, the use is no longer spontaneous, and permission must be sought.

Cumulative effect. This test limits the number of times a work can be used without seeking permission from the creator. This is because, even if the quantity used is small, repeated use may harm the market for the work.

Simplified Fair Use Guidelines

Type of materials	Amount
Excerpted prose	1,000 words or 10%
Complete prose	2,500 words
Poetry	Complete poem if less than 250 words and if printed on not more than two pages 250-word excerpt from a longer poem
Illustration	1 per book or periodical issue
Music	Excerpts of no more than 10% of a complete work, provided that they do not constitute a "performable" unit

- You may not copy more than one complete work or two excerpts from the same author
- You may not copy more than three times from the same work or volume, except for newspapers or other current news publications, for which there is no limit
- You may not copy the same item from term to term
- You may not copy "consumables" such as workbooks and study guides
- Each copy you make must include a copyright notice

These amounts and guidelines are based on the multiple copying guidelines outlined in the Agreement on Guidelines for Classroom Copying and the Guidelines for Educational Use of Music

Last, there are the Fair Use Guidelines for Educational Multimedia, an interpretation of the fair use doctrine written to help educators and students act responsibly when creating multimedia projects for educational purposes. These guidelines offer more specific limits as to how much of a work can be used, under what circumstances, and for how long. The online use of copyrighted materials enabled by these guidelines effectively parallels classroom use by requiring that access to the materials be limited to classroom participants, and also limiting the length of time the materials can remain online. Though their use may mean toning down your objectives – most notably, you cannot allow non–class members to view the site, and the materials cannot stay online indefinitely – you can probably justify some unauthorized use of copyrighted materials on your course site by following these guidelines.

Simplified Fair Use Guidelines for Educational Multimedia

Type of materials	Amount
Text	10% or 1,000 words
Images	No more than 5 works from any one artist
Music	10% or 30 seconds
Motion media	10% or 3 minutes
Database tables	10% of 2,500 fields or cell entries

- You must include credit and copyright information on all copies
- Your project must include notice that the materials are included under the fair use exemption and are restricted from further use
- With restricted access, the materials may remain available for two years. On an unsecure network, you can use the materials for only 15 days

These amounts and guidelines are based on the Fair Use Guidelines for Educational Multimedia

Most of the copyrighted materials you currently use in the classroom without permission may meet the criteria and pass the tests defined above. Or the use may not be public enough to gain notice. In publishing a course Web site, however, you are making your classroom materials available for public use: the dissemination is broader, and the potential effect on the creator is greater, as are your chances of getting caught. Posting content on the Web is also more complex and time-consuming than photocopying a four-page journal article for classroom use. In the time it takes to fashion the materials for the Web, you could solicit permission from the copyright holder. Your safest bet is to show a "good faith" effort by always seeking permission, even if you post the materials before you receive a response.

The fair use doctrine has always been a subjective measure, balancing what is fair for the public against what is fair for the creator of a work. In the traditional classroom, educators have puzzled over fair use when using materials in class, creating copies of materials for classroom use, and distributing copies to students for their coursework. Now that many classroom transactions take place in the global medium of the Web, it is even harder to determine what is fair. Even the meaning of a copy is confusing on the Web: Every time a user requests a document from the Web server, are they making a copy? When you put copyrighted materials on your site, are you permitting multiple copies to be made?

Many institutions have evolved internal policies and guidelines based on an interpretation of the current law to help answer questions about what an instructor can and cannot use on an instructional Web site. Ask your institution's legal office for guidance regarding Web-based educational materials and the fair use doctrine.

HOW TO STAY LEGAL

You would probably not go through the effort and expense to create and print a poster using images you did not have permission to use. You would end up with a poster that you could not freely display without fear of penalty. Like a poster, a successful Web site is highly visible. If you include copyrighted images on your course Web site without permission, you cannot display the site freely without compromising yourself and your institution. With all the effort that goes into creating a Web site, you should be able to show and use your site without restriction. That is why you should make every effort to stay legitimate and include only materials you have the rights to use.

Ask permission. Given the unsettled questions that remain regarding copyright, fair use, and the Internet, the best strategy when you find materials you would like to use on your course site is to obtain permission from the copyright holder. This task is not always straightforward, however. On the Web, for instance, it is often hard to determine who the site author is, and often you cannot be certain that the site author is the legal owner of the materials you wish to use.

If you know who the copyright holder is, write a letter requesting permission to use the materials. Arguments that can influence your chances of using the materials include limiting access to the materials to the students in your class (see Chapter 4: *Reasons to limit access*) and a promise to remove the materials at the conclusion of the term. If you are unable to determine ownership, and the materials are critical to your project, try hiring an agent to locate the copyright holder and negotiate usage (see next entry). Otherwise, you are best off looking for other materials.

Hire an agent. Organizations such as the Copyright Clearance Center (CCC) will broker copyright transactions. To use CCC Online, you search their database for publisher's permission and fee information. If you locate materials you wish to use, you submit a permission request. Many of the titles in the database are "pre-authorized," which means if you're ready to pay the license fee, you can start using the materials immediately. For titles that need approval on a case-by-case basis, the CCC will contact the copyright holder and negotiate the transaction for you. There are several options to choose among, including the Electronic Course Content Service, which facilitates licensing for use in conjunction with online instruction.

Link to the materials. If the materials you wish to use are on the Internet, linking is a good way to offer Web-based content without violating copyright. Placing a simple link from your site to another site is not a copyright violation, so you do not need to seek permission from the site author.

Purchase rights. There are many online options for purchasing rights to use royalty-free or rights-controlled digital content. When you purchase royalty-free materials, you pay a one-time fee and can use them freely. Rights-controlled licensing usually places restrictions on how the materials can be used: for example, you may be able to license an image, but not for use on your course site home page, and only for a set time period.

Sample permission letter

[Date]
[Your name]
[Your institution]
[Your address]
[Your fax number]
[Your email address]

[Name of copyright holder]
[Address]
[Email address]
[URL]

Dear [copyright holder]:

I am on the faculty at [Your institution] and have been preparing Web-based instructional modules for use in my teaching. In the course of my research I found your outstanding materials, and I would like to be able to use them for my course site projects. I am writing to request permission to use the materials for the courses listed below. I would, of course, include full attribution with the materials. Also, if you prefer, access to the materials can be restricted to class participants.

I seek your permission to use the following materials in my [Course Name] course during the [Term] term with a class size of approximately [Number of students] students:

Item	Portions requested	Hold copyright?	Grant permission?
[Item description including URL, ISBN, Title, Author, and so on]	[Information about the portion you wish to use, such as the page URL or file name, chapter title, page numbers, and so on]	Y or N	Y or N

Please indicate above whether or not you hold copyright to the materials listed. If not, please supply contact information for the copyright holder below. If you are copyright holder, please indicate above whether or not you grant permission to use the materials. If you are granting permission, please sign below and provide the text that should appear in the credit line.

Many thanks for your time and assistance, and for your excellent materials.

Sincerely,
[Your name]

Permission to reproduce is granted for the purposes stated above.

The credit line should read as follows:

Signed: Date:

Make it yourself. Take your own photographs, record your own narration, play and record your own musical content. Working with your own content is the very best method for staying legal: you have complete control over how you use the materials.

Take from the public domain. Work that is not protected by copyright is considered to be in the "public domain." Much of what is public domain got there because it is old and the copyright has expired. There are also times when an author chooses to make materials available without restriction, as is the case with "freeware" computer programs distributed free of charge. Most government documents (pamphlets, papers, books, data, images, films) are in the public domain.

Under most circumstances, when republishing copyrighted materials, you need to include a credit line with the materials. This both provides proper attribution for the materials and affirms that you are using the materials with permission. A credit line might read something like this:

Used with permission of *The Chronicle for Higher Education,* from "Lost in Cyberspace? A Librarian Offers an Online Course on Search Engines," Kelly McCollum, February 23, 2000

Creating content
The principles of academic freedom allow educators to express their views in the classroom, and so faculty have prepared syllabi, given lectures, and conducted class discussions with little interference from their institutions. Now that courses take place in a fixed form on the Web, with substantial resource allocation, and are potential revenue sources, ownership of course materials has come into question. As the author of your course Web site, it is important that you establish ownership of the materials you produce. And as copyright holder, you need to take measures to ensure that your materials are protected.

OWNERSHIP
The ability to educate has become more lucrative in recent years, particularly in the field of distance learning. Educators can package their teaching into online courses and sell them to profit-making distributors of education. Educational institutions are waking up to the fact that their "wired"

instructors are gaining attention, and even making money, and that the institution is bearing at least a portion of the cost.

When faculty members publish journal articles for no financial gain or publish academic books with very little financial gain, the work is usually considered the property of the author. The institution provides resources – salary, computer equipment, books, research facilities – in exchange for the prestige and recognition gained by the faculty's good work.

With the increasing use of technology in teaching, the question of ownership begins to touch the classroom. For example, who owns a course? Because copyright applies to an idea that is "fixed," much of what traditionally takes place in the classroom cannot be "owned": the ideas expressed in lectures and class discussions, unless recorded somehow, are not fixed. However, more and more faculty are "fixing" their ideas as part of a course site on a Web server. Many online courses are made with extensive use of institutional resources: designers, programmers, expensive computing equipment. Some courses take place entirely online. What happens when the instructor leaves to go to another institution? Can he or she take the Web course for use in the new position? Can the college still use the online course? And what if a publisher wants to purchase the course for a distance-learning module? Who would be entitled to the revenue?

There are no simple answers to these questions. Institutions are just beginning to form policies and establish guidelines. If you are putting materials online – whether a simple course syllabus or a full-fledged online course – find out your institution's policy on ownership of online course materials. For large projects, in which many people and resources are involved, you may want to negotiate a formal agreement outlining ownership, revenue rights, and how the materials will be maintained over time. It is best to establish this agreement at the outset to protect yourself from surprises later in the development process.

PROTECTION

As a Web author you may want to take steps to ensure that your Web content is not vulnerable to infringement. To a certain extent, given the nature of the Web, the only way to protect your materials fully is not to put them on the Web. However, given that you're reading this book, you've probably decided that a Web site would benefit your teaching and are ready to take some risks. Nevertheless, you should consider some of the following options as ways to minimize your vulnerability.

Restrict access

You can restrict access to your Web pages either by providing on-campus access only or by requiring users to login before viewing your content (see Chapter 4: *Limiting access*). This method does not ensure that your content will not be copied. It is a safeguard, not a guarantee: it reduces your exposure by reducing the number of viewers at your site.

Watermarking

Watermarking is a method for attaching ownership information to visual content, such as images or video. Various watermarking methods are available, some more robust than others. Photoshop provides a method in which you register contact information with Digimarc Corporation, the company that provides the service, and are assigned a creator ID number. Before putting your image on the Web, you use Photoshop to embed the contact ID in the image. Then, when users download and open your image in Photoshop (or any other Digimarc-enabled application), they see an indicator that means that the image is copyrighted, at which time they can get your contact information using the creator ID and contact you to ask for permission to use the image. This system clearly is not foolproof: it assumes a respect for ownership, which, for someone who has already downloaded and opened an image in Photoshop, may not be a factor.

Another method is to embed a visible watermark into your visual content. An indelible mark reduces the desirability of your visual content to potential pirates because it cannot easily be removed.

Without watermark

With watermark

Disable download

We might not be having this discussion about watermarks and ways of pursuing copyright violations if the browser software didn't make it so easy to act irresponsibly. It could take someone many hours and expensive equipment to create a Web video of a laboratory procedure, but it takes only a few seconds for a user to save that video to disk. Most content displayed on a Web page is easy to pilfer. Text can be selected, copied, and pasted or saved from the file menu. The menu that displays when you hold down the mouse button over an image has a selection, "Save this Image as...," which saves the image to your computer. The QuickTime media format has a "Save as QuickTime movie..." menu choice right on the controller bar.

You can discourage or disable download on some types of content. Media files that are streamed (see Chapter 3: *Multimedia*) do not provide an easy method for saving to disk. If you are using downloadable QuickTime, you can include the KIOSKMODE attribute in your HTML code that disables the pop-down menu: <EMBED SRC="example.mov" WIDTH="240" HEIGHT="200" KIOSKMODE="true">. Or you can hide the controller (CONTROLLER="false") altogether, but users can still get the pop-down menu by holding down the mouse button over the movie image.

Standard GIF (Graphics Interchange Format) or JPEG (Joint Photographic Experts Group) image files displayed used the IMG SRC tag are hard to protect. One less than elegant method for protecting images is to display them as background graphics. Holding down the mouse button over a background graphic does not produce the image pop-down menu. This solution may work for individual content images – photographs, paintings, diagrams – but not for images that must work within a layout.

None of these methods is guaranteed to protect your work from being copied to the desktop. Savvy Web users can usually find a way to your content. These techniques just make the path a little more convoluted.

Notice and registration
Web pages are protected by copyright as soon as they are created. You do not need to display a copyright notice on your Web pages in order for them to be protected. Including notice, however, informs viewers that the work is copyrighted, which would eliminate the claim of innocent infringement in the case of copyright violation. Neither do you have to register your Web site with the U.S. Copyright Office to be protected. However, in the case of successful litigation, works registered promptly after publication are eligible for more reparations.

It is a good idea always to include a copyright notice on your Web pages and in the HTML code of your pages, not so much because it strengthens your position in case of infringement, but because it clearly defines your rights as author. Ownership on the Web is a mysterious thing: browser software makes copying so easy, and we have all been confused at times about what is and what is not legally available for copying. Including copyright notice removes this uncertainty: copying Web content that displays explicit copyright notice is considered willful infringement.

Registration of copyright is prudent for large Web projects. Consider the scope of your project: Is it something you would publish without registration in another medium? A course syllabus hardly requires registration, but the course site equivalent of a textbook is another matter. Registration of copyright is a simple matter of filling out forms and sending in a small fee (currently $30). Keep in mind that works must be registered within three months of publication to be eligible for statutory damages and attorney's fees.

Publishing student work

If you use your site to post students' work, do you need their permission? The answer is yes. Placing, for example, a student's essay on your course Web site constitutes making a copy, and reproduction rights are exclusive to the author of the work: the student. Some institutions have a policy that states that work done to fulfill course requirements is the property of the institution, in which case, because the students have already assigned rights to the institution, you do not need to secure their permission (as long as your course site is also "owned" by the institution). Your best course is to ask your legal office about the policy at your institution and how they would like you to proceed. If you need to get explicit permission from your students, work with them to draft a permission form and have students sign it before posting their materials on your Web site.

Summary

Many people assume that because information is available on the Web it is somehow free. This may be true in some cases – many people who publish on the Web do so in the spirit of sharing – but unless a statement to that effect accompanies the materials, downloading and using materials on your Web site is copyright infringement. The same applies to materials you scan from a book, capture from an audio CD, or digitize from videotape: just because the technology enables their use does not negate the rights of the creator.

After reading this section on copyright, you should have some sense of how you can respect the intellectual property rights of others when incorporating copyrighted materials on your course Web site. You should also be attending to your own property rights as a Web site author and considering methods for protecting your materials from infringement.

Questions to ask at the end of this section include:

- Are you confident that you have the rights to use the materials you plan to include on your site? If not, are you seeking permission?
- Do you know who owns the rights to the materials you create for your course Web site? If you own the rights, do you plan to register copyright?
- If you leave your institution, will you be permitted to take the course site with you?
- Do you plan to implement any of the methods described in order to protect your materials from Web pirates?

Now that you have reviewed content types, create a checklist to track the status of the content items you plan to use on your course site. List the items from your content inventory and add any new items you are considering having read this chapter.

- Texts. List the texts you plan to use on your site, and indicate the status for each item.
- Online resources. List all Web sites, databases, texts, and other materials you have located online with the resource name and URL. Note whether you intend to contact the site author. For sites that are integral to the course, provide a backup (another site, printed materials). Also list any other resources you plan to provide, such as downloadable documents, and note their availability.
- Multimedia. Itemize any media content you want to use on your site. Indicate the current location of the materials – film, tape, digital format, not yet recorded. Because acquiring multimedia content can be time-consuming, it may be wise to prioritize these items.
- Copyright. Review your Web site outline and make a checklist of the items for which you need to obtain permission. List the information you have available to describe the materials – full title, author, publisher, copyright date, ISBN (International Standard Book Number), contact information. Use the checklist to keep track of the status of your permission requests.

Sample copyright checklist			Permission letter	
Item	**Portions requested**	**Contact information**	**Sent**	**Received**
On Book Design Richard Hendel	Text of chapter 1 (pp. 9–86)	ISBN: 0-300-07570-7 Yale University Press PO Box 209040 New Haven, CT 06520-0940	X	
NYC Access Richard Saul Wurman	Scan of 2-page spread	ISBN: 0-9604858-5-6 ACCESSPRESS Ltd. 672 S. Lafayette Park Place Los Angeles, CA 90057		
Chambers for a Memory Palace Donlyn Lyndon and Charles W. Moore	Scan of 2-page spread	ISBN: 0-262-12182-4 MIT Press 5 Cambridge Center Cambridge, MA 02142-1493		
Interaction of Color Josef Albers	2 color plates	ISBN: 0-300-01846-0 Yale University Press PO Box 209040 New Haven, CT 06520-0940	X	

REFERENCES

Blatner, David, Glenn Fleishman, and Steve Roth. 1998. *Real world scanning and halftones: The definitive guide to scanning and halftones from the desktop.* 2d ed. Berkeley, Calif.: Peachpit.

Boettcher, Judith, and Rita-Marie Conrad. 1999. *Faculty guide for moving teaching and learning to the Web.* Mission Viejo, Calif.: League for Innovation in the Community College.

Carter, Mary E. 1996. *Electronic highway robbery: An artist's guide to copyrights in the digital era.* Berkeley, Calif.: Peachpit.

Cavazos, Edward A., and Gavino Morin. 1994. *Cyberspace and the law: Your rights and duties in the on-line world.* Cambridge, Mass.: MIT Press.

Gorman, Robert. 1998. Intellectual property: The rights of faculty as creators and users. *ACADEME* May–June: 14–18.

Kelsey, Logan, and Jim Feeley. 2000. Shooting video for the Web. *DV* February. http://www.dv.com/magazine/2000/0200/videoforweb0200.html (18 February 2000).

Kitchens, Susan A. 1998. *The QuickTime VR book: Creating immersive imaging on your desktop.* Berkeley, Calif.: Peachpit.

Lawrence, Steve, and C. Lee Giles. 1999. Accessibility of information on the Web. *Nature* July: 107–109. [See also http://www.wwwmetrics.com]

Lynch, Patrick J., and Sarah Horton. 1999. *Web style guide: Basic design principles for creating Web sites.* New Haven and London: Yale University Press. [See also http://info.med.yale.edu/caim/manual]

McCormack, Colin, and David Jones. 1998. *Building a Web-based education system.* New York: Wiley & Sons.

Niederst, Jennifer. 1999. *Web design in a nutshell: A desktop quick reference.* Sebastopol, Calif.: O'Reilly.

Nielsen, Jakob. 1995–2000. *The alertbox: Current issues in Web usability.* http://www.useit.com/alertbox.

———. 2000. *Designing Web usability: The practice of simplicity.* Indianapolis, Ind.: New Riders. [See also http://www.useit.com]

Schlein, Alan M. 1999. *Find it online: The complete guide to online research.* 2d ed. Edited by James R. Flowers, Shirley Kwan Kisaichi, and Peter Weber. Tempe, Ariz.: Facts on Demand. [See also http://www.deadlineonline.com]

Simpson, Ron. 1998. *Cutting edge Web audio.* Upper Saddle River, N.J.: Prentice Hall.

Sullivan, Danny. 1996. *Search engine watch.* http://www.searchenginewatch.com.

Talab, R. S. 1999. *Commonsense copyright: A guide for educators and librarians.* 2d ed. Jefferson, N.C.: McFarland.

Tate, M., and Jan Alexander. 1996. Teaching critical evaluation skills for World Wide Web resources. *Computers in Libraries* December: 49–55. [See also http://www2.widener.edu/Wolfgram-Memorial-Library/webeval.htm]

Terran Interactive. 1995–99. *Media Cleaner Pro 4 User Manual.* San Jose, Calif.: Terran Interactive. [See also http://www.terran-int.com]

———. 1999. *How to produce high-quality QuickTime.* San Jose, Calif.: Terran Interactive. [See also http://www.terran-int.com/QuickTime/Article]

United States Copyright Office. 1999. *Copyright basics.* Washington, D.C.: Library of Congress. [See also http://www.loc.gov/copyright]

Williams, Robin. 1998. *The non-designer's Web book: An easy guide to creating, designing, and posting your own Web site.* Berkeley, Calif.: Peachpit.

Zinsser, William. 1998. *On writing well: The classic guide to writing nonfiction.* 6th ed, revised and updated. New York: HarperReference.

3 Creating the site

It is simplicity that is difficult to make.
– Bertolt Brecht

THE TASK OF CREATING A WEB SITE can be approached in many ways, and the success of each method may have more to do with one's working style and preferences than with methodological effectiveness. What is certain, however, is that you must have an approach. Web sites that are built page by page, without a unifying design and structure, lack coherence and are hard to maintain. The approach outlined here is similar to building a house: you move systematically from designing to framing to finishing. To create a Web site using this method, first you create a page design template for your pages and then you use the template to construct a framework for the site. Once the framework is solidly in place, you can add the Web site content.

This chapter offers a basic approach to setting up a Web site, as well as guidance and techniques for laying out pages and effectively integrating text, images, and multimedia. The method you use to create your site will depend on the software tool you choose. If, for example, you are using courseware to create your Web site, you may have little control over page layout, in which case the techniques outlined in the section on page design may not apply. Or, as another example, the method used to put text and graphics on a page will vary depending on whether you're using a visual Web editor or writing your own HTML code. Thorough coverage of the "how-tos" for each tool is beyond the scope of this book, but the general approach and techniques laid out here are generally applicable. For suggestions of useful how-to books and online guides, see the Bibliography.

ESTABLISH A PAGE DESIGN
The first step in site creation is to decide on a design approach. Here you establish the visual identity and logical screen layout that you will use throughout your course Web site.

Page design serves two important functions: first it should engage readers, and once it has captured their attention, it should help them make their way through the information. Engaging the reader means making your pages visually appealing: a page with nothing more than a solid block of text is not inviting, nor is one cluttered with overly bold graphics and text. In the first case the eye is repelled by a lack of contrast, in the second it is overwhelmed by too much contrast and a lack of organization. An appealing document attracts the reader's eye by providing enough contrast to make the document interesting while conveying a solid visual organization.

A well-designed Web page has just enough contrast to be inviting and convey document structure, but not so much as to appear cluttered and disorganized.

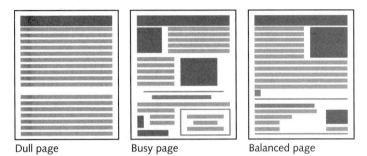

Dull page   Busy page   Balanced page

Once you have captured the reader's attention, you will need to employ various graphic design devices to help users navigate your document. Contrast and emphasis direct the reader's attention by prioritizing the information on the page. Space, alignment, and proximity define relationships among page elements such as text and graphics. Applying these devices consistently makes the reader's passage through the information predictable.

Idiosyncrasies of Web design

The Web has characteristics that at first glance may seem untenable to anyone who wants design control over their documents. When publishing on the Web, you are working in a diverse environment in which the actual look of your pages depends on the user's hardware and software configuration. You are also working with a fairly primitive design tool – HTML – which was intended to specify the structure of documents, not their appearance. Thus, if you want a measure of control over page layout, you will need to use HTML in ways it was not originally designed for. You must also be prepared to relinquish some control to your users and create flexible designs that will work in a variety of settings.

STRUCTURAL VERSUS VISUAL LOGIC

Many Web pages are not well designed. This is not necessarily because Web authors are inept or have no design sense. The fault lies more with the medium than with Web page creators. Hypertext Markup Language, was written to describe document structure in the abstract. The idea behind HTML was to divorce content structure from visual design, so that documents could be viewed on any computer system using any browser software without relying on such visual features as fonts and screen size for readability. Also, because this structural description is part of every HTML document, Web pages are "machine-friendly": computers can "read" HTML documents to compare and analyze texts, allow search engines to catalog pages, and accommodate visually impaired users. Because of structural markup, you have *some* chance of locating relevant pages from the billions of pages on the World Wide Web.

The trouble with a purely structural document description is that communicating information involves more than information alone. Communication also involves supplying visual cues that define relationships and establish hierarchies of importance. The framers of HTML paid only incidental attention to visual structure, designating such things as different point sizes for headings and an indent for bulleted lists. Unfortunately, although HTML's tools for structural markup are adequate, its visual characteristics are exaggerated – too big, too bold – and produce clumsy-looking documents in which everything is emphasized and nothing stands out. For this reason, Web authors who are conscientious and stick with straight HTML – defining document structure using basic HTML tags – cannot help but produce poorly designed pages.

DEFINE YOUR OBJECTIVES

Now it's time to examine your motivation for creating a course Web site and to develop and refine your ideas within the context of what's possible in your situation. The Web can enhance learning or ease the burden of administering a course in many respects. Take time now to define your purpose for creating a course site - what challenges you are hoping to meet, what tasks you are hoping to simplify - and how you intend to combine the Web and the classroom.

Goals and objectives

You may have embarked on this project because a colleague is having great success with his or her course site and you hope to achieve similar results. Or maybe your institution is requiring that all courses have Web sites or your students are demanding Web access to course materials. Or perhaps you see the Web as a solution to a teaching challenge you've been wrestling with for years. Whatever the motive, now is the time to clarify your goals and objectives for using the Web in your curriculum.

Look around

One of the best ways to define your Web teaching approach is to look at other teaching sites. Although some course Web sites are not open to the public, many are, which means you can peek into online classrooms and see how others are using the Web to teach. Your impressions of other teaching sites will help you form your own approach.

Explore the Web at other institutions to locate course sites in your discipline, or any instructional sites that seem to share your goals. Use your own critical thinking to evaluate the sites: identify where they succeed and where they fail. Look for new ideas or approaches you may be able to incorporate into your own online method. Bookmark those sites that you find particularly effective. Remember to evaluate what the site offers, not its aesthetics. Last, consult colleagues at your institution who have experience using the Web to teach. Ask them to demonstrate their Web-based materials and explain their approach. Such demonstrations are likely to stimulate your ideas.

Ask questions

Many questions need to be addressed before you develop your own site. The answers will guide your development efforts.

Audience profile

- What hardware and network connections are your students working with?
- What software are they using?
- What is their comfort level with technology?
- Do they expect Web access to course materials?

A Web page that uses purely structural HTML is a poorly designed document. Excessive white space makes it hard to see the relationships between items. And the many big and bold items obscure the relative importance of the page elements.

Most Web authors who care about visual design do not follow standard structural markup when designing Web pages. In fact, once graphic designers discovered the Web, they shifted the emphasis from structural to physical markup – using HTML codes to describe physical aspects of a document as opposed to document structure. For example, in most browsers the visual properties of a first-level heading in HTML using the <H1> tag are big and bold with a large margin above and below the text.

Plan your site

The success of your Web site depends as much on how well you organize your content as on the content you offer. A jumbled, incoherent presentation of materials is not likely to be popular with students, no matter how valuable the content. And Web sites, because they are by nature works in progress, soon become unmanageable when created ad lib. Without a clear outline of your content from the start, you may find yourself with an unruly collection of pages you cannot update and maintain. A careful review and classification of your content can be painstaking work, but the rewards are better site usability and ease of maintenance.

From a design standpoint, this heading is all wrong. The type is too large and heavy, and the heading is not close to the text it describes. The purpose of a heading is to provide a landmark so that readers scanning a document can locate relevant sections. To do this well, the header text must be close to the section it heads and must have *just enough* contrast for it to be differentiated from the body text and other page elements. In a complex document, headings of different sizes and weights must work to provide a visual hierarchy that reflects the information hierarchy contained in the document.

Adhering to strict HTML has many benefits: pages index better with search engines and can be accessed and read by all users and all devices. Indeed, compliance with HTML standards has become an "issue" because noncompliance may exclude certain users' access to information (visually impaired users, for example, will have difficulty "reading" Web pages that do not use standard HTML). However, if your goal is to control the design of your Web pages, you will have to leave behind many of the structural tags and concentrate on physical markup. For example, instead of using heading tags (<H1>, <H2>, <H3>, and so on) to define your visual hierarchy, use physical type styles to set the font face, size, and weight of the headings.

It is important to note in this discussion that a somewhat recent specification, Cascading Style Sheets, or CSS, is intended to address the design inadequacies of structural markup. Cascading style sheets work with HTML structural tags, which means that you can format your pages using strict HTML and then use style sheets to define the physical characteristics of the elements: for example, you can set all your <H1> tags to be bold, 12 point,

DEFINE YOUR OBJECTIVES

Now it's time to examine your motivation for creating a course Web site and
refine your ideas within the context of what's possible in your situation. The
enhance learning or ease the burden of administering a course in many respec
now to define your purpose for creating a course site - what challenges you
meet, what tasks you are hoping to simplify - and how you intend to combi
the classroom.

Goals and objectives

You may have embarked on this project because a colleague is having great s
or her course site and you hope to achieve similar results. Or maybe your in
requiring that all courses have Web sites or your students are demanding We
course materials. Or perhaps you see the Web as a solution to a teaching cha
been wrestling with for years. Whatever the motive, now is the time to clari
objectives for using the Web in your curriculum.

Structural markup

```
<!DOCTYPE HTML PUBLIC "-//W3C//DTD HTML 4.0 Transitional//EN">
<HTML>
<HEAD>
<TITLE>Structural Markup</TITLE>
</HEAD>
<BODY>

<H1>DEFINE YOUR OBJECTIVES</H1>
<P>Now it's time to examine your motivation for creating a course Web site and
to develop and refine your ideas within the context of what's possible in your
situation. The Web can enhance learning or ease the burden of administering a
course in many respects. Take time now to define your purpose for creating a
course site - what challenges you are hoping to meet, what tasks you are
hoping to simplify - and how you
intend to combine the Web and the classroom.</P>

<H2>Goals and objectives</H2>
<P>You may have embarked on this project because a colleague is having great
success with his or her course site and you hope to achieve similar results.
Or maybe your institution is requiring that all courses have Web sites or your
students are demanding Web access to course materials. Or perhaps you see the
Web as a solution to a teaching challenge you've been wrestling with for
years. Whatever the motive, now is the time to clarify your goals and
objectives for using the Web in your curriculum.</P>
```

DEFINE YOUR OBJECTIVES

Now it's time to examine your motivation for creating a course Web site and
refine your ideas within the context of what's possible in your situation. The
enhance learning or ease the burden of administering a course in many respec
now to define your purpose for creating a course site - what challenges you
meet, what tasks you are hoping to simplify - and how you intend to combi
the classroom.

Goals and objectives

You may have embarked on this project because a colleague is having great s
or her course site and you hope to achieve similar results. Or maybe your in
requiring that all courses have Web sites or your students are demanding We
course materials. Or perhaps you see the Web as a solution to a teaching cha
been wrestling with for years. Whatever the motive, now is the time to clari
objectives for using the Web in your curriculum.

Physical markup

```
<!DOCTYPE HTML PUBLIC "-//W3C//DTD HTML 4.0 Transitional//EN">
<HTML>
<HEAD>
<TITLE>Physical Markup</TITLE>
</HEAD>
<BODY>

<FONT FACE="Times New Roman">
<FONT SIZE="+1"><B>DEFINE YOUR OBJECTIVES</B></FONT><BR>
Now it's time to examine your motivation for creating a course Web site and to
develop and refine your ideas within the context of what's possible in your
situation. The Web can enhance learning or ease the burden of administering a
course in many respects. Take time now to define your purpose for creating a
course site - what challenges you are hoping to meet, what tasks you are
hoping to simplify - and how you intend to combine the Web and the
classroom.<BR><BR>

<B>Goals and objectives</B><BR>
You may have embarked on this project because a colleague is having great
success with his or her course site and you hope to achieve similar results.
Or maybe your institution is requiring that all courses have Web sites or your
students are demanding Web access to course materials. Or perhaps you see the
Web as a solution to a teaching challenge you've been wrestling with for
years. Whatever the motive, now is the time to clarify your goals and
objectives for using the Web in your curriculum.<BR><BR>
```

The visual characteristics of document elements largely cannot be controlled using a purely structural HTML description. To control headings, for example, you must use physical markup tags to define the font size and weight of the section headings.

Times New Roman. However, at the current time, full use of CSS is limited by inconsistent and incomplete browser implementations.

Given the goals of this section – to establish an inviting page design and a visual hierarchy of importance – strict adherence to HTML is not an option. Thus, we will not work toward structural purity but instead focus on creating effective page designs that work across platforms and browsers. Until new technologies such as CSS mature and can be used more fully, producing polished Web pages means drawing techniques from a mixed bag of strict HTML, CSS, adaptations, workarounds, and compromises.

VARIABILITY

Although creating a printed document – particularly one that uses color – involves many unknowns, once that document is printed the guesswork ends: for good or bad, when you mail your flyer or hang up your poster you know that everyone who sees it sees the same thing. One of the hardest aspects of designing Web documents is that there is no way to nail down your design so that all viewers have the same view of your pages. The Web was designed so that users could customize their view of documents: for example, users can set their preferred font for reading comfort and resize a document's width to make full use of their monitor's dimensions. Under this model, the importance of the user's preferences outweighs those of legibility, readability, and aesthetics, because a customized view can easily obscure design conventions. If, for example, a user chooses fuchsia as his or her preferred background color, the legibility of the documents will be significantly impaired.

Users can set their Web viewing preferences to override many of your design choices. In this example, the user has chosen to view pages using a preferred font and background, text, and link colors, and has asked the browser not to load style sheets or images.

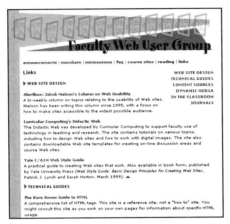

Actual page design

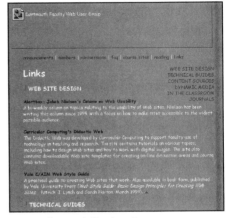

Page with user-defined preferences

The trick, then, when designing a Web page is to maintain enough control over the layout to communicate your message effectively. Because you cannot predict the setup of each user, you must create a flexible design that works across configurations. To do this, you first need to understand the variables that influence how a Web document is displayed.

Screen size. Computer monitors come in varying sizes, typically from 13 to 21 inches. The physical dimensions of a computer monitor are not the primary determinant of screen size, however, because a single monitor can display at different resolutions. For example, a 17-inch monitor can be set to display the standard 13-inch monitor resolution of 640 × 480 pixels. Indeed, many computers come configured to display at 13- or 14-inch settings, and some users do not realize that they can increase their monitor's resolution.

Color. Although it is safe to assume that most users have color monitors, the number of those available colors varies from 256 to 17 million. As with screen resolution, many users have the minimum color settings, not realizing that higher settings are available. Also, colors do not display consistently on different monitors and platforms. For example, images that look good on a Macintosh look dark on Windows, while images that work on a Windows display look washed out on a Mac.

Screen clutter. Web documents must share screen space with other interface elements from the operating system and browser software – menus, buttons, and scroll bars. Depending upon the user's set preferences, system and browser clutter can occupy as much as 10 percent of the screen's real estate.

Window size. A standard Web page layout will adapt to fill the user's browser window. This means that when a user resizes the browser window, page elements such as text and images reflow to fill the new dimensions. There is no way to predict how users will have their browser window sized when they visit your Web page.

User preferences. Browser software allows users to customize their view of the Web. For example, users can define the font used to render Web page text. Even if you program your pages to use a specific font, your design could be overruled by the user's browser preferences, which means that a page carefully designed using 12-point Times New Roman could be displayed in 24-point Comic Sans.

Browser inconsistencies. In their battle to gain the largest user base, the major browsers have differed in their implementation of HTML. As a result, an HTML tag that displays one way in one browser can look quite different in another. Browser developers have also developed propriety extensions to HTML – tags that are not part of the HTML standard but that add desired functionality for Web authors. These include such features as the MULTICOL Navigator tag for creating column layouts and the BGSOUND tag in Internet Explorer to add a background sound that plays automatically when a user visits a page.

Fonts. Web pages display using fonts that reside on the user's computer. Thus, you cannot use a nonstandard font such as Garamond or Gill Sans to lay out your Web pages and expect that all users will have that font installed in their system. For consistent display, you need to choose from the limited list of standard cross-platform fonts (see *Type,* below).

With so many variables, there is simply no way to have total control over how your Web page will look when displayed in a user's browser window. Some designers, in an effort to gain control of the medium, develop pages that are so precious that only a select audience can view them. You need to take into account the variability of the Web and to design flexible documents that are legible and accessible to all users. In what follows we will cover methods for ensuring that your Web documents display at their best advantage to the widest audience.

Layout grid

The primary purpose of a layout grid is to establish a visual framework for your information. Design grids underlie most well-designed publications, and though the tools for Web document design are much less flexible than those used for print or multimedia authoring, it is still possible to create effective layouts using HTML. Pages that are created ad lib with no underlying structure are a jumble of text and graphics – hard to make sense of and not inviting to the eye. A well-implemented layout grid produces a balanced-looking page and provides visual cues about the hierarchy of importance for the information.

An underlying design grid brings order to a page by delineating elements and establishing consistent lines and divisions.

No grid   Page with layout grid

TABLES FOR LAYOUT

If you simply place a block of text on a Web page, the width and flow of the text block varies depending on the dimensions of the viewer's browser window. Whenever the user resizes the window, the text reflows to fill the new dimensions. This "feature" of the browser is a "bug" when it comes to Web page design. To truly *design* a document – arrange text, images, and graphics on a page according to typographic conventions – you need to be able to create a stable layout.

Currently, the only way to establish a layout grid is by using HTML tables, though Cascading Style Sheets, once fully and consistently implemented by the browser software, will provide much-needed layout control. Tables were originally developed to present rows and columns of tabular information. Once graphic designers started creating Web pages, they co-opted tables and put them to use as a tool for page layout. By placing page elements into table cells and then making the table invisible, they could control such things as placement, white space, and alignment. Today the use of tables for page layout is widespread. Indeed, most WYSIWYG design tools allow you to position text and other elements on a page and the software generates the invisible tables that render the layout.

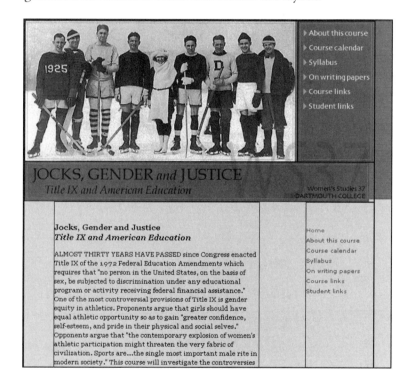

To position elements on a Web page, use HTML tables to construct a layout grid for the page, as in this example shown with the borders of the underlying table visible. The grid allows for control over the positioning and alignment of page elements and also limits the line length of the main text column.

Line length

A common problem on Web pages is that the text line length, or *measure,* is too wide for comfortable reading. On a large monitor where the text flows to fill the width of the browser window, line length can become unmanageable. When reading a block of text, the eye moves from the left margin to the right and then jumps back to the left margin to begin the next line. If the distance from left margin to right is too great, the eye must make a big shift to return to the left margin, and in this trek from left to right, the reader can easily lose track of the beginning of the next line. Keeping your line length to no more than 75 to 80 characters on a line will prevent reading from becoming physically uncomfortable and tiring.

Putting text into a table cell allows you to designate a width for a text block. Given the variables detailed above (see *Variability,* above), it is not possible to have full control over line lengths, but limiting the text cell width to about 360 to 400 pixels should result in a comfortable measure.

Space

One of the hardest things to control on a basic Web page is space. For example, the browser defines the amount of space before and after a section heading, and that amount is often too much to show the connection between the heading and the paragraph that follows. Good graphic design requires the careful application of space to distinguish related from unrelated page elements and to add contrast and visual interest. Control over space is essential to providing the visual cues that help readers grasp how a document is organized.

You can use tables to define page margins, columns, and gutters (the space between columns) and to associate related page elements.

You can use invisible tables to control space on the page. In this example, in addition to defining the page sections, tables are used to create gutters, for instance, between the navigation column and the main text block. Tables are also used for the hanging indent on the *Science* citation and to indent the section navigation links.

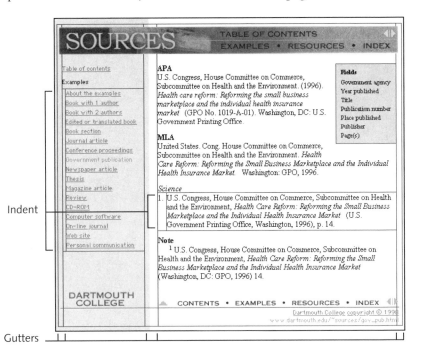

Types of layout tables

Like text, tables expand and collapse to adapt to the dimensions of the browser window. This flexibility means that Web users can customize their view of a document to make full use of their monitor dimensions or simply set a comfortable window size. It also means that Web designers who adopt tables hoping to control their layouts have to work with a tool that is flexible by default. One approach is to create designs that work in a flexible setting. Another approach is to design tables that adhere to a fixed layout grid. The best method is to create a combination layout using both fixed and flexible tables, so that you control aspects of the page while making full use of the available screen space.

Flexible. Tables need no special definition in order to be flexible. With no dimensions specified, tables will automatically size to the minimum dimensions needed to accommodate their contents.

Also rate the item for feasibility: for example, a video segment from a VHS tape of the movie Amadeus will have a low feasibility ranking because of copyright restrictions. Last, rate the item's availability: the above example would also rank low for availability because the content would have to be digitized and processed before it could be made available on the Web.

Item	Description	Priority	Feasibility	Availability	Comments
Course information	General course information, including hours and meeting location, information about the instructor and office hours, grading policies, etc.	1	1	1	Text currently in Word format
Course schedule	A weekly outline of the class topics and activities	1	1	1	Text currently in Word format
Assignments at-a-glance	A calendar showing when assignments are due	3	3	3	Not sure if program is available for this feature: check with computing support
Required reading	A list of the required readings for the course and the dates due	1	1	1	Text currently in Word format
Lecture notes	PowerPoint presentations	2	1	2	Not sure how to do this on the Web
Illustrations	Scans of print materials used as example sessions				Many of these items are under copyright: would cause site
Links	An annotated list of links to all sites us discussion				
Critiques	Description of Web site critique assign where students can post links and their				
Discussion	Class discussion area				
Portfolio	Links to student projects				

Having completed this step, you may want to revise your cont and leave all content items you are committed to including, eith

for example, a video segment from a VHS tape of the movie Amadeus will have a low feasibility ranking because of copyright restrictions. Last, rate the item's availability: the above example would also rank low for availability because the content would have to be digitized and processed before it could be made available on the Web.

Item	Description	Priority	Feasibility	Availability	Comments
Course information	General course information, including hours and meeting location, information about the instructor and office hours, grading policies, etc.	1	1	1	Text currently in Word format
Course schedule	A weekly outline of the class topics and activities	1	1	1	Text currently in Word format
Assignments at-a-glance	A calendar showing when assignments are due	3	3	3	Not sure if program is available for this feature: check with computing support
Required reading	A list of the required readings for the course and the dates due	1	1	1	Text currently in Word format
Lecture notes	PowerPoint presentations	2	1	2	Not sure how to do this on the Web
Illustrations	Scans of print materials used as examples during class sessions	3	3	3	Many of these items are under copyright: would course site use be permitted under fair use? How do I get them

If you simply place text in table cells without specifying dimensions, the table will size to accommodate its contents and automatically adjust to fill the browser window.

Although this random approach works well for tabular content, tables used for layout normally require width specifications in order to function as a page grid. Flexible layout tables use percentage values to adapt the page to the browser window while retaining the proportions of the layout.

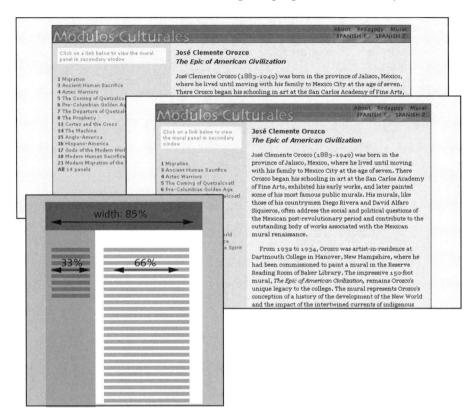

One of the greatest challenges of Web design is to construct flexible layout tables that adhere to design conventions but also adapt to a variety of displays. A major drawback of using a flexible layout is that it is hard to preserve a comfortable text line length. Another challenge is making sure when page elements move around on the page that the overall visual organization of the page is not lost.

Fixed. In a fixed-width layout table the columns are defined using absolute measurements. This type of table is "fixed" because it will not reflow to fill the width of the browser window.

Putting your content into a fixed-width table means that your page layout will be stable no matter what size the user's monitor or browser window is. Designing in a stable environment means that you can define where elements appear on the page and have greater typographic control over such factors as line length and spacing.

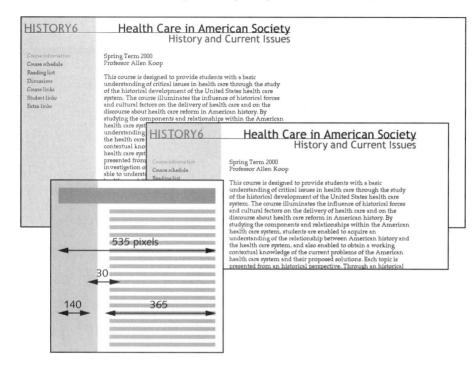

Fixed-layout tables defined using pixel values remain stable no matter how the browser window is sized.

Although the control offered by fixed-width tables is advantageous in many ways, there are also disadvantages. On a small monitor, a too-wide table means that parts of the page are positioned offscreen, and users must scroll horizontally to see the entire page. On a large monitor, fixed layouts positioned against the left margin look unbalanced against the blank right portion of the browser window.

Combination layouts. The trend in Web page design is to fashion page grids that are both fixed and flexible. This method produces pages that contain stable page elements but fill the screen regardless of monitor or window size. There are different ways to create combination layout tables, one of which is to define absolute values for elements that need to be stable, such as the navigation column, and leave the remaining table cells, such as that of the text block, undefined.

By combining flexible and fixed tables, you can create a layout that adapts to fill the user's browser window but where elements that need to be a certain width, such as the navigation column, remain fixed.

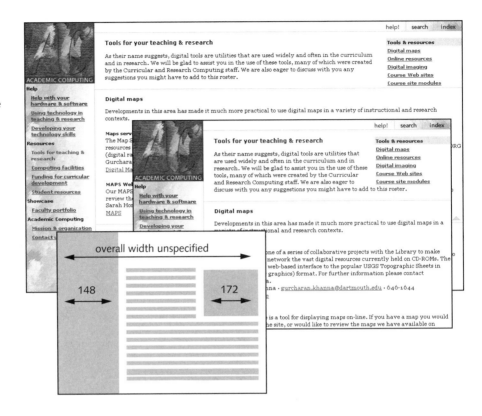

To use this approach, you have to be prepared to give up control over some elements on the page. In the example above, the text column is flexible: it reflows to fill the space. Because the exact positioning of elements in the text block is less crucial to the design, the only real compromise is that you cannot control line length. Elements that do require absolute positioning, such as the navigation column and the gutter between the navigation column and text, remain stable on the page.

In summary, if you use fixed tables for page layout you can be sure of where page elements will appear, but your pages will look unbalanced on large monitors (you can remedy this somewhat by centering the layout table on the page). If you use flexible tables, you will not have control of positioning or line lengths because undefined tables resize to fill the display. The best approach is to combine methods and put elements that require absolute positioning in fixed table cells and allow the remainder to expand and collapse to fill the browser window.

PAGE DIMENSIONS

Two main concerns when establishing a layout grid for your Web pages are how the materials will look onscreen and how they will look when printed. It is worthwhile to note that, as the Web moves onto portable devices and into the living room, Web designers will have to design for such devices as handheld organizers and cellular telephones, as well as for the television screen. Here, however, we will focus on mainstream Web devices: the computer screen and, secondarily, the printed page.

Safe areas

Designing for a varied audience means that you must make sure your page design works on all monitor sizes. Although some users with large monitors may grumble if your design does not fully use the screen, you should not exclude users by designing pages that will not display properly on small monitors.

Be sure to design flexible pages that display well on all monitors and, for pages that are likely to be printed, that print easily. To accomplish this, you'll need to use a flexible layout and keep all images within the safe area dimensions detailed below.

Screen. Designing for the "lowest common denominator" monitor dimensions of 640 × 480 pixels remains the safest route if you want to ensure that your layout fits on all monitors (if scroll bars and system and browser interface elements are taken into account, the actual screen-safe dimensions are 595 × 295). Web authors often make the mistake of designing pages that don't fit on a standard monitor. Designs that exceed the width dimension force users with small monitors to scroll horizontally as well as vertically to see the full layout.

If you are using a fixed layout for your page grid, make sure that the table width does not exceed the screen safe-area dimensions detailed below. Also, when designing graphics for your pages, keep your design within the safe-area dimensions. If you are using flexible tables, you

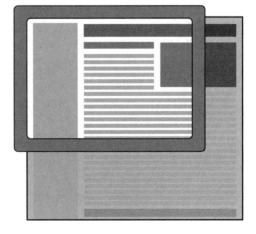

A common mistake is to design page layouts that look great on large monitors but cannot be easily viewed on smaller monitors.

needn't worry about the pages fitting on small monitors, because they will automatically adjust to accommodate different monitor sizes (as long as the graphics are not too wide).

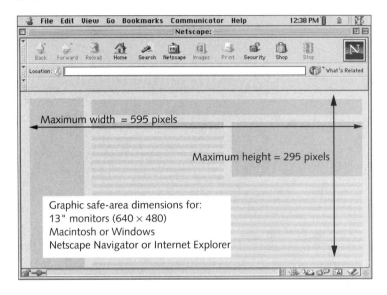

Print. Pages designed to make full use of screen real estate often fare poorly when printed using a standard vertical print layout. When printed, Web pages that use a wide layout grid normally lose a portion from the right side of the page, and the missing content from the right margin is printed on additional pages. In this case, the only way to obtain a readable printout is to scale down the page, which reduces the readability of the printed text.

Flexible pages print fine, as long as page graphics do not exceed the print-safe dimensions detailed below. The browser automatically adjusts the layout to fit on standard letter-sized paper. If you are using a fixed layout, however, you will need to limit the width of your tables and graphics to fit within the print-safe dimensions (535 pixels wide).

Printing may not be a primary concern for many of the pages in your course Web site. Students are not likely, for example, to print pages from online discussion, but they may wish to print lecture notes, articles, or the course syllabus. For lengthy documents or any documents that you expect will be read offline, design the pages so that they print properly. (If designing to accommodate both screen and print becomes unwieldy, consider offering a link to an easy-to-print version.)

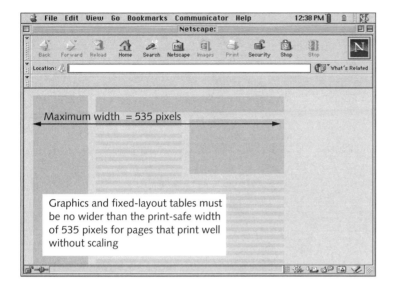

If you think your pages are likely to be printed, design your pages to print well without scaling. Make your graphics no more than 535 pixels wide, and if you are using fixed-width layout tables make sure the table width does not exceed the print-safe dimensions.

Within the browser window:

Maximum width = 535 pixels

Graphics and fixed-layout tables must be no wider than the print-safe width of 535 pixels for pages that print well without scaling

Vertical design

It is also important to design for vertical screens of information. Be sure your navigational links and document summary appear within the safe height dimension, because this is what the reader sees as the page is loading. Users should be able to determine what the page is about and where else they can go without having to wait for the page to load completely.

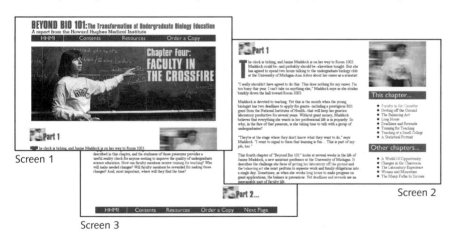

Screen 1

Screen 2

Screen 3

This article is broken up into three "screens." The first screen provides site navigation options and establishes the subject and tone of the document. The second screen begins the text and offers links to related pages. The final screen contains the page footer with site links and a link to the next page of the document.

Site graphics

Signature graphics give a Web site its unique identity. A site that consists only of text – text links, textual content, text titles and headers – has no visual identity to set it apart from other text-based sites and no distinguishing "look and feel" to establish its tone. A text-only site is a collection of pages with no visual similarity that must assert its identity through content alone.

Without some sort of graphical interface, basic text pages lack any visual uniqueness to set them off from other text-based pages.

DEFINE YOUR OBJECTIVES

Now it's time to examine your motivation for creating a course Web site and to develop and refine your ideas within the context of what's possible in your situation. The Web can enhance learning or ease the burden of administering a course in many respects. Take time now to define your purpose for creating a course site - what challenges you are hoping to meet, what tasks you are hoping to simplify - and how you intend to combine the Web and the classroom.

Goals and objectives

You may have embarked on this project because a colleague is having great success with his or her course site and you hope to achieve similar results. Or maybe your institution is requiring that all courses have Web sites or your students are demanding Web access to course materials. Or perhaps you see the Web as a solution to a teaching challenge you've been wrestling with for years. Whatever the motive, now is the time to clarify your goals and objectives for using the Web in your curriculum.

Look around

One of the best ways to define your Web teaching approach is to look at other teaching sites. Although some course Web sites are not open to the public, many are, which means you can peek into online classrooms and see how others are using the Web to teach. Your impressions of other teaching sites will help you form your own approach.

Explore the Web at other institutions to locate course sites in your discipline, or any instructional sites that seem to share your goals. Use your own critical thinking to evaluate the sites: identify where they succeed and where they fail. Look for new ideas or approaches you may be able to incorporate into your own online method. Bookmark those sites that you find particularly effective. Remember to evaluate what the site offers, not its aesthetics. Last, consult colleagues at your institution who have experience using the Web to teach. Ask them to demonstrate their Web-based materials and explain their approach. Such demonstrations are likely to stimulate your ideas.

By contrast, a well-designed graphical interface that uses a consistent set of site graphics establishes the site's unique purpose and identity. Graphics add visual interest to the page and set the tone for your materials. Applied consistently, site graphics unify the pages in the site. And navigational graphics – graphics with linked "hot spots" – let users move around your site with ease.

The signature look of *Kairos* is applied consistently throughout the different sections of the site.

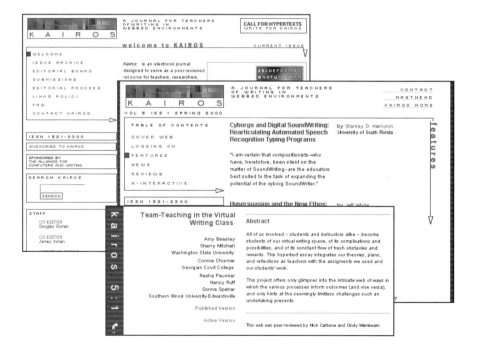

In this section we will cover the different types of site graphics and their purpose and function. The section below on adding image content (*Working with images*) has more information about Web images but is directed at modifying images for use as site content, not at graphic design. For details about designing Web site graphics, consult the sources listed in the Bibliography under *Multimedia*.

HEADERS

A Web page header is the top area of a page that normally displays the site title and primary site navigation options. A graphical page header adds more visual interest, and establishes more visual identity, than a simple text heading. Used consistently throughout the site, a banner graphic unifies the pages and establishes a signature graphic identity. Incorporating site links into a graphical header gives your users multiple navigation options in a small space. On a Web page, which on some monitors displays only a half a printed page's worth of information, the header must be used economically and to full advantage.

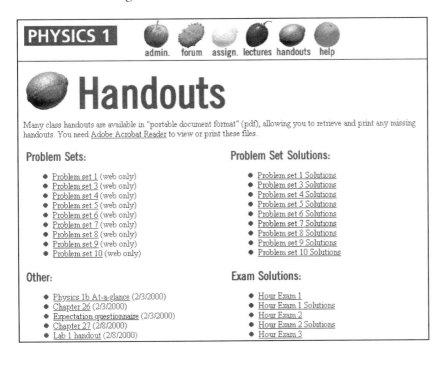

This page header displays the site title and provides access to the main site navigation links. A graphical header sets the tone and, when used consistently, unifies the pages in the site.

FOOTERS

The most important function of a Web page footer is to allow users who have scrolled to the bottom to navigate easily to other pages in the site. The footer should be visually similar to the header graphic in order to maintain consistency and site identity. A page footer normally has site navigation links and source information, such as details about the origin of the page and how to contact the author.

Each page footer on the Voice of the Shuttle site contains links to the other main sections of the site, as well as site origin information and several contact options.

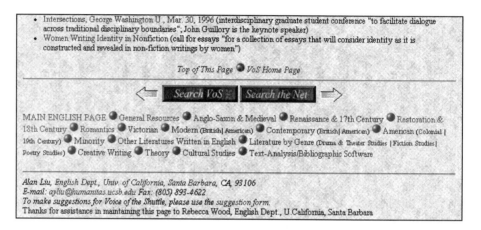

COVER GRAPHICS

Cover graphics, or splash screens, can be a delight or a nuisance. Like the cover of a book, a site cover is intended to attract users and establish a tone for the site. But Web sites are not like books, lined up on a shelf and competing for notice. People are drawn to Web sites more by the information they offer than by their aesthetics. Web sites should give users quick access to substantive content. For many users, a site cover is just an annoying mouse click between them and the information they seek.

Being enticing should probably not be a priority when you create a course Web site. Your student audience has already made a commitment to learning your materials, and if part of that learning process takes place on your course Web site, you don't need "eye candy" to lure them in. That said, a graphical home page can be pleasing and fun, and it can give your site a unique look. If you do use a site cover, just be sure to offer many link options along with your images, and ensure that the links are obvious so that users know where to click.

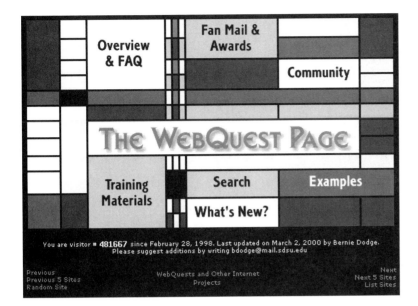

The WebQuest cover graphic is visually engaging while providing users with many navigation options. The graphic also fits nicely on smaller monitors.

BACKGROUND GRAPHICS

A graphical background is an image that loads behind the Web page content: page elements such as text and graphics "float" in front of the background image. Background graphics are unique in that they "tile" across the page. This means that you can use a small image – a one-inch textured square, for example – as a background graphic, and the image will repeat both horizontally and vertically to fill the browser window. With background graphics, you can add visual interest to a page using a *very* small file that loads quickly.

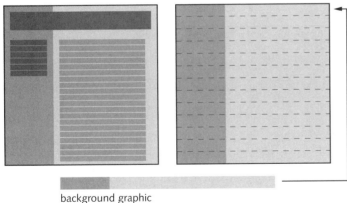

background graphic

The colored sidebar that is used as a background for the popular navigation column interface is actually a wide graphic strip that repeats down the page to fill the browser window.

Background graphics can be tricky. A complex background can impair the legibility of your content by reducing the contrast between the background and text, as well as by adding visual complexity to the page. Used carefully, however, background graphics can enliven pages, and they can delineate page sections: for example, to provide the colored background for the left-column navigation interface used in many sites. If you do use a background graphic, choose one that won't interfere with the content of your page, and make sure that it is a very small file so that it doesn't unduly lengthen the download time.

Background graphics can add visual interest to a page, but take care that they do not interfere with the legibility of your content.

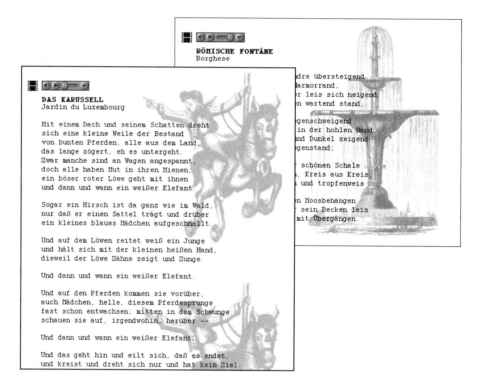

Navigation

In Chapter 1, *Planning,* you created a navigation system for your course Web site. The system contains site links to appear on every page, page-level links pointing to page content and related pages, and site guides such as paging links or links to an index or contents page. Your page layout should incorporate the links from your navigation system.

In creating a page design template, you need to incorporate a navigational interface that includes any site links, page-level links, and other navigational devices, such as paging buttons or a search field. Your navigational interface could be simple text links or complicated graphic rollovers or popdown menus. Whatever the method, the finest attributes of a navigation system are clarity and ease of use. The goal of a navigational interface is above all functional, not aesthetic. Don't create menus that, though clever or visually pleasing, actually impede movement.

Here are two common navigational devices:

Scan column. Site links can be provided in a left or right column on the page known as a "scan column." Using a navigational scan column has two main advantages: it provides convenient access to other site content, and by narrowing the main column of the page, it limits the width of the text block (see *Line length,* above).

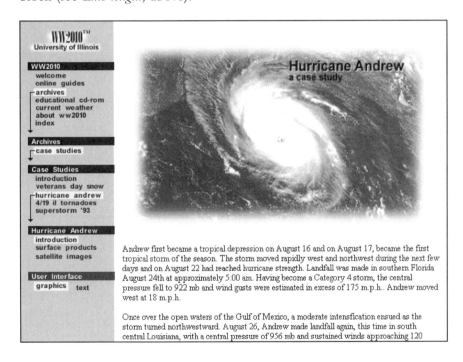

A left-column navigation bar is a good way to provide multiple link options in a small space, and by dividing the screen, it narrows the main text column to a comfortable reading width.

Button bar. Many sites use a navigational button bar, either as a horizontal site header or footer (or both) or as a vertical graphic along the right or left margin of the page. Button bars serve multiple purposes. First, because they are graphical, they help establish a signature identity for the site. Second, when button bars include a contextual marker, they can situate users within the overall site. Last, a graphic button bar with an underlying image map allows for many links in a small space.

Button bars usually include the site title and links to the other main site sections. They provide mobility and establish a visual identity for the site.

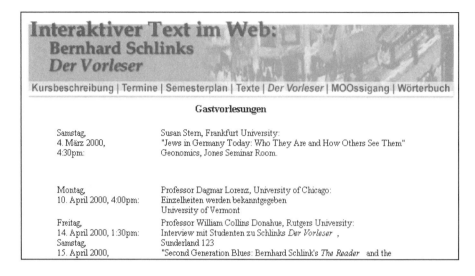

IMAGE MAPS

A graphic image map enables "hot spot" links in a graphic, so that when users click on the graphic they are taken to another page. If you are creating a navigational interface using graphics, you will need to create an image map that defines the "hot" areas and destinations for all your menu choices.

The page header on the Sources site is an image map with "hot spots" that link to the main sections of the site and paging buttons that support sequential navigation.

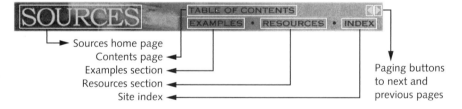

Sources home page
Contents page
Examples section
Resources section
Site index

Paging buttons to next and previous pages

CONTEXT CUES

One task of a navigation system is to give users site orientation cues. Text links make it easy to provide context: simply remove the link from the link text, then apply a subdued color to the text, something that tells the user, "Because you are here, this link is not active." Whatever the method, the object is to visually differentiate the link for the current page from the other active links.

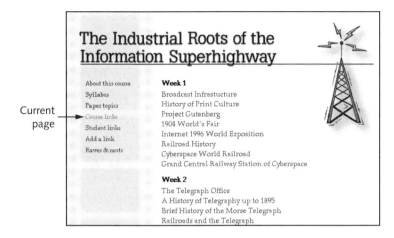

Current page →

One way to provide context for the user is to deactivate and change the color of the navigation link for the current page.

TEXT ALTERNATES

Navigation can be provided using buttons, bars, columns, and animations, but it is critical that you design your navigation system for all users. If your site's navigation interface uses graphic menus, always provide an alternate navigation route that uses basic text links. Users without graphics capabilities, such as those using text-only browsers or visually impaired users, will not be able to navigate your site if you provide only graphic menus.

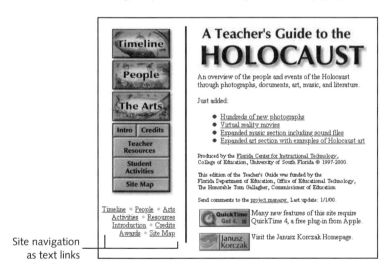

Site navigation as text links

If you use graphical menus, always provide alternate text links for users who for whatever reason cannot see your graphical links.

RELATIVE ADDRESSING

Most linking on Web pages is done using relative, as opposed to absolute, pathnames. A link using an absolute pathname contains the full URL of the linked page, for example, "http://www.yourschool.edu/yourcourse/syllabus.html." A link based on relative addressing describes a linked page's location relative to the directory location of the current page (for more on Web directories, see *Organizing your Web directory,* below). For example, a link to a page at the same level of your course directory would simply contain the file name (a link to "readings.html" on the "syllabus.html" page). A link to a page in a subfolder of your course directory would include the folder name in addition to the file name ("discussions/week1.html" because the week 1 discussions page is in a folder called "discussions").

Links created using relative addressing describe the location of the linked page relative to the location of the current page.

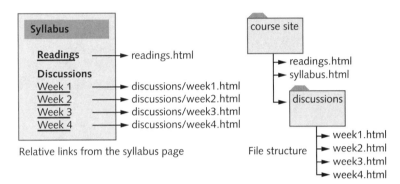

Relative links from the syllabus page   File structure

The benefit of using relative addressing is that it keeps your site portable. Because the host (www.yourschool.edu) and the account (yourcourse) are not part of the link, you can move your site into a different account or to another level within your account (yourcourse/spring2000) or even to a different host altogether, and the navigation links will still work.

Summary

In this section we discussed the peculiarities of designing Web documents and covered strategies for working within the medium to produce well-designed pages that display clearly across a variety of user configurations. We discussed the function of a graphical interface and reviewed different types of site graphics. We also covered methods for implementing the navigation system defined in Chapter 1.

Questions to ask at this first stage of Web site creation include:

- Will you use structural or physical markup to create your Web documents?
- When designing a page grid, which best accommodates your design goals, a flexible approach, a fixed approach, or some combination of the two?
- Which site graphics will you use to define your graphical interface?
- How will you implement your navigation system? Will you use graphic menus, text links, or both?

Design page "mock-ups" using representative examples from the content that you gathered in Chapter 2. Work up site graphics and try out designs for the graphical interface of your site. Experiment with arranging the content and site graphics on the page. Be sure to include all site- and page-level navigation links defined in Chapter 1, as well as links to any site guides that are part of your sitewide system. Show your sketches to colleagues and potential users, and then refine your designs based on their feedback. Your goal is to create a layout (or layouts) that will accommodate the different types of content you plan to use on your site and to establish the site's look and feel. At the end of this exercise you will have a page design template (or templates, if your content requires more than one layout) to use in the next step – constructing a framework for your site – and later to "plug in" your content.

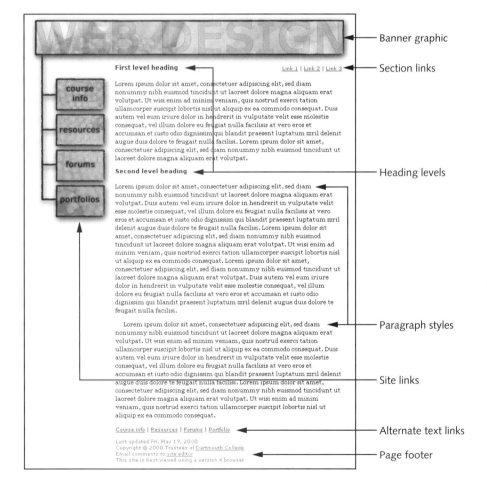

Banner graphic

Section links

Heading levels

Paragraph styles

Site links

Alternate text links

Page footer

Your page template should include site graphics, navigation links, and page information such as a copyright statement and a contact link. You can also create a style sheet to go with your page template: in this example, the text styles are set using a style sheet. When designing a page template it is convenient to use filler text where your actual content will appear.

CONSTRUCT A FRAMEWORK

In this step you will frame your site. Using your site map as a blueprint, you will create all the pages in your site and connect them following your navigation system. The pages themselves will be constructed using the page design template created in the previous section. As with framing a house, where the structural rafters and beams must be firmly in place before finishing can begin, make sure that the framework of your Web site is solid and complete before starting to add content.

Organizing your Web directory

A solid framework requires carefully organized and named files. You will need to create a logical system for organizing files at the start to avoid having your site management become unwieldy later when you want to add or update pages: links will break, or you might find that you've saved several versions of the same file in different locations or with different names. A Web site directory tree can easily become a tangle of branches, with subfolders inside subfolders inside subfolders. Devise a system that works for you, and try to keep the levels to a minimum.

CREATING FOLDERS

The easiest way to organize files is to use your site map as a guide and create folders and files following the hierarchical organization of the site. Say, for example, that you have a category called "Course Documents" and within that section have four separate pages, "Course Information," "Course Calendar," "Required Readings," and "Course Links." In your Web site directory, create a folder called "documents" and place the pages

Set up your file directory following your organizational site map, creating folders for each category and for similar content types such as video, images, or site graphics.

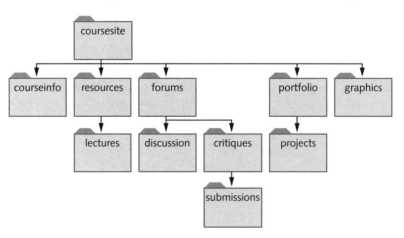

"info.html," "calendar.html," "readings.html," and "links.html" in that folder. You might also want to make subfolders to group similar items such as site graphics or video and image files.

Making pages

Having established a logical file directory structure, use your page design template to create pages. At this step you are merely creating a framework, so don't be concerned yet with adding page content. Simply open the template file in your Web authoring tool of choice, and save files to correspond to those pages detailed on your site map. Be sure to save the files in the appropriate folder in your file directory.

NAMING FILES

When making Web pages, you need to name your files according to established conventions so that different types of computers can read them. You also need to choose descriptive names so that you will be able to locate pages in your directory. Consider also how easy the name is to communicate. Try to imagine explaining to a user where to go to find your page: for example, www.webteachingguide.com/File_Names.html" spoken would sound like "w, w, w, dot, webteachingguide, dot, com, slash, uppercase F, then i, l, e, underscore, uppercase N, then a, m, e, s." Chances are the user would have to try several times before successfully locating the page. The best approach is to keep file names as simple as possible (www.webteaching guide.com/filenames.html).

- Case. You *can* mix lowercase and uppercase letters in a file name, but it is not advisable. Filenames are case sensitive, so users need to type them correctly to receive the page.
- Spaces. Don't use spaces in filenames because some computer systems cannot recognize them.
- Special characters. Use only letters, numbers, underscores, hyphens, and periods. To minimize confusion, stick with letters and numbers whenever possible.
- Suffixes. Web pages must have the ".html" or ".htm" suffix. Media files also need to have the proper suffix, for example, ".gif" for GIF files, ".jpg" or ".jpeg" for JPEG files, ".mov" for QuickTime movies. The Web server and the browser software need the file suffix to determine what to do with the file in the browser.

Name the home page of your site "index.html" (or "index.htm" or "default.html" depending on your Web server's configuration). Web servers are normally configured to look for and send the index file when a user requests a Web directory. For example, when a user types "www.webteaching guide.com" into the location bar of the browser, the Web server sends them "www.webteachingguide.com/index.html." This convention simplifies the process of finding pages: users do not have to type in long URLs but instead can easily get to the main page of a site and then find the page they're looking for using the site's navigation links.

Use your page template to create files for all the pages in your site. Be sure to observe naming conventions, and keep your file names simple and descriptive.

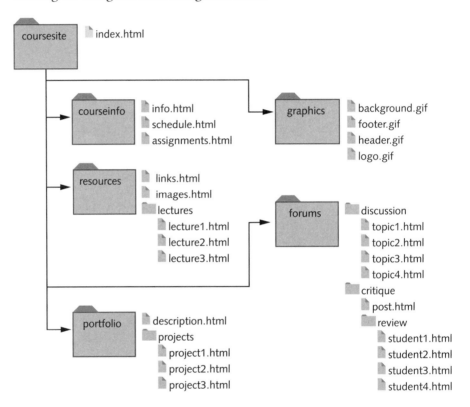

Customizing individual pages

The next task in creating a framework is to create unique titles and establish the linkages between pages. Right now you have an organized collection of identical pages that may or may not work together functionally due to broken links. At the end of this step you will have a functional framework into which you can begin adding content.

PAGE TITLES

A page title is the text that displays in the window title bar when a Web page is displayed in the browser. An effective page title situates users and describes the content of the page: for example, the class discussion page on your course Web site might include the name of your institution and course number to identify the site and "Class Discussion" to describe the contents of the page.

Descriptive page titles also help in the following circumstances:

Bookmarks. When a user decides to bookmark your page, the text you have designated as the page title is the text that appears in the user's bookmark list. When you are deciding on page titles, imagine what the text will look like in a long list of bookmarks. Choose a descriptive title, so that users will remember why they bookmarked your page.

Search engines. Most search engines use page titles as the primary descriptor when indexing your site (see Chapter 4: *Listing with search engines*). This means that a page titled "Music 36: Contemporary Music: Syllabus" is more likely to be the result of a search on "contemporary music" than is "Music 36: Syllabus." If you want to be visible to users of search engines, create page titles that contain the main topic of your materials.

Use a consistent approach when establishing page titles for the pages in your site. For example, if you decide to include your course name in the title, be sure to include it on all pages.

CHECKING LINKS

In designing your page template, you designed a navigation interface for your pages that included site links, page-level links, and other navigational devices such as paging buttons or a search field. Now you need to make sure that those links function and point to the correct locations. If you are using page-level links, you will need to customize them for each page: for example, if you are using paging buttons in your navigational interface, you will need to designate the correct filename for the previous and next pages. This final stage of framing your site is like hammering all the nails solidly into place, so that the structure stands as a single unit. Make sure that all your links work and point to the appropriate pages, so that you can navigate the site without encountering broken or misdirected links.

Summary

In this step we created a file directory structure following the hierarchical structure of our site organization. We then created individual pages using the page design template from the previous section, taking care to name the files according to standard naming conventions. Finally, we gave all the pages unique page titles and customized each page to function within the site's navigation system.

Having constructed your site's framework, consider the following questions:

- Do all your links work? Are all your pages titled? Did you use descriptive titles?
- Is the framework sound? Is it flexible enough to house all your content?

Ask a couple of representative users to sit down with the site and try out the navigational interface. Pretend that there is content in place, and ask them to complete such activities as locating information or performing a task online. Have them "think aloud" while interacting with your site (see Chapter 5: *Do-it-yourself assessment*). Use their feedback to uncover flaws in the usability of your design.

The time to fix usability problems is now, before you add content. You don't want to spend time and effort molding your content to fit into a flawed design. If you find in your own interaction with the framework, or by observing others work with it, that something is not quite right, go back now and fix it before moving to the next step of adding content.

ADD CONTENT

In the final stage of creating your course Web site, you will take the content you gathered in Chapter 2, *Developing content,* and plug it into the site framework. Here we will explore how to get your content in place with style and effect. You will need to modify each type of content to fit your page layout and the medium of the Web.

Working with text

Text on the computer screen is inherently inferior to that on the printed page. Screen resolution is far lower than print resolution, which means that the computer screen renders type at much lower quality than you see in books or other printed materials. The physical aspect of reading on the screen is also not as comfortable as reading from a page. For these reasons, as an author of Web documents, you should do all you can to make your text as readable as possible.

As mentioned at the beginning of this chapter, there are currently two ways to approach text formatting: basic HTML and Cascading Style Sheets. Only certain properties of CSS are implemented consistently across browsers at the time of this writing, though CSS support should be more robust in the future. Until then, you will need to format your text using either HTML alone or some combination of HTML and CSS. This section covers general text formatting and offers examples of both HTML and CSS.

ALIGNMENT

The way text interacts with space strongly influences the readability of a page. Alignment influences the way text sits within the page margins. A justified alignment, for example, creates a symmetrical page with straight margins, whereas other alignment options create asymmetrical, or ragged, margins.

The following alignment options are available on the Web:

Justified. Justified text is set flush with the left and right margins to create a solid rectangle of text. To create a single-width text block, page layout software uses hyphenation and fine adjustments to letter- and word-spacing that spreads the text out evenly over every line. But even with sophisticated software and high-resolution output, many printed documents that use justification have uneven spacing and excessive or inappropriate hyphenation.

It will be some time before justification can be used effectively on a Web page. Web browsers contain none of the tools of page layout software for adjusting text on a line. Also, the relatively coarse resolution of the computer monitor cannot support the fine adjustments needed to make justification work. Though you *can* justify text on a Web page, it is not possible to do it well and so should be avoided.

Centered or right-justified. A centered or right-justified text block results in an irregular left margin. When we read, we anchor our tracking to the straight vertical line of the left margin. Our eyes sweep across the line to the right and then return to the anchor of the left margin. When you center or right-justify text blocks you sacrifice that straight left margin, which means that readers must search for the beginning of each new line.

Centered or right-aligned text works for display type, such as section titles, and short text passages, such as image captions. These alignment options should not be used for extended text passages, however.

Left-justified. The most readable text alignment is left-justified. Text that is aligned flush with the left margin maintains the straight vertical anchor that enables easy reading. The resulting uneven right margin does not interfere in any way with legibility and even adds visual interest to the page.

A common approach is to use centered headings over left-aligned body text. Yet this pairing of symmetrical title with asymmetrical text creates an unbalanced page: the symmetry of the heading contrasts with the ragged right margin of the text block. Centered headings work well over justified text, but justification is not a viable option on the Web. The best approach is to use left-justified alignment for both your text blocks and your headings.

Centered or right-aligned text creates a ragged left margin that impairs readability, and although justification is an option for formatting paragraphs, the fine letter-spacing required to make justification work is not available on the Web. For best results, use left-aligned text throughout your pages.

DEFINE YOUR OBJECTIVES

Now it's time to examine your motivation for creating a course Web site and to develop and refine your ideas within the context of what's possible in your situation. The Web can enhance learning or ease the burden of administering a course in many respects. Take time now to define your purpose for creating a course site - what challenges you are hoping to meet, what tasks you are hoping to simplify - and how you intend to combine the Web and the classroom.

Goals and objectives

You may have embarked on this project because a colleague is having great success with his or her course site and you hope to achieve similar results. Or maybe your institution is requiring that all courses have Web sites or your students are demanding Web access to course materials. Or perhaps you see the Web as a solution to a teaching challenge you've been wrestling with for years. Whatever the motive, now is the time to clarify your goals and objectives for using the Web in your curriculum.

Look around

One of the best ways to define your Web teaching approach is to look at other teaching sites. Although some course Web sites are not open to the public, many are, which means you can peek into online classrooms and

Justified

DEFINE YOUR OBJECTIVES

Now it's time to examine your motivation for creating a course Web site and to develop and refine your ideas within the context of what's possible in your situation. The Web can enhance learning or ease the burden of administering a course in many respects. Take time now to define your purpose for creating a course site - what challenges you are hoping to meet, what tasks you are hoping to simplify - and how you intend to combine the Web and the classroom.

Goals and objectives

You may have embarked on this project because a colleague is having great success with his or her course site and you hope to achieve similar results. Or maybe your institution is requiring that all courses have Web sites or your students are demanding Web access to course materials. Or perhaps you see the Web as a solution to a teaching challenge you've been wrestling with for years. Whatever the motive, now is the time to clarify your goals and objectives for using the Web in your curriculum.

Look around

One of the best ways to define your Web teaching approach is to look at other teaching sites. Although some course Web sites are not open to the public, many are, which means you can peek into online classrooms and

Centered

DEFINE YOUR OBJECTIVES

Now it's time to examine your motivation for creating a course Web site and to develop and refine your ideas within the context of what's possible in your situation. The Web can enhance learning or ease the burden of administering a course in many respects. Take time now to define your purpose for creating a course site - what challenges you are hoping to meet, what tasks you are hoping to simplify - and how you intend to combine the Web and the classroom.

Goals and objectives

You may have embarked on this project because a colleague is having great success with his or her course site and you hope to achieve similar results. Or maybe your institution is requiring that all courses have Web sites or your students are demanding Web access to course materials. Or perhaps you see the Web as a solution to a teaching challenge you've been wrestling with for years. Whatever the motive, now is the time to clarify your goals and objectives for using the Web in your curriculum.

Look around

One of the best ways to define your Web teaching approach is to look at other teaching sites. Although some course Web sites are not open to the public, many are, which means you can peek into online classrooms and

Centered headings/left-aligned text

DEFINE YOUR OBJECTIVES

Now it's time to examine your motivation for creating a course Web site and to develop and refine your ideas within the context of what's possible in your situation. The Web can enhance learning or ease the burden of administering a course in many respects. Take time now to define your purpose for creating a course site - what challenges you are hoping to meet, what tasks you are hoping to simplify - and how you intend to combine the Web and the classroom.

Goals and objectives

You may have embarked on this project because a colleague is having great success with his or her course site and you hope to achieve similar results. Or maybe your institution is requiring that all courses have Web sites or your students are demanding Web access to course materials. Or perhaps you see the Web as a solution to a teaching challenge you've been wrestling with for years. Whatever the motive, now is the time to clarify your goals and objectives for using the Web in your curriculum.

Look around

One of the best ways to define your Web teaching approach is to look at other teaching sites. Although some course Web sites are not open to the public, many are, which means you can peek into online classrooms and

Left-aligned

One characteristic of Web typography is excessive white space: paragraphs have a full line of space between them, lists are excessively indented, headings float too far above the text they describe. White space is good, but when overused it disrupts the logical flow of content and makes things appear choppy. It obscures relationships between page elements: with so much space around everything, elements that form logical groups appear unconnected.

It is hard to control white space in a Web document, even when using style sheets. In fact, the space around type elements is probably the property most inconsistently implemented across browsers. To control white space, Web designers have adopted a workaround of using a transparent single-pixel image and adjusting its attributes. For example, when you define section heads using the HTML heading tag, there is too much space between the heading and the following paragraph: the header "floats" unconnected on the page. If instead you place a line break after the heading text and add an invisible spacer graphic between the heading and the subsequent paragraph, you can adjust the spacing around the image to create a *slight* division between the elements while maintaining a visual connection.

Spacer graphics

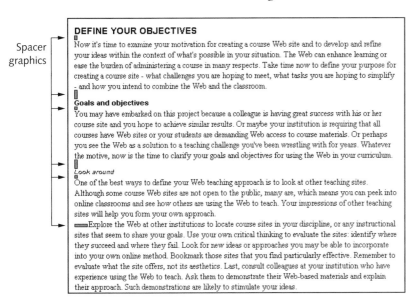

You can use a transparent single-pixel image and adjust its vertical space (VSPACE) and horizontal space (HSPACE) attributes both to control the space between headings and paragraphs and to create a first-line indent.

This may not necessarily be good HTML practice, but until there is consistent browser support of CSS, the invisible spacer graphic is the only reliable way to control white space in a Web document.

Leading

Leading is the distance from one baseline of text to the next. This vertical space has two important functions: it separates the ascenders and descenders of the type, and helps the eye find the left margin and location of the following line. Too little leading, especially when combined with a wide text block, can make it hard to locate the next line while reading.

Basic HTML offers Web designers no control over leading, and leading as interpreted by the browser is too tight for comfortable reading. If you use CSS, however, you can designate leading values in your style definitions. The convention is to set standard blocks of text with an additional two points of leading above the type size: for example, 10-point type with 12 points of leading (10/12). Additional leading increases the readability of wide text blocks, and because most line lengths on the Web are long, you may want to use more space, perhaps an additional half or full point (such as 10/13). Certain typefaces also work better with increased leading, such as large or dark type or sans-serif faces.

One of the best features of Cascading Style Sheets is that you can increase interline spacing, or leading, which will greatly improve the readability of your text passages.

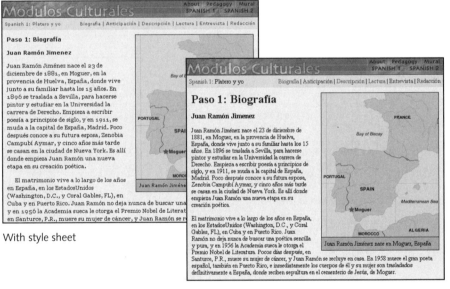

With style sheet

With basic HTML only

Marking paragraphs

If you use the standard HTML <P> tag to mark paragraphs, a full *white line,* or hard return, is inserted between paragraphs. The most economical way to mark a paragraph is to use a first-line indent instead of a white line – a convention used in most printed literature, as it is in this book. The use of the first-line indent for marking paragraphs keeps the text block intact, free of unnecessary gaps and interruptions.

Using basic HTML, the only way to add a first-line indent is through a workaround. One approach is to use a line break (<BR>) to mark the end of your paragraph and then insert a few nonbreaking spaces ( ) before the first line of the next paragraph. Another method is to use an invisible spacer graphic and adjust its horizontal space attribute (HSPACE="8"). If you are using CSS, you can use the text-indent property for your paragraph style (text-indent: 8pt), though as of this writing this does not work consistently across browsers.

TYPE

Controlling the appearance of type on a page goes against one of the original intentions of the Web. The aim was to allow users to control their viewing environment, and whether users chose to read their Web pages in Times or Tekton was up to them. Web page authors, however, have realized that to communicate effectively on the Web, there needs to be some way of controlling the most elemental aspect of typographic design: the type itself. Recent versions of HTML allow authors to control type on their pages. The options, however, are limited, and users can still override page-defined fonts by setting their browser to enforce their preferred settings.

Choosing a typeface

Selecting the right typeface for your Web page is simple because you have a limited set to choose from. Fonts are not part of your Web page, so for the user to see your pages rendered using your specified typeface, the font you list needs to be installed on the user's hard drive. This narrows your typeface choices to the cross-platform fonts that are standard on most computer systems.

Some standard fonts – Helvetica, Times – were designed for print use, and they don't fare well onscreen: screen resolution is coarse in comparison with print, so the legibility of type with a small "x-height" (the height of the lowercase "x" in that font) suffers onscreen. For pages that will be both viewed onscreen and printed, it is best to use Times New Roman – a traditional typeface that has been adapted for the screen. Pages to be viewed onscreen work well with a font such as Georgia, which was designed specifically for screen legibility. However, Georgia's large size and exaggerated x-heights look awkward in print. A good choice is to use a serif type such as Times New Roman or Georgia for body text and a sans-serif face such as Verdana or Arial for links and navigation text.

When choosing a typeface, you are best off selecting from the limited set of *useful* standard cross-platform fonts. Also note that there is a marked difference in font size for Macintosh and Windows display.

Arial
Selecting the right typeface for your Web page is simple because you have a limited set to choose from. Fonts are not part of your Web page, so for the user to see your pages rendered using your specified typeface, the font needs to be installed on the user's hard drive.

Georgia
Selecting the right typeface for your Web page is simple because you have a limited set to choose from. Fonts are not part of your Web page, so for the user to see your pages rendered using your specified typeface, the font needs to be installed on the user's hard drive.

Times New Roman
Selecting the right typeface for your Web page is simple because you have a limited set to choose from. Fonts are not part of your Web page, so for the user to see your pages rendered using your specified typeface, the font needs to be installed on the user's hard drive.

Trebuchet
Selecting the right typeface for your Web page is simple because you have a limited set to choose from. Fonts are not part of your Web page, so for the user to see your pages rendered using your specified typeface, the font needs to be installed on the user's hard drive.

Verdana
Selecting the right typeface for your Web page is simple because you have a limited set to choose from. Fonts are not part of your Web page, so for the user to see your pages rendered using your specified typeface, the font needs to be installed on the user's hard drive.

Windows

Arial
Selecting the right typeface for your Web page is simple because you have a limited set to choose from. Fonts are not part of your Web page, so for the user to see your pages rendered using your specified typeface, the font needs to be installed on the user's hard drive.

Georgia
Selecting the right typeface for your Web page is simple because you have a limited set to choose from. Fonts are not part of your Web page, so for the user to see your pages rendered using your specified typeface, the font needs to be installed on the user's hard drive.

Times New Roman
Selecting the right typeface for your Web page is simple because you have a limited set to choose from. Fonts are not part of your Web page, so for the user to see your pages rendered using your specified typeface, the font needs to be installed on the user's hard drive.

Trebuchet
Selecting the right typeface for your Web page is simple because you have a limited set to choose from. Fonts are not part of your Web page, so for the user to see your pages rendered using your specified typeface, the font needs to be installed on the user's hard drive.

Verdana
Selecting the right typeface for your Web page is simple because you have a limited set to choose from. Fonts are not part of your Web page, so for the user to see your pages rendered using your specified typeface, the font needs to be installed on the user's hard drive.

Macintosh

Type size

Different platforms display type sizes differently. On a Macintosh, for example, 12-point type looks about the same size on the screen as it would printed. On a Windows machine, however, 12-point type looks 2–3 points larger than on a Mac – the equivalent of 14- to 15-point printed type. To get the equivalent of 12-point type on a Windows machine, you would have to set your font size to 8 points, which would be illegible on a Macintosh.

This difference in type size rendering can have a big impact on your page layout, so it is important to check your pages on different systems. If you're designing your pages on a Windows machine, you might find that the type size you've chosen is too small to be legible on a Mac. It's one thing for your type to appear large and clunky on the "other" platform, but some sites designed on Windows machines are unreadable on Macintoshes.

Plan your site
The success of your Web site depends as much on how well you organize your content as on the content you offer. A jumbled, incoherent presentation of materials is not likely to be popular with students, no matter how valuable the content. And Web sites, because they are by nature works in progress, soon become unmanageable when created ad lib. Without a clear outline of your content from the start, you may find yourself with an unruly collection of pages you cannot update and maintain. A careful review and classification of your content can be painstaking work, but the rewards are better site usability and ease of maintenance.

Content inventory
The first step in designing your site is to create a list of items you want to include as content on the site. A content "item" should be the most detailed category of information that needs to be accessed individually. For example, "Composers' biographies" is not a content item,

Windows

Macintosh

When choosing a type size for your text, make sure that it is legible across platforms. Though small, this 8-point Arial is readable on a Windows machine, but it is illegible on a Macintosh.

Specifying fonts

To specify a typeface in your HTML document you need to define a *fontset*. A fontset is a list of "suggested" fonts for the browser to use to render the type on your pages. They are only suggestions because the pages will render using the user's default font if the fonts listed are not on the user's hard disk or if the user has chosen to override page-specified fonts. The fontset list is in order of preference – your first choice first, then your second, and so on. If you end your list with the general font specification (serif, sans-serif), systems that have none of the fonts in your fontset will at least render the type using the correct style.

```
HTML: <FONT FACE="georgia, times new roman, serif">Specifying fonts</FONT>
CSS: H1 {font-family: verdana, arial, sans-serif}
```

Although you can specify a font size for your text, it is best to leave the control of that setting to the user. If you exert too much control over type size, you may exclude users who cannot read the text at the size you specify. The best approach is to create flexible layouts that can accommodate varying type sizes.

There may be times, however, when you want to control the size of particular text elements in relation to other text on the page. For example, you may want the page footer text – copyright, last-updated date, and contact information – to display smaller than the main text. In this case, you can specify font size in relative terms: the following code displays the footer text 2 points smaller than the body text.

```
<FONT SIZE="-2">Footer text</FONT>
```

Typographical emphasis

A reader is guided through content by typographical landmarks such as headings and toward items of importance by emphasized words or phrases. These devices for adding emphasis are time-honored and work by contrasting these items from surrounding body text.

When incorporating contrast into your pages, add one typographic device at a time. Don't, for example, make your headings large, bold, and all caps. To differentiate headings from the main text, keep them the same size but make them bold, or keep them the same weight but make them slightly larger than the main text. You'll be surprised how little contrast is necessary to guide your reader's attention *when it is used sparingly.*

Capitalization. Capitalized text provides emphasis because its shape differs from regular text: a word set in uppercase is a SOLID RECTANGLE, unlike words set in upper- and lowercase. Novice designers commonly use capitalized text inappropriately. A block of capitalized text is hard to read, because part of reading is recognizing words by their shapes. A capitalized word has no distinctive shape and so must be interpreted letter by letter.

NOW IT'S TIME TO EXAMINE YOUR MOTIVATION FOR CREATING A COURSE WEB SITE AND TO DEVELOP AND REFINE YOUR IDEAS WITHIN THE CONTEXT OF WHAT'S POSSIBLE IN YOUR SITUATION. THE WEB CAN ENHANCE LEARNING OR EASE THE BURDEN OF ADMINISTERING A COURSE IN MANY RESPECTS. TAKE TIME NOW TO DEFINE YOUR PURPOSE FOR CREATING A COURSE SITE – WHAT CHALLENGES YOU ARE HOPING TO MEET, WHAT TASKS YOU ARE HOPING TO SIMPLIFY – AND HOW YOU INTEND TO COMBINE THE WEB AND THE CLASSROOM.

Capitals can be used for emphasis, but limit their use to such things as titles and section headings.

Italics. Italicized text provides emphasis because it is shaped differently from plain roman text. But it is hard to read, particularly at low screen resolution, so you should not italicize long text passages. Use italics to follow stylistic conventions – italicizing book titles, for example – or to stress single words or foreign-language terms within the text block.

Bold. Boldface provides emphasis because it is darker and heavier than body text. Bold text within the text block can be disruptive because it stands out so much as to draw the reader's eye. Large blocks of text set in bold lack contrast and lose effectiveness. Bold text is best reserved for headings and subheads.

Small caps. Small caps are used frequently in printed documents for acronyms and subheads. With the limited typefaces available to Web authors, small caps can be achieved only by capitalizing the text and reducing the font one size.

```
<FONT SIZE="-1">SMALL CAPS</FONT>
```

Contrasting typeface. You can achieve typographic emphasis using a second typeface: subheads, for example, are often set in a sans-serif typeface to contrast with serif body text. You can also use a contrasting typeface within body text to provide emphasis, but be sure that it is not distracting.

Underlining. Underlining is used on the Web to indicate a link and so should be avoided as a device for typographical emphasis. Browsers underline links so that people who cannot see colors will know when text is a link. If you use underlining for typographic emphasis, the text will surely be confused with a link.

Color. Like underlining, colored text has a special significance on the Web, and if you include colored text on your pages, people are likely to think that it signifies a link and click on it. It is best to avoid using colored text on your Web pages; instead, add emphasis through a contrasting typeface or bold text.

CASCADING STYLE SHEETS

Styling Web pages using basic HTML formatting does have several benefits. If, for example, you use the <H1> heading tag to define your main headings, that structural information helps search engines determine the subject of your pages. This in turn means that a Web user is more likely to find your content than if you had used the <B> tag to apply bold formatting: the <B> tag has no structural significance. The trouble is that the <H1> tag produces big, overemphasized, clunky-looking headings that violate all the typographic conventions we've just covered. Web authors who want to fashion documents using visual logic have not been able to reap the benefits of using a standard HTML structural description.

Using Cascading Style Sheets, it is possible to design pages using structural HTML tags *and* control document presentation. Much like the "style" feature of word processing and page layout software, style sheets allow you to define styles for different elements, such as headings and subheadings, lists, and body text, and then use those styles to format the text on your pages. This means that you can use standard HTML tags to define the structural logic of your document and CSS to define its visual logic. For example, if you want your main headings to be bold but the same size as your body text, you can use the <H1> tag for the heading and then specify in your style sheet that <H1> headings should display as 12-point bold.

H1 { font-size: 12pt; font-style: bold }

A style sheet can be defined in the <HEAD> section of an HTML page, or you can link your pages to an external text file that contains style definitions for all the elements in your site.

Style sheet definitions can be included in the HTML document, or they can be applied by including a link to an external style sheet file.

Styles defined in the HTML document

Link to external style sheet

There are additional advantages to using CSS:

Consistency. If you design a "master" style sheet for your site, the styles will be implemented the same way on every page. For example, if you define a style for <H1> headings, that same style will be applied to every level-one heading on every page.

Convenience. You can link all your pages to a single style sheet document. Then, if you want to change the formatting of your <H1> heading, you can make the change in one place – the style sheet document – and the change is immediately reflected on all the linked pages.

Additional typographic controls. Certain typographic controls are available using CSS that are not available with standard HTML. The most notable of these is line spacing (see *Leading,* above), but you can also specify such things as letter spacing, indents, and margins.

CSS may seem like the perfect solution to the irreconcilable differences between structural and visual logic in Web page design. As of this writing, however, the major browsers have not fully implemented current CSS specifications. Even the properties that have been implemented function differently on different browsers, so that pages that look just right in Internet Explorer look different in Netscape Navigator. Only a small subset of CSS properties can be used with some measure of confidence at this time. You may also find that some properties, even though inconsistently applied, produce acceptable results across browsers. Unless the browsers adopt a consistent implementation, using style sheets will involve both trial and error and cross-checks on different machines.

CSS elements for formatting text

Property	Possible values	Examples
font-family	font-family name: arial, times new roman generic family name: serif, sans-serif	H1 { font-family: verdana, arial, geneva, sans-serif;
font-weight	normal, bold	font-size: 14pt;
font-style	normal, italic	font-style: bold;
font-size	exact measure: 12pt, 3em	color: gray }
	relative value: larger, smaller	P { font-family: georgia, times new
	absolute size: x-small, small, medium	roman, palatino, serif;
color	color name: gray, black, red	font-size: 12pt;
	color hex code: #333333, #FFFFCC	line-height: 15pt;
line-height	percent: 150%	text-indent: 12pt }
	absolute value: 15pt	
text-indent	length: 12pt	
	percentage: 10%	
text-align	left, right, center	

Megan Williams: Mount Holyoke College

Megan Williams took a different approach when she taught Magic and Astrology in the Greek and Roman World at Mount Holyoke College, in South Hadley, Massachusetts. In Religion 212, students look at ancient literary texts that discuss magic and at remnants of spells and handbooks on magic written on lead and papyrus, all with a focus on understanding religious and philosophical attitudes toward magic. "I was nervous about teaching the course because the materials are difficult: hundreds of pages of incomprehensible gobbledygook. I wanted my students to learn how to read these weird old texts and try to see what they reveal about the social context in which they were produced." Instead of asking the students to write traditional research papers, she assigned one major project for the semester: to create a Web site. "I wanted to get the students to engage a topic closely in a small compass." She had each student select from a list of topics and then created small project groups at the beginning of the semester.

The students' first step was to create an outline and assign each person in the group a separate task. The second step was for each group member to write text for the site. Each student submitted a "polished draft," and Megan responded with detailed feedback. Then the group worked together to produce a "skeleton" of the Web site containing the graphics and structure of the pages but no content. At this stage, Megan worked at length with the students to help them refine both their writing and their site design. "I kept saying I wanted the sites to look really good. They didn't have to be complicated, but they did have to work, and they couldn't have spelling errors. In fact, one goal I did accomplish using the Web was that they revised their papers with much more care." In the final step, students added their text and image content to the site framework to complete their Web site.

The students' readiness for this type of coursework varied. "At the beginning of the semester about 30 percent of the students already had the basic tools they needed to do this project. Another 30 percent were enthusiastic about the idea, and were saying, 'I'm glad you're making us do this because I really need to learn it.' And the remaining students were grumbling. By the end of the semester at least 60 percent had a favorable response to the whole thing." Megan tried to assign at least one person with previous Web programming experience to each group. And as for those students who had little or no experience with the Web, Megan saw this project as an opportunity for them to learn essential skills. "Having to use this technology in the classroom setting is useful because it's going to become a basic feature of functioning cultural literacy over the next ten years, and somebody has to help them learn." With strong Web programming and design skills, Megan is unusually "techie" for a humanities professor, and she was able to guide her students not only with the content aspects of the project but also with the technical challenges.

Yet even though they were ultimately positive about the approach, the students uniformly agreed that the project was demanding: "They could probably have written three five-page papers in the amount of time and energy it took them to do these Web sites." But, says Megan, "Mount Holyoke students are very hardworking, so you can be demanding and they're not going to whine – at least, not too much."

Megan would approach two aspects of the project differently next time. First, she would structure the projects to be more collaborative. Megan wanted to limit the interdependence of the group, so that less productive individuals did not sour group dynamics. As a result, however, the projects were much less collaborative than she had hoped.

Because each student was responsible for an aspect of the project, they weren't required to interact enough to pull together as a group. "The cool thing about the Web is that it provides a tool where people can do collaborative work and see it coming together in a way that is strong and graphic. I'd like to keep exploring how to make that work better." Another area of focus next time around would be to help students use images effectively in their scholarly work. "I should have figured in time to gather images and to define text-image relationships." Megan still views the project work as successful, however. "Though I didn't get as much of the collaborative, multi-approach view on the topics as I would have liked, and I didn't get as much use of images and interpretation of material culture as I would have liked, I definitely got a lot more of each than if I had just assigned papers."

Megan has been using a Web site in every course she teaches. "I started out writing course materials in Word and then converting the documents to HTML for the course Web site, and then I thought, this is pointless. Now I write all my course materials as Web pages only." Megan got her technical foundation by attending a seminar on New Technologies for Teaching and Research at Princeton University. Funded by the Arthur Vining Davis Foundation and run by Professor Will Howarth of Princeton's English department, this intensive seminar is for budding educators who want to learn Web development for instructional purposes. The participants meet for two full days a week for six weeks. "I went into the seminar with a vague and poorly articulated sense of how to create a basic Web page using Netscape Composer and came out knowing a little bit of UNIX, feeling comfortable working with HTML, ready to try a little Perl programming...." Megan also participated in a weeklong Web development course at Mount Holyoke, sponsored by the Mellon Foundation, where she learned more Web design and basic Javascript programming. Her course sites contain the standard course materials – syllabus, list of readings, course requirements, descriptions of assignments. Megan found that even this elementary use of the Web has been advantageous. At Mount Holyoke, for example, she had little time to prepare her courses, and because she had never taught these courses before, placing her syllabi on the Web allowed her to start with general outlines and fill in details as the semester progressed.

Megan hopes to work on more ambitious Web projects in the future, including adding more interactivity on her sites and building a database of images. "There's such a huge gap between the simple text-and-image level I'm at now and creating something that's technically innovative. I feel as if I'm stuck using the Web as a substitute for paper rather than using it to do things you can't do on paper. I want a chance to bring the 'bells and whistles' of the technology together with well-defined pedagogical goals and generate really interesting and effective teaching tools." Megan Williams is representative of a new generation of educators who take for granted the use of the Web in the classroom. Her embrace of technology and enthusiasm about its potential may well be a catalyst for instructional innovation. ∎

Providing links

For a Web author, one of the most compelling aspects of creating Web pages is the ability to tap into the vast information resource that is the Web to provide links to related materials, glossaries, additional details, and interesting digressions. Placed carelessly, however, links can disrupt the narrative flow of your pages and even lead readers away from your site. To be effective and to minimize their disruptive effect, links must be offered with care.

PLACEMENT

Because links are colored and underlined, they contrast from the regular text on the page and draw the reader's attention. Also, since links lead elsewhere, they disrupt the flow of information. Although it is certainly worthwhile to include links, consider carefully where and how you offer them.

Location. Links in body text make reading difficult: because of their contrast with the surrounding text, they are hard to ignore. They also disrupt the narrative by inviting readers to leave. If you place a link in the middle of your text, many readers will follow the link before finishing your narrative.

If links supplement your content, place them at the bottom of the document; alternatively, place all links on a separate annotated "Links" page. Only in rare instances should you include links in the body of your text: most links are not important enough to justify the disruption.

Color. Brightly colored links within body text draw the eye in the same way as bold or CAPITALIZED text. If you do include links within the body of your text, use a custom link color that is similar to the color of the body text, for example, dark blue links with black text.

MAINTAINING CONTEXT

Links are also disruptive because they eliminate context. When users click a link, the content of their browser window is replaced by the linked page. If you use links to point away from your site, many readers may never make their way back. You can help your readers by giving context to the links on your pages and by making it easy for them to return to your site.

Annotation. Following a link can be an adventure, sometimes an adventure leading nowhere: if your readers do not know what *you* found relevant at the linked site, they might follow the link and not know what to look for once they get there. When you post links on your Web pages, provide an accompanying annotation. Explain the connection and relevance of the linked materials on *your* pages so that readers know in advance where they are going and why you are sending them there.

Secondary window. One common approach to maintaining context is to open related sites in a second browser window using the TARGET="main" attribute of the link tag. Users can explore the supporting site and then close the window to resume with your content.

This approach has limitations, however. Many users navigate using the history feature of their Web browser (the Back button or the Go menu). Opening the supporting site in another window creates a history for the new window that does not include your site. Also, some users will not notice that another window was opened and will not know how to return to your site.

Working with images

You are now ready to begin optimizing your Web graphics for network delivery and cross-platform display. Publishing color on the Web is simpler than it is on paper in many ways. But preparing images for Web publishing does entail special considerations. For example, Web graphics must be designed to work under variable conditions, such as on different monitors and over varying Internet access speeds. Also, because the images are delivered via a network, there are definite limitations to file size. In preparing images for your Web site, it pays to work within the medium. Calculate carefully, and prepare your images to display properly under variable conditions and to reach your users regardless of the speed of their Web connection.

Although producing color images on paper is far more complicated than it is on the screen, an understanding of print will better prepare you to design images for the Web. We begin, then, with an overview of the factors involved in creating printed images.

How print images work

Photographs, because of the material they are printed on and the method used to develop them, are termed continuous-tone images because you cannot distinguish divisions, or gradations, between colors (in black-and-white photos, these gradations are different values of gray). Printed images, because of the way they are produced, are not continuous-tone images. The devices typically used in the printing process – printing presses and laser output devices – cannot produce continuous tones: imagine inking plates for hundreds of colors! Instead, printers create the *illusion* of many colors using halftone dots. Most printed images are made up of rows of dots of varying sizes, called *halftone screens,* which produce the appearance of multiple tones when printed.

Printed images produce tonal variation using rows of dots of varying shapes and sizes called halftone screens.

Enlarged detail of halftone grid

Printed color images are produced by combining two or more halftone screens using different inks. In full-color printing, four printing inks (cyan, magenta, yellow, and black, abbreviated as CMYK) are combined to create the color spectrum. The inks are not actually mixed to create color but are laid down separately in dots of varying patterns and sizes, and the viewer's eye does the mixing when viewing the final printed image.

In CMYK printing, four printing inks (cyan, magenta, yellow, and black) are laid down using dots of varying patterns and sizes to create the illusion of full color.

Cyan

Magenta

Yellow

Black

The quality of a printed image is greatly influenced by the refinement of its halftone screen. The finer the screen, the less apparent the dot pattern, because there are more dots per area and they are closer together. A high-resolution imagesetter, which can produce a high number of dots per inch, will accommodate a fine halftone screen.

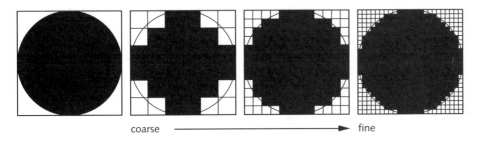

coarse ⟶ fine

The quality of a printed image depends on the refinement of its halftone screen and the resolution of the output device. A high-resolution device can accommodate a finer halftone screen, which means smoother shapes and a greater tonal range.

Here are the different types of resolution that affect printed images:

Dots per inch (dpi). Dots per inch is the value that measures the resolution of an output device. Most desktop printers have a resolution of 300 to 600 dots per inch. Imagesetters used for offset printing can print 1,200 or more dots per inch. Dots per inch, or *output device resolution,* is often confused with image resolution (see *Pixels per inch,* below).

Lines per inch (lpi). Lines per inch is the value that measures *halftone resolution.* The appropriate halftone resolution is dependent on output device resolution, printing paper, and, for offset printing, printing factors such as the type of printing plate and the quality of the press and press person.

Pixels per inch (ppi). Pixels per inch measures the resolution of the image. *Image resolution* measures all the sample points that represent color and value in your image. The more pixels your image is divided into, the greater resolution your image has.

When preparing a document for printing, the standard rule of thumb is to set the image resolution at twice the halftone resolution. Thus, for an image to be printed on a 600-dpi laser printer, which can accommodate a 65-lines-per-inch halftone screen, the image resolution should be about 130 pixels per inch.

Resolution on the Web

Images display differently on a computer screen than on a printed page. Whereas printed images are composed of dots of varying size and color, computer images are composed of square pixels: white and black pixels for basic text, different-colored pixels for color photographs and artwork.

Images on the computer are displayed using a grid of square pixels with each pixel shaded differently to create the illusion of continuous tone.

Enlarged detail of pixel grid

Unlike in print, where image resolution varies according to output device, on the Web there is one-to-one correlation between the resolution of an image and the resolution of its output device, the computer monitor. When a computer image is used for print, its pixels must be translated to halftone dots. An image displayed on screen needs no such transformation: a 72-pixels-per-inch Web image will display at full size on a 72-ppi monitor. If the image has more resolution than the screen – say, 100 ppi – the display will be larger than expected or look distorted as the Web browser tries to eliminate the extra pixels.

Because Web images display onscreen, there needs to be a 1:1 correlation between image resolution and monitor resolution. An image with more pixels per inch than the average display monitor will appear larger than expected.

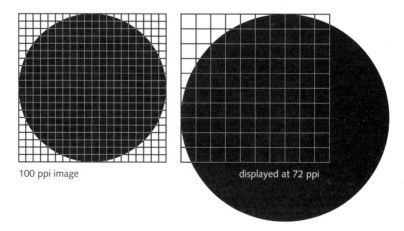

100 ppi image   displayed at 72 ppi

Another difference is that the computer monitor is a comparatively low-resolution output device: the typical monitor resolution is 72 to 96 pixels per inch. Printed images can contain more than 300 ppi of information (see *Resolution for print,* above). Maintaining the 1:1 ratio between image and monitor resolution means that Web images are normally resolved at 72 ppi, less than one-fourth of the standard image resolution used for high-quality offset printing.

Print resolution = 300 ppi

Screen resolution = 72 ppi

A screen image – normally resolved at 72 pixels per inch – has far fewer image samples, or pixels, than a standard printed image.

Web color

One area where Web imaging surpasses print is color. First, full-color printing is expensive, whereas Web color is essentially free. Second, the computer screen is superior to the page in several ways. As opposed to print color reproduction, in which the four inks cyan, magenta, yellow, and black are combined to give the illusion of full color, most monitors display at least 256 colors using the RGB (red, green, blue) color system, so an image viewed on the computer screen can display many more colors than a printed image. And whereas printed color images depend on reflected light, on the screen, color comes straight from the light source – the monitor. Because they are "transilluminated," screen images can display a broader range of contrast and intensity than printed images.

The downside of color on the Web is that, unlike in print, where colors are "fixed" on a page, each monitor displays color differently, so you can never be certain that your users will see your color images just as you see them on your monitor. In general, images on a Windows or Unix machine appear darker than images on a Macintosh. As a result, images designed on Windows look washed out on a Mac, and images designed on the Macintosh look darker on a Windows machine.

File size

The Web and print also diverge in the matter of file size. Given today's adage, "Disk is cheap," file size is normally not a consideration when one is creating images for print. Large image files can easily be stored on the high-capacity hard disks that come standard with today's desktop machines, and transported as needed using removable storage devices. Web images, however, need to be small so that they can move across the Internet briskly enough to reach the user before he or she tires of waiting. Small file size is particularly important for users connecting to the Internet via modem. For this reason Web graphics must be compressed and scaled.

PREPARING IMAGES

In Chapter 2 you gathered images for use on your site. Now it is time to modify those images for use on your Web pages. In this step you will learn how to prepare images that fit into your layout and are optimized for cross-platform display.

The image editing techniques are illustrated in this section using Photoshop, Adobe's popular image editing software. Photoshop is the standard tool for designing and manipulating graphics. The methods described here, however, are standard image editing techniques, so if you're using other software, though it may work a little differently, it should have the same functionality.

Before you begin producing images for your site, you'll need to customize your work area for creating Web images.

RGB color. Because Web images are displayed on a computer monitor, work with images using the RGB color mode, which is the monitor's model for creating color. Always use full-color RGB, even if you have to change the color mode later on (see *Saving images,* below).

Pixels. Image dimensions are dependent on the resolution of the output device, and the output device for Web images is the computer monitor, so start thinking in terms of pixels instead of inches or centimeters (see *Resolution,* above). Set your software to use "pixels" as the standard unit of measure so that your graphics can be sized and adjusted for the monitor.

Also, when creating images for the Web, always save a copy of the original full-size, full-resolution, full-color source file. The original image file will take many downward steps in its passage to the Web. If you save your original you can always return to the high-quality, unmodified version if needed. Also save all intermediate files either in Photoshop format or using a non-lossy compressed format such as TIFF. Do not save your images in a compressed Web file format until you have finished modifying them.

Scaling

The first step is to scale the image to the dimensions you will use on your page. Beginning Web designers often mistakenly include images that are too large for the layout or are at too high a resolution and then use the HEIGHT and WIDTH attributes of the image's HTML tag to scale each graphic to fit the page. This approach fails on two fronts. Even though the image now looks smaller on the page, its source is a large graphic file, and users must wait for this seemingly small image to load. The other problem is that images scaled using HTML usually look bad onscreen: often the proportions are off or the browser doesn't display the selected pixels cleanly.

Whenever possible, scale your graphics to fit within a single browser window. Images that are too wide require users to scroll in order to view the entire image, and they do not print well on standard letter-sized paper (see the safe-area dimensions detailed in *Page dimensions* for specifics about image size).

Use Photoshop's Image Size controls to scale the image to fit on your Web page. Be sure to set the image resolution to 72 pixels per inch.

Set the pixel dimensions to fit within your layout

Resolution for Web images should be set to 72 pixels per inch

Be sure to save a copy of your original full-size, full-resolution source file before scaling. Working from the copy, scale the image to fit into your layout. The actual dimensions depend on how you want the image to appear on the page, but be sure to set the resolution to 72 pixels per inch.

Optimizing images

Having scaled your image to fit your layout, take a few moments to adjust the image for optimal display. Done carefully, these three easy steps can make a world of difference in improving how your image looks onscreen.

Tonal correction. Tonal correction is a way of optimizing the color range in an image and is particularly important when working with photographic images. Tonal range describes the way image samples are distributed across the spectrum, from shadows to midtones to highlights. For example, low-contrast images are those where color samples are concentrated around the midtone area of the spectrum. Tonal correction is the process of selectively spreading out the image samples to increase the visible detail in an image. You can use Photoshop's Levels slider to make tonal corrections.

In the uncorrected photograph on the left, the image samples are concentrated around the shadows and midtones. The image on the right shows the photograph after using Photoshop's Levels adjustment to redistribute the image samples to span the spectrum, thereby increasing the tonal range of the photograph.

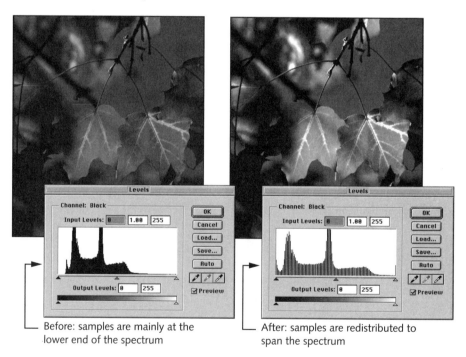

Before: samples are mainly at the lower end of the spectrum

After: samples are redistributed to span the spectrum

When making tonal adjustments to an image, keep in mind you are see-ing only one version of how the image will appear on the Web. As ex-plained above, every monitor displays color differently, and the differences are particularly marked between Macintosh and Windows displays. You can use Photoshop's Gamma controls to switch between the gamma settings of your monitor and the typical gamma settings of the "other" platform. By viewing an image under both conditions, you can settle on a middle ground tonal adjustment for your image.

Saturation. Adjusting image saturation using Photoshop's Hue/Saturation controls will make the color in your images more vibrant. Be sure to boost saturation in small increments and preview the results: too much added sat-uration could produce a strange-looking image.

You can use the satu-ration slider in Photoshop's Hue/ Saturation controls to *slightly* boost the strength of the color in your images.

Before

After

Move the slider to the right
to increase saturation

Sharpening. You can make your photographic images look crisper onscreen by using Photoshop's Unsharp Mask filter. Unsharp masking is a process of locating the edges in an image and increasing the contrast between the edge and the surrounding image. Scanned images in particular benefit from sharpening, because the scanning process often introduces image blur.

Unsharp masking sharpens an image by increasing the contrast around edges.

Before unsharp masking   After unsharp masking

SAVING IMAGES

File size is a major challenge when using images in a networked environment. An uncompressed image file can take up many megabytes of disk storage. To be delivered using limited Internet bandwidth to users with modem connections, Web image files must be sized in the range of bytes or kilobytes, not megabytes.

Uncompressed image files are too large to be delivered over the network to users with varying Internet connection speeds. To reduce file size, Web image files must be compressed.

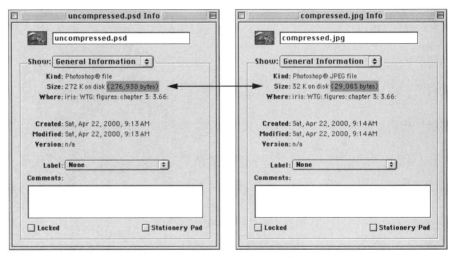

Uncompressed = 277K   Compressed = 29K

The challenge of Web image file formats is to apply compression to an image to remove redundant or less relevant data without significantly degrading image quality. The most commonly used Web image formats, Graphic Interchange Format (GIF) and Joint Photographic Experts Group (JPEG), each has its own method for compressing image data.

GIF format

The GIF format was introduced by CompuServe specifically to transmit images across the network. GIF compression uses the LZW (Lempel Zev Welch) compression algorithm, which is designed to remove redundancies in data storage. In the case of images, LZW compression works very well for images with large areas of a single color. In its simplest form, the compression scheme identifies the first occurrence of the color and then stores the color value along with the number of times it appears in succession.

When applying LZW compression to images that contain gradations of color, each color change must be saved, which represents an increase in file size. Also, the GIF format supports only 8-bit, or 256-color, graphics, which is inadequate for images that contain a broad range of color. For both these reasons, the GIF format is best used for diagrams, illustrations, and site graphics, not for photographic images.

Diagrammatic images and illustrations are better suited to GIF compression than are continuous-tone images like photographs.

The GIF format has the following characteristics.

Indexed color. A full-color RGB image can contain millions of colors. When you create a GIF image, you must reduce the number of colors to a maximum of 256. To create an indexed color image using Photoshop, you change the color mode from RGB to Indexed Color. Photoshop then generates a 256-cell color *palette* made up of the colors that are most used in the image. In the conversion process from full to indexed color, image colors that do not make it into the color palette are simulated using a combination of the available colors.

An effective method for reducing file size for GIF graphics is to reduce the number of colors in the color palette. For example, with simple images, such as interface graphics, you can reduce the number of colors down from 256 without a perceptible loss of image quality.

18 colors: 4,827 bytes

8 colors: 4,019 bytes

Interlacing. An interlaced GIF graphic displays progressively in the browser while the image file is downloading. Interlacing is particularly important for large graphics because it allows users to preview an image without having to wait until it downloads fully.

Transparency. You can designate a color or colors in a GIF image to be transparent when displayed on a Web page. Using transparency in an image means that the background of the page can show through.

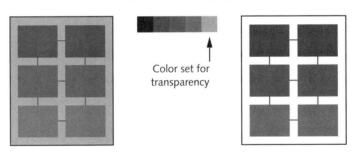

Color set for transparency

JPEG graphics

JPEG files are full-color images compressed using a "lossy" compression scheme – lossy because in the process of squeezing the image, data is discarded. The algorithm is selective about the type of image information it removes, so even highly compressed images retain what the algorithm determines are critical details and lose only the more "unnecessary" data.

Because the JPEG format supports full-color (24-bit) images, it is a better choice than GIF for photographic images or complex illustrations. JPEG also achieves much higher compression ratios than GIF, particularly for photographic images: a photograph compressed using JPEG will be two to three times smaller than one using GIF compression. Where JPEGs are problematic is with images with hard edges or high-contrast images, such as photographs shot against a plain background or graphics that include text. Using JPEG compression for images with sharp color boundaries will produce JPEG "noise" around the boundary edges.

Enlarged detail of JPEG

The JPEG compression algorithm can produce blocky patterns and pixel "noise," particularly in areas of sharp contrast such as around the edges of these tulips.

These factors influence the display of JPEG graphics:

Quality. When using the JPEG format, you can use the quality settings to control the amount of compression that is applied to your image. Of course, the higher the quality setting, the larger the file, and for a Web image, the aim is to squeeze the data enough to reduce file size significantly. When saving JPEG graphics you will need to experiment with the quality settings to achieve the smallest file size while maintaining image integrity.

Progressive JPEGs. As with interlaced GIFs, progressive JPEGs write image data to the screen as the image is downloading so that users can preview the image as it loads.

Save your originals!

Before saving your image files in either of the formats described, be sure to *save an original, uncompressed version*. If you keep only the GIF file, you won't have a full-color version. If you save only the JPEG file, all you'll have is a compressed version of the image, and if you do any further editing and re-save the image, its quality will suffer substantially (JPEG loss is additive: each time you modify and resave a JPEG there is further image-quality loss). Keep an archive of uncompressed images in case you later want to resave using a new format or modify an image.

IMAGES ON THE PAGE

Once your images have been optimized and saved in a Web file format, you can start plugging them into your pages. How you do this depends on how you are using images — as site graphics, as illustrations to support textual content, as the primary content. Your task at this stage is to incorporate the images into your page design so that they integrate well with other site content.

The approach you take in incorporating graphics into your Web page layout depends on the function of the images.

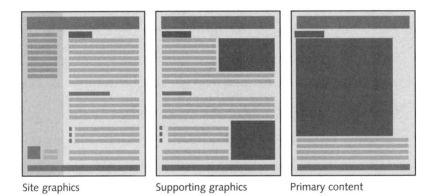

Site graphics   Supporting graphics   Primary content

Thumbnails

If you are presenting large, high-resolution images on your site you may want to use a two-image scheme using thumbnails linked to the full-sized images. In this approach, you save a thumbnail version (maybe about 100–130 pixels high) for every image and present the thumbnails with a brief description on a main page of your site. That way, users can browse the thumbnail page and then click a thumbnail only when they want — and are willing to wait for — access to the full-sized image. This interface to large graphics means that users do not endure lengthy download times for images that may not be relevant to their needs.

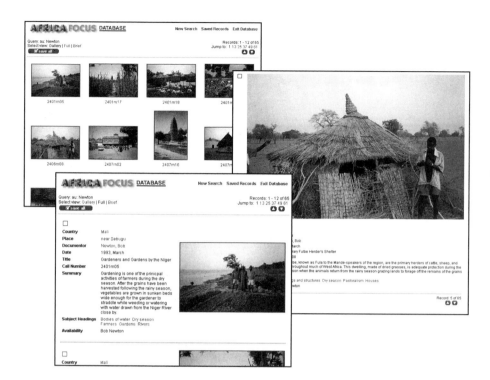

The thumbnail interface to the image collection on the Africa Focus Web site provides three options for viewing search results. Users can select images by clicking the corresponding checkbox, then have the selected images sent to their email account.

Image HTML

When putting an image on a Web page, it is important that you include the following details in the image source code:

Height and width. Although an image *will* display without its dimensions defined in the source code, it is best to include the HEIGHT and WIDTH attributes. If you leave them out, the browser must actually load the image before it can determine how much space to allot on the page. By contrast, when you supply the image dimensions, the other page elements can load into place while the image is loading. The user can see the layout and begin to read without waiting for the images to download.

Alternate text. The ALT attribute is essential for visitors who for whatever reason are unable to see your images. Some users have browsers that do not support images or have a slow Internet connection and therefore turn their browser's image display off. Visually impaired users use software that reads them Web pages. The text you supply using the ALT tag is what shows (or is read) when the image is not displayed.

Paul Christesen: Dartmouth College

Professor of classics Paul Christesen got involved with the Web while addressing larger issues in classical studies. The classics department at Dartmouth College, in Hanover, New Hampshire, has been rethinking its approach. "We're concerned about building a curriculum that blurs the distinction between different kinds of data. One problem that has always been an issue for classical scholars is that people tend to specialize in one particular body of information: historians are text-driven, archaeologists specialize in artifacts, literature people read a specialized subcategory of text. And there has been a general sense that we could all use the other bodies of information quite handily and that this would be better for the students because it would assemble a more complete and, I think, more entertaining picture for them. So we've been trying to encourage students to be more broadly defined in their field of information." To this end the classics department introduced Theories and Methods in Ancient History. Designed for midrange classical studies, this course exposes students to the various bodies of evidence people studying the classical world use, along with the relevant methodologies for interpreting them.

Promoting a multidimensional curriculum, however, raises basic discrepancies regarding information access. If students were supposed to be looking at multiple bodies of information, they had to have access – outside class time – to the information. Says Paul, "The literary people and the historians have tended to photocopy and hand out texts, and so it was feasible to ask students to read them before class. The archaeologists have found themselves in a more complicated position because they want students to look at artifacts, or images of artifacts, which generally students can't look at before they come to class." This deficiency has meant that classicists have had some difficulty in getting students to consider visual data to the same extent as textual data. "Here we are saying that images are 'texts' and that you can read this form of information exactly as you can read Thucydides and Herodotus, but what you're actually saying to the student is, 'You have two-and-a-half minutes to look at the slide – okay, that's it, you'll never see it again.' That's a problem; it doesn't encourage students to take images seriously."

Paul was assigned to teach this new course, and his first task was to bridge the access gap, so that when students were studying image-based texts, such as artifacts, they had easy access to high-quality images before class. Paul used the Web to distribute the 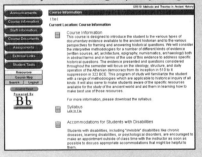 images: "It was not feasible to do in any other way as far as I could tell" (the other options being grainy photocopies or a shared study slide collection). To construct the Web site, Paul used the CourseInfo courseware tool, and offered, along with course handouts and other materials, access to the image collections. In preparing the images, Paul used LivePicture technology, which allows Web users to view images at high resolution.

Having addressed the problem of access, Paul set about assembling the image collections. Because the focus of his course is interpretation rather than content, he felt that standard textbooks had too much interpretive information to be useful. For his course, he needed image collections with just enough text to allow the students to interpret the images on their own. Because he was using the Web, he decided to create custom image sets, choosing just those images that focused on what he wanted his students to see. This flexibility, however, came at a significant cost. In eschewing textbooks in favor of a custom approach, he found that he had to create supporting materials to go along with his image collections. "I had this wonderful set of images, but how was I going to link them? What I ended up doing was writing the text around the images, so that they all tied together very well, but what I had written was pretty much a chapter in a textbook, and that was shockingly time-consuming."

The demands of this endeavor proved to be too significant. The next time he creates a course Web site he will assemble an image collection, but with minimal text. And although he acknowledges that this approach is "less than optimal for the student," as a junior faculty member he has other obligations. "Academic institutions simply haven't had the time to come to terms with the Web yet. We need to figure out how writing Web content fits into existing requirements to produce publishable scholarly work. Until we figure that out, there is a disincentive to engage in this sort of behavior, because, with the institution

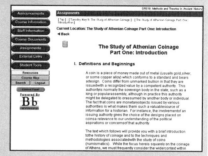

rewarding other sorts of behavior, and with only so many hours in the day, Web course development inevitably gets short shrift."

In spite of the time demands, Paul is pleased with the results of his endeavor. The custom image collections have allowed students to make much more rapid progress since they work only with images that are directly relevant to the course. And having the images online means that it is much easier to make side-by-side comparisons. Paul has found that his students are doing much more comparison work: "You can't ask for more than that." An unanticipated benefit has been that the number of images students use in their coursework has increased. "It hadn't occurred to me to that this would have ramifications for the shape of their own work, but they've become much more interested in using images within their own work as well."

But, says Paul, the students were "a little creaky in the beginning." They weren't used to having part of their coursework be to make sure that their systems were properly configured. "I understood their complaint, which was, this is a part of the learning process with which they never really had to deal with before. This was not just having your pencils ready, but having your technology group ready to do the work you needed to do." The next time he uses the site, he will be more proactive about making sure the software requirements are clearly defined and that students have plenty of help in getting up and running. And although he acknowledges the additional challenges of using technology, he did not yield to the students' resistance. "When I talked to them, we talked about how technology gives us pedagogical possibilities that require effort on both my part and their part. They haven't done it before and I haven't done it before, but that doesn't mean we shouldn't do it, it just means we have to learn how to do it."

The pivotal moment for the students came one day during class in a technology classroom. "We were talking about a particular bird that was on one of the vases, and I asked them what the bird was and what it was doing there. One of them said, 'It's carrying something in its claws, what do you think that is?' and I said, 'Well, let's find out right now.' And on the big screen this little tiny detail on the vase can be four feet high, and they can see incredibly small details, and they said, 'Gee, we know what that is now.' And you could sort of hear the gears grinding in their heads: 'Hmm, wow, that was kind of interesting.' Things got much easier after that little incident." ■

Multimedia

The considerations involved in putting multimedia files on the Web generally concern the need to create files that are small enough to move across the network and don't place unreasonable demands on the user's machine. Raw audio and video take huge amounts of data. For the Web only a small percentage of that data can be used so that users can begin working with the materials without unreasonable delays or uneven playback. The key is to strike a balance between the amount of movie data needed to maintain quality and the capacity of the typical network connection and desktop machine of your target audience.

FORMATS

Multimedia content on the Web can be delivered in several ways. The two most popular multimedia architectures for the Web are QuickTime from Apple Computer and RealMedia (RealAudio and RealVideo) from RealNetworks. Both options are fully cross-platform and work with a variety of formats, including Video for Windows, WAVE (.wav), and AIFF (Audio Interchange File Format) files. These multimedia architectures are composed of various software extensions and a player application – QuickTime Player and RealPlayer. You can include QuickTime and RealMedia content directly on a Web page, though Web authors commonly set up RealMedia content to play using RealPlayer. For both options, the basic software components are free for download, and both have an inexpensive upgrade option that gives users better-quality playback and additional features.

For this discussion, however, we will focus on QuickTime. QuickTime is cross-platform, and the QuickTime plug-in comes as part of most browser software, which means that users don't have to perform any special installations to view QuickTime content. The more recent QuickTime versions support streaming and have special compression options designed specifically for low data-rate delivery. QuickTime also offers a wide range of media types, including interactivity and VR panorama and object movies. It is because of these strengths and its broad user base that QuickTime is currently the most widely used Web multimedia format.

DATA RATE

The key issue when preparing media content for the Web is determining the appropriate movie data-rate limit for your audio and video content. The data rate is the amount of data required to represent one second of movie time and is normally measured in kilobytes per second (KBps). A typical Web video, for example, has a data rate anywhere from 8 to 80 KBps. If you consider that the goal with still images is to keep file size down – ideally below 50 kilobytes – think about the demands of pumping out a still image of that size every second! The objective when preparing Web media, then, is to reduce the movie data rate as much as possible while maintaining some degree of quality.

You'll need to weigh the following when determining the suitable data-rate limit for your target audience:

Connection speed. For real-time movie playback, the movie data rate needs to be lower than the connection speed of the typical user. For example, if your users are connecting to the Internet with 56.6 modems, which are capable of receiving about 7 KBps, for real-time playback the movie data rate will need to be about 4–5 KBps (the movie rate needs to be lower than the access speed to allow for Web congestion). If you are using downloadable-format media files and don't object to delays, you can set the movie data rate higher than the user's connection speed.

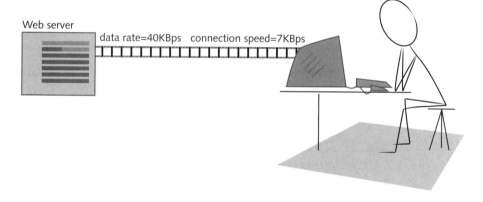

As long as your users don't mind waiting, you can get better-quality media by using a downloadable format that allows you to set the movie data rate higher than the user's connection speed.

CPU (Central Processing Unit). Some of the best audio and video compression options are "CPU-intensive" and require a high-end computer for smooth playback (see *Compression,* below). This means that even if the data rate is right for your users' connection speed, they may not be able to play your movies if their computer's processor cannot keep up with the demands of playback. When compressing media for the Web, test your movies, especially those that use CPU-intensive compression, on different machines.

COMPRESSION

One approach to reducing a movie's data rate is to reduce the quality of the materials. For example, you can downsample audio from 16 to 8 bits or reduce the frequency from 44.100 to 22.050 kHz. With video, you can scale the movie size from full-screen, 640 × 480 pixels, down to, say, 240 × 180, or display fewer frames per second. Using this method, less data is needed to reproduce the materials, so the file size and data rate are reduced, though so is the quality of the materials. Used alone, however, this method is not sufficient. Even after substantial downsampling, media files are still too big for network delivery, so they must also be compressed.

Media compression is achieved using codecs, or compression algorithms that handle the *co*mpression of media files and the *de*compression at playback. Codecs work by removing redundant or "less important" data from a file. For example, video compresses well when shot against a single-color background, because the codec will identify the redundant color pixels in the image and save only the area coordinates and color. Conversely, an image with a detailed background – such as a backdrop of bushes or trees – will be difficult for the codec to generalize. Also, video that contains minimal motion compresses well because the codec saves only the differences from frame to frame. Thus, a static shot of an interview, for example, will compress better than one with a lot of camera movement and motion.

Video compression algorithms reduce the amount of movie data using temporal compression, where only data that changes between frames is stored, and spatial compression, which generalizes movie frames to remove redundant image data.

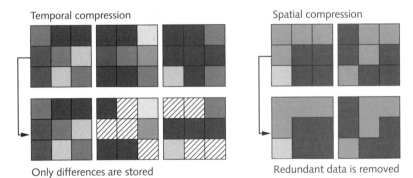

Temporal compression

Only differences are stored

Spatial compression

Redundant data is removed

A primary benefit of using compression is that you can do less downsampling and use compression instead to lower the data rate. With audio files, for example, compression alone is sometimes enough to lower the data rate for Web use, in which case you can keep the audio settings at CD-quality. This option does not hold true for Web video. Given the high data demands of video, it is currently not possible to use compression alone to reduce the image data to a range suitable for the Web.

Although they are thought of largely as a means for limiting data transfer rates, codecs play an important part in multimedia playback. With compressed media, decompression needs to happen fast enough for the movie to play in real time on the user's computer. If the data rate is high, the demands of real-time playback may be too high for low-end machines. For example, with a 15-fps video, each frame needs to decompress in less than 1/15th of a second for smooth playback. A slower computer may not be able to keep up with decompression and playback at that rate, in which case frames will drop and movie playback will stutter. It is crucial to consider both the average connection rate *and* the typical processor of your users. Be sure to test your Web media under typical viewing conditions.

DELIVERING MULTIMEDIA

In a typical Web session, the files associated with a page – the image files, the HTML documents – are downloaded from the server and stored on the hard drive or in memory on the user's machine. When a Web page includes multimedia content such as audio or video, the files tend to be much larger than even a large image file, so the demands on the user's machine increase. For example, a 10-minute video, even when heavily compressed for the Web, can require 10–20 megabytes of storage. These large files also mean long delays as the files traverse the network from the server to the user's machine. And even if you want to view only a small segment, you have to wait for the entire movie to download.

To make these interactions less tiresome, most large files, such as image or movie files, have a progressive download feature that allows users to begin interaction with the content before it is fully downloaded. The interlacing feature described above under *Saving images* is one example of a progressive approach. With downloadable audio or video content, progressive download means that users can start to play the movies once a small portion of the file is received.

Streaming technology was devised to try to manage the data demands of multimedia. With streaming media, data is sent to the user in a continuous stream, but only a small amount, or buffer, is actually stored on the user's machine. The stream is played directly from the buffer to the display, and once a segment plays, it is discarded to make room for the incoming stream, greatly reducing the storage demands on the user's machine. Streaming also provides random access, so users can start viewing at any point in the movie. The shortcoming of streaming media is that, in order to play back in real time, the movie data rate needs to be low enough to stay below the user's connection speed. To keep the data stream manageable, the movie quality of streaming media tends to be lower than that of its downloadable counterpart.

Streaming media files can be accessed anywhere in the stream, and they play directly from the buffer to the page and are then discarded. Downloadable media must be downloaded from the beginning, and the entire file is stored on the user's machine. If there is a network glitch, a streaming file will lose data, whereas with downloadable media, the download will pause and resume once the network has cleared.

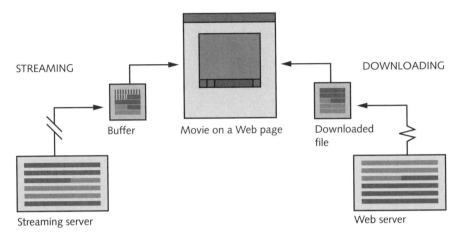

STREAMING   Buffer   Movie on a Web page   Downloaded file   DOWNLOADING

Streaming server   Web server

Strengths of downloadable multimedia

- Quality. Playback is not dependent upon connection speed, so you *can* put high-quality video on your site: it will just take longer to load.
- Data integrity. Downloadable media will arrive intact on the user's machine.
- No special server. You can put downloadable QuickTime on a regular Web server.

Weaknesses

- Storage demands. Downloaded movies are stored in memory or on the hard drive of the user's computer. Even a 10-minute video clip takes up many megabytes of storage.
- Lengthy download. For users connecting to the Internet via modem, a 3-minute video clip could take 10 minutes to load. With QuickTime's progressive download feature, or "fast start" QuickTime, users can begin playing a movie soon after the movie begins to download. As long as the download speed is faster than the movie data rate, playback should continue uninterrupted.
- No random access. Movie data is downloaded in sequence, so even if you want to view only the last few minutes of a movie, you must wait for the entire movie to download.

- Saving. Because the movies are downloaded, they can be saved on the user's machine and potentially misappropriated.

Strengths of streaming multimedia
- Buffering. Only a buffer is actually saved on the user's machine, so the storage demands are minimal.
- Random access. If you want to begin viewing in the middle of a movie, you use the movie controls to move forward and then click "play." The server sends the media stream beginning from your requested starting point.
- Cannot be saved. With streaming media, users can save only a pointer to the actual movie source, not the movie itself, which makes copyright violation difficult.

Weaknesses
- Not enough quality. Because of the requirements of real-time playback, streaming media quality is often inferior to that of downloadable media. Playback suffers if the network bogs down or the computer can't keep up with the data stream: the movie stutters and drops frames, affecting both image quality and playback. Also, to keep the data rate below the user's connection speed, the overall movie quality must be lower than with downloadable media.
- Requires streaming server. Streaming media needs a special streaming media server to manage the flow of data between it and the user.

COMPROMISES

The process of preparing audiovisual content for the Web is all about making compromises. With so much data involved, you have to make choices about what information can be removed or degraded without destroying your message. If, for example, you want to use the Web to provide audio clips to your students, you may decide that the quality of the audio is paramount. In this case, you may opt for large files and lengthy downloads with no sacrifice in quality. Or with video content, you may decide that smooth motion is critical, in which case you could prepare the video using a high frame rate, but lower image-quality settings and set a small frame size.

Preparing Web multimedia is a delicate process of balancing the needs of your content with the limitations of the medium. After working with your materials and experimenting with different approaches, you may decide that the compromises are too great: that the quality loss is so significant that it renders the materials useless. In this case you may need to find an alternative method for delivering your multimedia content.

PREPARING CLIPS

Too often media content is captured in digital format and put on the Web without special processing. Considering the overhead that is involved with Web media, both on the authoring end and from the user's perspective, optimizing the quality is well worth the effort. A few minor tweaks and adjustments can turn messy, poor-quality video and audio into something worth waiting for. In this section we will cover some quick and easy adjustments to your Web multimedia that will greatly enhance the quality of your final product.

The illustrations and examples of multimedia processing shown below all use the media compression tool Media Cleaner Pro (MCP), from Terran Interctive. The MCP interface greatly simplifies the process of preparing media content and produces superior results.

Optimizing audio

Audio is commonly overlooked when multimedia clips are being prepared, though a weak or noisy audio track can be more intrusive than jerky motion or poor image quality. The best time to adjust the audio signal for digital multimedia files is at capture time, but if you find yourself with digital audio that lacks amplitude or needs to be cleaned up, there's still hope. You can use MCP, or an audio editing program such as Sonic Foundry's Sound Forge or Macromedia's SoundEdit 16, to filter out the noise, boost amplitude, and greatly improve the overall signal.

Normalizing an audio track boosts the amplitude by locating the loudest peak in the audio signal and amplifying the file to make that peak's volume 100 percent.

Original audio track

Audio track after normalizing

Video preprocessing

In a few easy steps you can clean up your video before compressing and saving it. Not only will these methods improve the quality of your video, but they will also improve compression. Remember that detail makes compression difficult. If your video has unnecessary detail, such as video noise or interlacing artifacts, then the codec has to work hard to compress it. If you preprocess your video to remove unnecessary details, the codec can focus on compressing the actual video, not its blemishes. And better-looking video will result.

Trim clips. Make sure that your video starts and ends with a high-quality frame that looks good out of the context of the movie. When downloading video, the first movie frame is what the user sees while the movie is loading, and the last frame remains on the screen once the movie has finished playing. These frames need to look good as still images.

Cropping. Video captured from analog source often has noise around the edges: an ugly border of black or messy pixels. In preparing Web video, you should crop the image to remove any video noise. If the original has a lot of unnecessary detail around the edges, you can also crop the movie to better frame the video.

Original image   video noise   Image cropped to remove border

When processing video, be sure to crop the image to remove any black or messy pixels from around the border of the image.

Image quality. As with still images, you need to adjust video image quality for optimal onscreen and cross-platform viewing. Try boosting the contrast for a more vibrant image, and adjust the gamma settings for greater consistency across platforms.

As with still images, you can greatly improve the quality of your Web video by adjusting the brightness, contrast, and saturation of the image.

Original image

Image with color values adjusted

Interlacing. Some video source may be interlaced, containing two images (or fields) of alternating odd and even lines (see Chapter 2: *Images from video*). You can recognize interlacing by the horizontal stripes that appear around objects, particularly in areas of high contrast. To remove interlacing image artifacts, use MCP's de-interlace filter to blend the fields.

You can use software to remove video interlacing artifacts – the horizontal stripes that appear around objects – particularly when there is motion in the video.

Original image with interlacing

Image adjusted to remove interlacing

PROCESSING CLIPS

Having adjusted your media source, you are ready to process the file for Web use. This step reduces the file size and data rate for Web delivery. This data-reduction process is like reallocating funds from different accounts (or robbing Peter to pay Paul?): data is removed from an area where its absence may not be noticed and reallocated to address a more critical need.

Generally speaking, when you allot more data to a specific aspect of a movie, there must be a decrease in quality elsewhere. For example, if you opt for a large video frame size, such as 320 × 240 pixels, the quality of the video image will degrade. The first step, then, when processing media content, is to assess the demands of your materials. You need to determine which aspects can bear compromise and which cannot. You may decide, for example, to devote more data to smooth motion than to image quality or to favor the audio track over the video. When preparing Web media you will need to experiment with different settings to determine those that best meet the requirements of your materials.

Audio
When processing audio, experiment with the following settings to find the best solution for your materials:

Single-channel audio. Audio files can contain multiple channels, but each additional channel adds to the file size. Make sure you don't use stereo settings for mono source, and even if you are working with multiple-channel audio, consider switching to mono to reduce the data.

Sample rate. If your source audio is sampled at 44.100 kHz, you can use software to resample to a lower frequency, such as 22.050 kHz. For voice-only audio, you may be able to reduce the sample rate as far as 11.025 kHz.

Sample size. CD-quality audio has a sample size of 16 bits. For some materials, such as a good-quality interview or narration, you may be able to reduce the audio to 8-bit samples, depending on the compression you use, though in most cases the degradation in quality is too great.

Compression. QuickTime offers low data-rate codecs for audio compression, including the QDesign Music Codec for compressing music and Qual-Comm's PureVoice for compressing voice-only audio. If you compress audio using QDesign you may be able to keep your settings at CD quality (44.1 kHz, 16-bit, stereo), and have the compression lower the data rate. Bear in mind, however, that CPU-intensive codecs like QDesign may be too demanding for playback on low-end machines (see *Compression,* above).

Video
When processing video for the Web, you will need to work with the following elements to reduce the movie data rate.

Audio. For video that contains an audio track, you can downsample and compress the audio as explained above to reduce the overall data rate.

Frame rate. Standard TV-quality video has a frame rate of 30 frames per second (29.97, to be precise). This frame rate enables motion on television to look smooth. On the Web, you can reduce the video data rate by reducing the frame rate to 15 fps or fewer. You will need to experiment to find the right frame rate for your materials. For example, the frame rate for a low-motion video sequence, such as a "talking head" interview, can be as low as 6–10 fps. When choosing a frame rate, make sure to choose a number that is an even divisor of the frame rate of your source materials (for 30-fps NTSC video, choose 15, 10, 7.5, 6, 5, and so on).

Frame size. Frame size influences all other factors. For example, with a large frame size, the amount of data needed to represent each frame is greater because the frame is bigger. The data rate required to support the frame rate of a large-sized movie thus needs to be higher or the image quality will suffer. Full-screen video is 640 × 480 pixels, but the data rate needed to display these dimensions cannot be supported on the Web. Large Web video is generally quarter-screen, 320 × 240. If you are developing video for users connecting via modem, you will need to scale your video down as small as 160 × 120 (or smaller!).

Quality. Adjustments to image quality can reduce the data rate. For example, introducing a slight blur into a video simplifies the image, which makes for better compression. Some codecs also allow adjustments to image quality that affect the movie data rate: with a lower image-quality setting, more compression is applied to the image, resulting in reduced image quality and a lower data rate.

Compression. The QuickTime codec most commonly used for Web video is the Sorenson Video codec. Sorenson maintains good image quality at low Web data rates. Like QDesign, however, Sorenson is processor-intensive. Use Sorenson only at data rates lower than 100 KBps, and be sure to test your movies on different machines.

MULTIMEDIA ON THE PAGE

Careful and conservative is the best approach to take when putting multimedia on your Web pages. For a Web user, multimedia comes with a big overhead – special plug-ins, long waits, potential system crashes. When designing an interface for your multimedia content, set it up so that users get only the media they want when they want it and can control their interaction with the files.

Placement

Don't put multimedia on the main pages of your site. People exploring your site should not be forced to wait for large and possibly irrelevant media files to load. High-bandwidth materials like audio and video should be offered only in response to an informed user choice. Offer access to media content via links from the main site, and provide ample description of the materials along with the links. Also be sure to explain any software requirements needed for viewing, so that users can perform any required installations before visiting the pages.

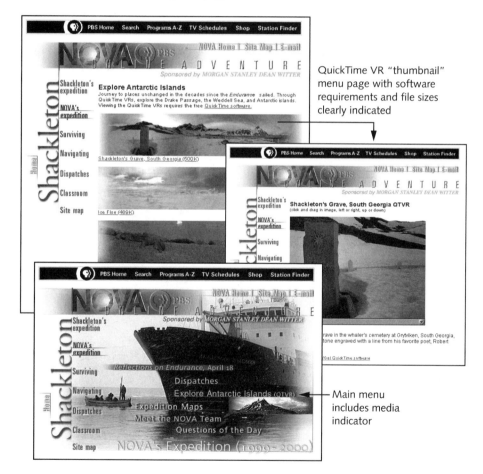

QuickTime VR "thumbnail" menu page with software requirements and file sizes clearly indicated

NOVA offers an excellent interface to its media-rich sites. Users can see what types of materials are available and can choose which files to download depending on their connection to the Internet.

Main menu includes media indicator

User control

Have you ever loaded a Web page that included background music in a public setting, such as the public library? Web authors often make the mistake of including media files on a page without offering the user any controls. Assuming that all users will want to experience your multimedia (or are in an appropriate setting to do so) can be a fatal error in Web design. In the library setting, the only way to stop the music may be to close the Web browser window without getting a chance to look at the page content.

Let interaction with your Web multimedia be entirely user-driven. Always include a media controller with your media content, and avoid prescribed playback options such as looping and autoplay. For example, with autoplay, when a Web page is loaded and enough of the media file is available, the movie begins to play automatically without the user pressing Start. This can be intrusive, particularly for pages that have other elements, such as descriptive text: the user might want to read the text before playing the movie, or he or she might *only* be interested in the text. Design your multimedia interface so that media files play only when the user explicitly elects to initiate playback.

Summary

At the end of this step you will have integrated the materials gathered in Chapter 2 into your Web site framework. For each content type – text, links, multimedia – you established an effective approach to displaying the materials on the page, and you applied that approach consistently across all the pages in your site. You also took steps to prepare your images and media for Web delivery and for optimal cross-platform display.

Things to consider at the end of this process include:

- Have you used a consistent typographic approach on all the pages in your site?
- Have you checked your site on different display monitors? Do your images and video look good (or good enough) on both Macintoshes and Windows machines?
- Have you tried loading your media-rich pages using a desktop machine and an Internet connection that match your typical student's setup? Do your image and media files download and display fast enough?

At the conclusion of this process, you will have a Web site that is ready to use, even if it is not completely populated with content. This is a benefit of starting with a site framework instead of building the site page by page. As long as the links function and the page connections are set, you can start using your site before all the content is in place: just insert an announcement that there is "content to come" on the empty pages, and fill in the materials as they become available. Your users will tolerate incomplete pages much better than they will broken links.

Now that you have a real site in place, with real content, ask a few students to review your site and monitor their interactions. Look for areas where the site design or navigation fail – where users are unsure of what to do next, appear lost, or follow a link that yields unintended results. See how they navigate the site: Do they use the site links or the browser back button? Or do they bypass all navigation and go directly to the search feature? If your site is fairly complete, you might consider conducting a more formal usability test to uncover flaws in your design (see Chapter 5: *Do-it-yourself assessment*) before implementing the site in the classroom.

At this point you should also update your content list to assess the status of each content item. Is the item on the site? Is it awaiting copyright permission? Does it still need processing? As your site grows and evolves, use your checklist to manage your site inventory and to track the status of content items.

REFERENCES

Blatner, David, Glenn Fleishman, and Steve Roth. 1998. *Real world scanning and halftones: The definitive guide to scanning and halftones from the desktop.* 2d ed. Berkeley, Calif.: Peachpit.

Bringhurst, Robert. 1996. *The elements of typographic style.* 2d ed. Point Roberts, Wash.: Hartley and Marks.

Castro, Elizabeth. 1998. HTML 4 *for the World Wide Web.* Berkeley, Calif.: Peachpit.

Day, Rob. 1995. *Designer Photoshop.* 2d ed. New York: Random House.

Lie, Håkom Wium, and Bert Bos. 1997. *Cascading Style Sheets: Designing for the Web.* Reading, Mass.: Addison-Wesley.

Lynch, Patrick J., and Sarah Horton. 1999. *Web style guide: Basic design principles for creating Web sites.* New Haven and London: Yale University Press. [See also http://info.med.yale.edu/caim/manual]

Microsoft Corporation. 2000. *Microsoft typography.* http://www.microsoft. com/typography/default.asp.

Niederst, Jennifer. 1999. *Web design in a nutshell. A desktop quick reference.* Sebastopol, Calif.: O'Reilly.

Stern, Judith, and Robert Lettieri. 1999. *QuickTime Pro for Macintosh and Windows.* Berkeley, Calif.: Peachpit.

Terran Interactive. 1995–99. *Media Cleaner Pro 4 User Manual.* San Jose, Calif.: Terran Interactive. [See also http://www.terran-int.com]

———. 1999. *How to produce high-quality QuickTime.* San Jose, Calif.: Terran Interactive. [See also http://www.terran-int.com/QuickTime/ Article]

Waggoner, Ben. Making great Web video. *DV* (October 1999). http://www.dv.com/magazine/1999/1099/webvideo1099.pdf (18 February 2000).

Williams, Robin, and John Tollett. 1998. *The non-designer's Web book: An easy guide to creating, designing, and posting your own Web site.* Berkeley, Calif.: Peachpit.

4 Using the site

I may not have gone where I intended to go, but I think I have ended up
where I intended to be.
– Douglas Adams

Y OUR COURSE WEB SITE is a tool, and a tool by itself has little effect.
For your effort to pay off, you need to incorporate the site into your teaching method effectively. This chapter explores ways to use your course Web
site successfully both within and outside class.

Your course site is useful only if your students work with it. Depending
on the nature of the site, your students may be more or less inclined to
consider it part of their learning method. If the perceived gain in using the
site is significant, you may not have to do much selling; students enrolled in
your class know that they need to learn the materials, and they are likely to
readily adopt any tool that expedites that effort. If the course site serves a
more supplementary role, you may find that you need to coax them into
using it. Integrating the site into your classroom teaching and maximizing
its visibility will increase its chances for success with your students.

Many course Web sites are designed as resources for both classroom use
and student use outside class. In fact, using the Web in class is an excellent
way to promote student use of your course site. Yet with so many components involved – hardware, software, network, projection – and so many of
them beyond your control, it is important to acknowledge that something
might go wrong and prepare accordingly. If you plan to use the Web as part
of your classroom teaching, be sure to practice with the classroom technology setup and prepare your presentation to avoid glitches.

A final consideration when using the Web is whether you want your online classroom to be part of the *worldwide* Web or whether you want your
site to follow the more intimate model of the traditional classroom. Each
approach has its benefits, but if you choose to host only your students, you
will need to restrict access to your course Web site.

ESTABLISH THE SITE
Student participation is one of the wildest wildcards in the success of a
course Web site. As the saying goes, you can lead a horse to water, but you
cannot make it drink. There is no magic formula that will guarantee stu-

dent participation short of inflicting a penalty on nonparticipants. Perhaps the most important factor in encouraging participation is your own attitude toward the site. If you regard the site as an adjunct, your students will perceive it as additional and unnecessary work with little influence on what many consider to be the most important learning outcome: their grade. For students to take a course site seriously, you must make it clear that *you* consider it essential by integrating the site into your teaching method.

Promoting your site

Unless your site has content or features that significantly enhance their understanding, students may not use your course Web site for much more than checking a meeting time or posting a perfunctory comment to the discussion area. The best way to avoid failure is to offer students a Web site with substantive content.

Even if you have created a site that *you* know is valuable, your students may still not begin using it. The Web is not (as yet) an established medium as are books, labs, and lectures. For example, when you assign your students a book to read, they approach the task with a basic understanding of why and how to read books. The Web is another matter. Certain areas of the Web are somewhat predictable – notably, commercial sites – but educational Web sites are far from standardized. In other words, you know why you go to an online bookstore: to buy books. You cannot expect students to know *why* they would use your course Web site.

Also, do not assume that your students know *how* to use the Web. Make sure they understand how you are using the Web site to teach, and guide them on how to make best use of the site.

Give a site tour. If you have the requisite classroom technology, display the site during one of the first class sessions. Give your students a full tour of the site, making sure to emphasize the aspects that you feel are particularly valuable. Make sure they are comfortable with the technology, so they don't get hung up later by technical aspects of using the site.

Include an FAQ. Establish a Web site FAQ (see Chapter 2: *Frequently asked questions*) that addresses any student issues with using the course Web site. Encourage students to report problems they have with the site, and include the problems with resolutions in the FAQ.

Use the site in class. Find ways to integrate the site into your classroom teaching. Even if you don't have the resources to display and work with the site in class, you can still use it in class – for example, use class time to address questions that were raised in discussion on the Web site.

Give credit. If you consider your Web site to be an essential part of your students' learning experience, find ways to reward those who use it – for example, include questions based on content from the site on exams, or base a percentage of the grade on Web site participation.

Make them "look it up." When students ask you directly about something that is available on the site, such as information about scheduling, don't answer: send them to the Web site instead. Condition them to turn to the site first; it's likely to be more available than you are, and if you use the site to cover the basics, you'll be free to focus on more challenging questions.

Encouraging participation

As with any conversation, online communication needs participants; without continuing exchange, conversation falters and dies out. This may occur in a course discussion area for a number of reasons:

- No community. Classroom dynamics play a large part in the success of online discussion – if there is little exchange in the classroom, there isn't likely to be much online. It is important to build community in class if you want online discussion to flourish.
- No motivation. If you give too little weight to discussion, students may not bother to participate. Make sure they know that online discussion is essential to your teaching method and that you expect them to participate.
- Unfamiliarity. Students new to online discussions may not participate because they are unfamiliar with the technology. Spend class time showing your students how to use the discussion area – how to read submissions and post comments.

Here are some methods for encouraging participation:

Participate. Online discussions can fail because the instructor is not involved or because he or she *is* involved. This factor depends on the dynamic that exists among the students in the class, between the students and the instructor, and the subject matter. Ask your students which they prefer, participation or no participation from the instructor. Decide whether you want an area where students discuss class topics freely or with the knowledge that they are participating for your approval. Trial and error may be the only method of discovering the appropriate level of participation.

Give credit. Encourage online discussion by offering course credit to those who are active participants in the course discussion area. A reward may provide the incentive needed to get the ball rolling.

Allow anonymity. If you find students are not participating, allow students to contribute using a pseudonym. Students may find it easier to discuss sensitive topics using an alias. Be sure they reveal their pseudonym to you at some time during the course so that you can reward their participation.

Encourage collaboration. Create assignments that require students to collaborate online. Have students meet together online in small groups to discuss a topic, or use the site for coursework critiques and roundtable discussions.

Be realistic. Keep your expectations for online participation consistent with the subject you are teaching. If the subject of your course is not one that provokes much face-to-face discussion, don't expect your Web site to be abuzz with conversation.

Getting listed

You can write the course site URL on the blackboard during the first class or include it on your handouts or email it to all your students, but everyone should also be able to find your site without knowing the address: students with handout-eating dogs, department chairs considering your petition for tenure, colleagues looking for ideas to use in their own teaching. An active effort to get listed in the appropriate forums is the best way to maximize your site's visibility.

Note that Web sites often get listed without any effort on the author's part. Your site may be discovered by one of the search engine "spiders" that crawl the Web looking for new sites to add to their index. Once indexed by a search engine, your site is one of the millions of potential sites that may be returned as a "hit" from a search query. Then a user may discover your site using the search engine and decide to create a link to your site from his or her own, and voilà! You're famous! Even so, a more proactive approach to publicizing your site will give you greater control over where and how your site is listed.

INSTITUTIONAL LISTING

Make sure that your site is listed on all relevant pages on your institutional Web site (departmental pages, course listings, and so on). Look around your school's site and identify potential pages, then contact the page authors and ask that they publish a link to your site on their pages.

RELATED SITES

Many sites are discovered by users following links from related sites. For example, for a site about classical music, you are likely to gain the notice of music scholars and enthusiasts if your site is included as a link on other classical music sites. In fact, the more links you have from related sites, the better your chances are of being found and indexed by search engines (see *Listing with search engines,* below).

Although much of this cross-linking happens by chance, you can take steps to get your site listed as a link on other sites. The biggest challenge may be finding contact information for the authors of the related sites. If you successfully identify a contact, send along a note with your URL and site description. Ask the author to post a link to your site, and offer to post a "reciprocal" link to their site on yours.

Some search engines allow you to search the Web for sites that have posted a link to your site. For example, typing "link:www.dartmouth.edu" in the AltaVista search field would return all sites containing a hyperlink to the Dartmouth College home page. Another way to find out which sites have links to your site is to review the Web server logs (see Chapter 5: *Server logs*). Each time a user requests a page from a Web server, information about the requestor is logged in the server log file. One tidbit the server can log is referrer information, or the URL of the page the user was on before he or she requested your page. If you visit the referrer URL, chances are that you'll find a link to your site somewhere on the page.

SPECIALIZED DIRECTORIES

A number of sites simply list directories of sites on specific topics. Many of these directories are vetted, which means that the sites listed have been reviewed and approved by some authority. For example, there are sites dedicated to gathering information and URLs for course Web sites. Users visiting these compilations can search for sites in their field to see how educators around the world are using the Web to teach. If you would like to list your course site in such a forum, first identify the compilations that pertain to your field, then follow the submission procedures detailed on the site (a professional organization's Web site for your discipline is one place to look for such compilations). Make note of the places where you've listed your course site so that you can keep your listing current (that is, edit or remove the listing based on the status of your site).

Listing with search engines

A search engine is a database of Web pages that users can search to locate information, buy merchandise, do research, or book a trip. The database is compiled by a software "spider" that "crawls" the Web looking for new or changed pages, whose information it adds or updates in the second component: the index. Users searching the Web interact with search engine software that scans the index for matches and returns the results to the user, usually sorted in order of relevancy, or relatedness, to the search query.

In a study conducted in February 1999, Steve Lawrence and Lee Giles report that approximately 85 percent of Web users use search engines to find information. They estimate there are about 800 million pages on the Web (there will likely be twice that number by the time you read this). The bad news is that they determined that no search engine indexes more than about 18 percent of those pages and that there is a marked bias about which 18 percent are indexed: many search engines follow links to discover new pages and so are more likely to find popular sites that have many links to them. Even for sites that are listed, there is the great challenge of getting noticed on a long list of search results. How good are your chances of being found if your course site on John Milton is result number 10,000 on a user's search for "milton?"

Given these statistics, the utility of search engines for course Web site authors is uncertain. For commercial sites, the advantage of listing well with search engines is considerable, but for your course Web site you may be inclined to leave it up to chance and hope that your site will someday be discovered by a spider. If you wish to actively pursue search engine listings, your greatest effort should be directed at garnering links to your site from other sites (see *Related sites,* above), because that will greatly increase your chances of discovery. You can register your site for indexing with all the search engines. Last, you can take several measures to optimize your pages in the event that your site gets indexed.

REGISTERING YOUR SITE

Most search engines have a feature whereby Web authors can register their sites for indexing. To register your course Web site, go to the search engine home page of your choice (see Chapter 2: *Search engines*) and look for a link that leads to a submission page. Registering does not assure your site a position in a search engine's index, so many search engines offer anxious Web authors an easy way to find out whether their URL is listed. Say, for example, that your course site URL is "www.myschool.edu/music101." If you type "url:myschool.edu/music101" into the Infoseek search field, any of your pages that are in the Infoseek catalog will be returned because their URL contains "myschool.edu/mus101."

OPTIMIZING YOUR PAGES

Getting indexed is only the first challenge in having your pages represented on the Web. It is far too easy to get buried in the vast collection of Web pages that have content that is related in some way to the content of your pages. Several measures will help ensure that users who are seeking materials such as those you offer on your site can find your pages.

Keywords

When optimizing pages for Web search engines, the term *keywords* signifies the word or words that best describe the content of your Web document. This is not to be confused with the keywords used when searching, for example, a library catalog, where many keywords are used to describe every topic covered in a document. In the search engine context, keywords are really *key words:* two or more words that best describe the entire document. Using the library catalog analogy, keywords are more in the category of document subject than keywords.

Keywords are relevant to Web content for an important reason: whereas library catalogs are created by library catalogers, search engine "catalogs" are created largely by computers. The search engine software "reads" Web pages and makes calculations based on frequency and location: frequency being how often a word or phrase occurs in a document, and location being where in the document the phrase occurs (a phrase that appears repeatedly at the beginning of a Web page is considered more relevant than those appearing at the end of a page). The search engine uses these measures to define the subject of a Web page. For example, if a user is looking for pages on "Medieval and Renaissance music," and your page has that exact phrase as the page title, and the phrase appears several times in the first section of the page, a link to your site is likely to appear toward the top of the user's search results page.

The best way to define keywords for your content is to predict what search string users would enter to find your content, for example, "Nietzsche and anti-Semitism" or "Molecules and radiation." Keywords function best when they are specific: for example, choose "Biography of John Milton," not "Milton Bio," for a site dealing specifically with the life of the author John Milton.

Once you've defined your keywords, use them consistently throughout the site. For example, the text that appears inside the <TITLE> tag is considered a primary descriptor of page content by many search indexes. Use the full text of your keywords as the page title:

<TITLE>Biography of John Milton</TITLE>

Search engines also index the content of pages, giving extra attention to text at the beginning of the page. Use your keywords as often as makes sense in your text, particularly in the headings and first paragraphs of the page. Also, when you refer to keywords in the text, do not truncate them. For example, write, "*John Milton* was a misogynist," not "*Milton* was a misogynist."

META tags

META tags are special tags that appear in the top section of your HTML document. They are invisible in that they do not describe any physical aspect of the page, but they can be used for myriad purposes, one of which is to describe the content of a Web page for indexing.

The following are the main META tags that influence searching (note that not all browsers and search engines support all META tags):

Description. The description META tag controls the text displayed with your link on a search results page. Without a description tag, search engines cobble together a description based on the text of your page. For a page that begins with actual content, this method may be *somewhat* effective. But for pages that begin with other page elements such as tables for formatting or navigation links, the page description might look something like this:

[Chronology][About the times][Images][Links to online texts]Welcome to the Biography of John Milton Web Site! This site is a chronicle of the life and…

With a description META tag, you can control how (some) search engines describe your Web page, for example, this HTML code:

```
<TITLE>Biography of John Milton</TITLE>
<META NAME="description" CONTENT="A chronicle of the life and times of the
author John Milton, with extensive links to online Milton texts.">
```

yields this listing on the search results page:

Biography of John Milton
A chronicle of the life and times of the author John Milton, with extensive links to online Milton texts.

Keywords. The greatest utility of the keyword tag is that you can use it to list words that relate to your content but don't appear in the text of the page. For example, if you think your Biography of John Milton page might be of interest to theologians, listing "theology" in the keywords tag would mean they would see your page as the result of a search on that word:

```
<META NAME="keywords" CONTENT="theology, theologian, poetry, poet"]
```

Robots. This tag allows you to specify whether you want search engines to index the page (see *HTML exclusion,* below). Note that the default value for this attribute is "index," so you need to include the tag only if you *do not* want your page indexed.

```
<META NAME="robots" CONTENT="noindex">
```

Summary
This section detailed several strategies for promoting your course Web site, with the aim of encouraging student participation. The most effective ap-

proach is to make the site an integral part of your teaching method: use it in class, refer students to it, measure student progress with it. You can also increase your site's visibility by soliciting links from other sites and by registering the site with search engines.

At this stage, consider the following:

- How heavily do you need to promote your site to capture your students' attention? Should you give a site tour, or are course Web sites already part of your students' experience?
- How can you integrate the site into the classroom? How relevant is the Web-based content in the context of class lectures?
- Can you use the site to deflect the more common questions students ask relating to the course content?
- To what lengths will you go to encourage use? Is your course site essential enough that you are willing to offer credit for online participation?
- How much effort are you willing to expend to make your site visible? Is an institutional listing enough, or do you want your site to be found by Web users around the world?

THE WEB IN THE CLASSROOM

Many Web sites developed in education are designed either to supplement or to replace classroom teaching – that is, they are intended for use *outside* the classroom, in place of face-to-face interactions. Yet in the same way that instructors use such teaching aids as slides, overheads, or video in class, Web sites can be used to illustrate concepts or as part of classroom activities. Indeed, using a course Web site in class is a good way to promote its use by students outside class.

Classroom technology

Many institutions have fully equipped audiovisual classrooms with support for networking and computer projection. These classrooms, sometimes called technology classrooms, are the most reliable way to use the Web in class. The computer is fixed as part of the installation, so you can configure the system and browser with any special software or plug-ins you need before the term starts. Remember that you are most likely sharing the classroom with other instructors. See whether the computer can be configured to allow users to store preferences and files directly on the computer and activate them as needed.

Check with the media services department to determine which classroom technology is available. Even if you do not have technology classrooms, or if the classrooms are unavailable, media services may be able to provide a temporary setup in your classroom using portable equipment.

Preparing a Web-based presentation
The thought of fumbling around with technology in front of a classroom full of students is enough to scare many instructors away from using the Web as part of class, and justifiably so. Any added complexity compounds risks: an entire lecture can be thrown off when the slide projector bulb blows or a slide tray jams, or when the VCR eats the videotape. The Web is more complex than a slide projector or VCR. There are many more components to go wrong: the computer could freeze or crash, the network could be down, the projector could malfunction, the site that you planned to base your lecture on could have moved or been taken down for maintenance.

Here are some measures you can take to avert potential disasters:

Rehearse setup. Store any files and information you might need for your Web-based presentation (for example, URLs, preference settings, plug-ins) somewhere on the network, perhaps in your email account. Practice retrieving the files and configuring other computers: your home machine, a classroom computer, a colleague's computer. Knowing what's involved in setup and rehearsing the steps in advance will prepare you for public Web-based presentations.

Verify links. Before you decide to use an external Web site in class, contact the author of the site. Explain your wish to use it and ask the author's intentions regarding the site. If the author intends to keep the site active, go ahead and use it. If the response is noncommittal, try finding another site that might be more reliable. In general, choose sites that come from reputable organizations, such as sites at other educational institutions or sites sponsored by established organizations (see Chapter 2: *Finding Web content*).

Practice. There is no substitute for practice to assuage nervousness about using technology in the classroom. Some institutions provide a practice room for instructors to rehearse technology-based classroom presentations. These rooms have all the equipment of a technology classroom: the computer, network, peripheral devices, and projection. Instructors can use the room to practice configuring the classroom setup and running through their presentation.

A practice session can help you see what is entailed in customizing a technology classroom setup for your needs: Will you need to change the monitor resolution, add any system extensions or browser plug-ins, or change the sound output controls? It is also an opportunity to see your presentation displayed from a projector. If your institution lacks a dedicated practice room, try to schedule a time in your classroom when you can familiarize yourself with the setup.

Get help. Determine what department at your institution is responsible for setting up and maintaining classroom technology (media services, computing services, classroom management). Arrange for someone from the department to be in your classroom at the start of class to help with setup and get you off to a good start.

Contingency planning. It is important to acknowledge that contingency planning is a fundamental aspect of using the Web in the classroom. Anyone who has ever been caught without a spare knows the importance of having backup. The likelihood of having a virtual blowout during a technology-based presentation is greater than that of getting a flat tire while driving to work. When using the Web as part of your lecture, have a contingency plan so that you are not left stranded if there are problems with the technology: print the Web pages or make transparencies, save the pages on your local hard drive, prepare a backup lesson plan (see Chapter 2: *Using Web content*).

Pre-class checklist	
Browser preferences	Do you want to customize the way pages look in the browser? Do you want links underlined? What fonts do you want to use?
Additional software	Is all the software that you'll need for your presentation installed? For example, are all required browser plug-ins loaded? Are you using any nonstandard plug-ins?
Memory	Is enough system memory available to run your presentation? Is enough memory allocated to the browser application?
Monitor	Are the resolution and color settings right for your presentation?
Audio	Is the audio output functioning? Does the volume need adjusting?
Lighting	Is the room lighting suitable both for viewing the projected image and for taking notes?
Sites	Do you have bookmarks for the sites you will be using in class? Have you checked the sites to make sure they're available?

Summary

You should now understand some of what is involved in using your Web site as part of face-to-face classroom teaching. Classroom technology, in many shapes and sizes, is becoming more commonplace in higher education. Your first task is to assess what options are offered at your institution. If the possibility exists for you to use your site in class, you will need to prepare accordingly to avoid potential pitfalls.

   Questions to ask at this stage include:

- Do you have the institutional resources necessary to use the Web in class? Are technology classrooms available? If not, can you get a portable setup?
- Are you confident about using the Web in class? Are you ready to face technology glitches in front of a roomful of students?
- Will you be thorough in your own preparedness? If not, do you have support staff to step in when needed?

LIMITING ACCESS

One of the benefits of Web publishing is that you can make something as visible and accessible as a billboard, but only to a select audience. Although privacy seems to run counter to the philosophy of the Web – all information for all comers – in many instances you may not want your Web-based materials to be world-accessible.

   When considering privacy issues for your course Web site, first determine whether you have a need for restricting access to your materials. If so, evaluate the different restriction methods to determine which best accommodates your needs, and find out which ones are in use at your institution.

Reasons to limit access

Leaving your site open for worldwide access brings many benefits. Your students may do better coursework if they know that it is published in a widely viewed forum. Discussions may become more animated with input from students and scholars from around the world. Colleagues and students at other institutions can use a course site that is unrestricted. In short, access is one of the main advantages of the Web, and restricting access to your course content is a bit like tossing a wet blanket over the whole works.

   Yet there are many practical reasons to restrict access. If only your students have access to your site, you may have more choices about the materials you can display. Your content, and your students' work, is less vulnerable to misappropriation. And a Web forum that resembles its classroom counterpart may feel more protected to students, so they may be more inclined to participate.

COPYRIGHT

Educators have traditionally relied on the fair use doctrine to use copyrighted materials in their teaching both because classroom use of these materials (mostly) met the criteria of fair use and because there was little chance of discovery: no "moles" lurked in classrooms to spot instances of copyright violation. The Web is different. In most cases, using copyrighted materials without permission on a course Web site does not legally constitute fair use (see Chapter 2: *Copyright and intellectual property*). Also, a Web classroom is an open classroom, so there is a greater chance that unauthorized use will be detected (there are, indeed, Web "bounty hunters" who scout the Web for copyright violations).

Access restriction can be used to model traditional classroom use of copyrighted materials, where access to the materials is limited to class participants. For a course Web site, an implementation of this method would be to set up access restriction on the site and provide students with a course site login. Then, when a page is requested, users are prompted to log into the site, and those without a login are denied access to the pages (see *Authentication,* below).

When seeking permission to use copyrighted materials, access restriction can be a real selling point. You will have a much better chance of obtaining permission to use materials by ensuring that the content will be viewable only by your students or only within your institution. Also, some licenses for use, such as that from the Electronic Course Content Services from the Copyright Clearance Center, require that Web authors use site restriction to ensure that access to the licensed materials is limited to class participants.

PROTECTION

Web-based materials are generally up for grabs. This is more a characteristic of the technology – it's just plain easy to download stuff – than it is a disregard for intellectual property. However, you may not like the notion of someone playing fast and loose with your Web site materials. For this reason, you may want to limit access to your site to protect yourself and your students from infringement.

If, for example, you are posting student essays on your site, you may find that your students are reluctant to post their hard work on the Web if it can easily be downloaded and used by other students. Restricting access to areas where students post their work provides a safe haven for sharing and exchange; leaving these areas open could inhibit or squelch participation.

PRIVACY

The grand global scale of the Web has its place, but there are times when it's good to be parochial and to consider local interests first. Teaching and learning are not activities that we have traditionally performed in public. In fact, one of the often cited strengths of classroom teaching is the intimacy it fosters among students and between students and the instructor. Trying to replicate the character of the classroom on the *worldwide* Web is a bit like trying to have a meaningful conversation in front of thousands of people. By restricting access on your site you get the benefits of privacy while still making full use of the Web as a tool for teaching.

Certain things take place in the intimacy of the classroom that simply cannot happen in a crowd or in front of spectators, such as class discussions or student workgroups. An effective use of the Web in education, however, is to provide students with a convenient way to continue class discussions outside class. If you plan to use a discussion area on your Web site, consider restricting access to allow a greater sense of intimacy. Indeed, you may find that any online exchange of a personal nature will lag unless you restrict access to class participants.

Restriction methods

Access can be restricted on a Web site in several ways. The main distinction is the type of entry users must pass through to get to your content: some ask the user to log in, others check to see where the user is coming from and either let them in or block their entry. With most methods you can restrict access to certain areas of your site while leaving others accessible to the world.

The restriction method you choose will depend largely on the software installed on your Web server. If you are using a courseware tool, access restriction is likely to be a built-in feature of the software. If you are developing your own site, ask your computing support personnel about access restriction options.

Dana Flaskerud: Columbia University

The World Wide Web is an obvious tool for language instruction. The Web's global nature allows educators to tackle challenges that come with teaching a foreign language outside its cultural context. In addition, the computer's multimedia capabilities give them many options for presenting language-instruction materials. Says Dana Flaskerud, "Foreign-language teaching cries out for the use of technology." Dana is a graduate student at Columbia University. She teaches all levels of Spanish, as well as introductory Spanish and medieval literature. In fall 2000, she will become interim director of Columbia's language program. Dana began to use the Web after participating in Project 2001 at Middlebury College, in Middlebury, Vermont. Funded by the Mellon Foundation and run by Middlebury's Center for Educational Technology, this program trains instructors of foreign languages to integrate instructional technology into their curriculums.

Dana was excited by the possibilities the Web presented. Though she was a beginning teacher with only two semesters of teaching experience, she was frustrated with some of the established modes for language teaching. "I wanted to bring up the level of sophistication for class discussion. I didn't want to go around the room saying, 'Okay, you start the first paragraph,' and have each student read. That's how it went the first couple of semesters of teaching." Dana also saw the Web as a way to appeal to different types of learners. "I wanted to be able to address different learning styles, such as the global learner, who looks at things as a whole and appreciates skimming text, or the haptic learner, who likes to click the mouse and requires "hands-on" learning, or the visual learner, who can see the images and the glossed text." Another concern was student independence. "I was concerned about a task that takes one student five minutes and another student fifteen – how do you address student pacing problems in the classroom?" To address some of these shortcomings, she developed a curriculum around various "texts" that she found on the Web.

"One of my assignments is on *los toros* (bullfighting) in the context of cultural stereotypes. I send the students to one site that is totally anti-*toros* and to another site that is totally pro-*toros*. They have to read what they find at the sites and come up with a list of five pros and five cons, and then form their own opinion. This way they get different perspectives and can choose – learning is in their hands. I'm not giving them a predigested page or a *nota cultural* out of a book." The Web exercises are assigned as

WEEK 5: Feb 14 - 18: Chapter 9: Los hispanos en los Estados Unidos

Monday: Turn in Composition 2. TEMAS, Chapter 9 Grammar and vocab activities. TAREA: Read 261-264. Do "práctica" pg. 264. do "A" pg. 265 in Pasajes.

Wednesday: Chapter 9 Grammar and vocab activities. Pre-reading for Los inmigrantes. TAREA: Read 268-269 do "práctica" pg. 269. Do "A" pg. 269. Read 271-272. Do "A" pg. 272.

Friday: Reading: Los inmigrantes En Con-Textos . Turn in "preguntas de comprensión" in Con-Textos.

WEEK 6: Feb 21-25: Chapter 9: Los hispanos en los Estados Unidos, cont'd

Monday:

Wednesday: Presentations: André. Finish discussion of Los inmigrantes. Grammar points

Friday: Internet tarea 2: Spanglish. Everyone must prepare presentations / discussion questions. (Spanglish). Discussion leaders / presenters: Brian and Erin. Leer 273-275 y hacer "práctica" pg. 275. Hacer "ojo" pg. 281.

**On Friday, I will be screening the movie El Norte at 1:00 in 204 Lewisohn Hall from 1:00-2:30. Please tell me if you'll be there.

WEEKEND HOMEWORK: Watch: El Norte: answer Preguntas de comprensión y temas de discusión

WEEK 7: Feb 28 - Mar 3: Chapter 9: Los hispanos en los Estados Unidos, cont'd

Monday: Discussion of EL NORTE and Presentations: Ben

Wednesday: Continue discussion / review grammar. Presentation on El norte: Martin. Presentation on a comparison of El Norte y Los inmigrantes: Gaby

homework, but Dana integrates the topics from the texts into the classroom. "For example, *El Pais* has an article called 'Tentaciones,' and it's all about what young people in Spain are complaining about. We'll have a pre-reading exercise in class where I'll say, 'Okay, what are you guys complaining about?' We'll have a conversation for about ten minutes to start them brainstorming. Then I send them away with the link and they read the text at home. I set up a Web bulletin board where they brainstorm online: What are the most frivolous complaints, what are the most serious complaints? I have them write a response and then talk about their own complaints. I do this to get them not only to just read but to be able to *talk* about their reading and *write* about what they've read, so that everything is integrated."

Dana encourages her students to write freely on the bulletin board. "Their online writing is much more colloquial, which I don't mind. Some people would say that it really does matter: that they need to type it out and put the heading and follow the MLA guidelines. Obviously there's a place for that, but I don't think the place is Spanish 1. In our program we require them to write four formal compositions – it's just not natural, and it doesn't work. What does work is the electronic writing, and the *daily* writing, and my not necessarily correcting every grammar error they make."

The work of her project is twofold: locating Web sites and constructing exercises to go with them, and then creating her own Web sites. Dana uses Macromedia's Dreamweaver to create her course Web sites, and although it took "many, many hours" to learn, now that she is comfortable in the environment, she finds that using the Web saves her time with some of the administrative aspects of teaching. "Using the Web takes more time initially, but then it becomes so much easier. I don't think I could live without it now.

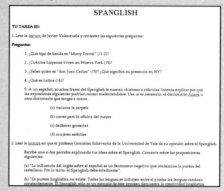

Even just for practical reasons, like posting assignments: I get so sick of the same excuses, like, oh, sorry, I didn't get the homework. I say, 'Sorry, it's there on the Internet and you have to get it.' And with email and conferencing, I don't get the same question twice. Since the answers are there on the site, I send my students there to read them."

Dana uses the Web for another repetitive task of teaching any language: grammar drills. Instead of using valuable class time for the sort of, "go around the room – you, you, you – fill in the blank-type of activities," Dana sends her students to sites with online grammar drills that provide instant feedback. Then, instead of doing drill sessions, she spends class time getting her students to "converse and discuss and communicate," using the grammar they've learned through the online drills.

This new approach has met with some resistance from other language instructors. "The other day a colleague said to me, 'Dana, now I know you are a great fan of these modern technologies and these MTV-style methodologies, but I tell you a good drill session is what they need!'" But in Dana's view, if technology is not part of the curriculum, the language program is outdated and lacks continuity. "I develop these materials for my Spanish 1 course, but then the students move on to someone else's class where they are not using the Web. We need to collaborate with one another if we're going to take this anywhere." She thinks that part of the trouble is that language instructors are overwhelmed by today's array of options. Textbooks now come with Web sites, CD-ROMs, videos, workbooks, and audio. With all these materials, "something has to give." But Dana suggests that "instead of thinking of all this as adding on to the traditional curriculum, we need to rethink our approach. We need to decide whether students would benefit more from these new paradigms." Many language teachers support the use of technology in the classroom, and Dana's students constantly cry for "more Web!"

Perhaps the real issue facing language instructors is not whether to use technology in their curriculum but a far more basic teaching goal: Where do educators want their students to be at the end of their four semesters of basic language instruction? Asks Dana, "Should they be able to conjugate verbs, or should they be able to communicate?" ■

AUTHENTICATION

One method for controlling access to Web-based content is to require users to identify themselves before allowing them access to pages. This portal requires users to enter a login and password, and their entry is checked for authenticity against a central database of users and passwords or against a class login of a single username and password.

A common implementation of this method is Kerberos authentication. When users request a page that is restricted using this method, they are prompted to submit their username and password. The server checks the information against a list of authorized users, and if the entry matches, users are issued a "ticket" and sent the requested page. If the server is unable to authenticate a user, it sends an error page instead.

When a Web page is restricted using Kerberos authentication, the user submits his or her account name and password, which are checked against a list of authorized users. If the account information is "authentic," the user is sent the requested page.

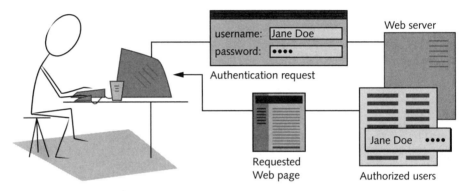

username: Jane Doe
password: ••••

Web server

Authentication request

Requested Web page

Jane Doe ••••

Authorized users

IP FILTERING

An IP address describes the location of a computer on the network. Every computer on the Internet has a unique IP (Internet Protocol) address. But all IP addresses at a single institution have certain commonalities. These shared properties make possible IP filtering, a method whereby only computers whose IP address match defined criteria can receive restricted Web pages. A sample IP address is 129.170.18.13, where 129.170 designates the network (Dartmouth College) and 18.13 defines the host (my computer).

To implement IP filtering, you configure the server to send your restricted pages only to computers with certain IP addresses. For example, to restrict access to on-campus users, you would set your criteria such that only computers on the campus network (129.170 in the example above) can view your content. When a user requests a page that falls within this restricted area, the server checks the requestor's IP and, if it meets the criteria, sends the requested page. If the IP does not match − for example, for off-campus users − the Web server sends an "access denied" page instead.

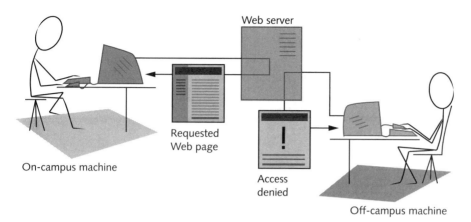

When a user requests a page that is restricted using IP filtering, the Web server checks the user's location. If the computer's IP address verifies that it is an on-campus machine, the server sends the requested page; otherwise, it sends an "access denied" page.

On-campus machine

Web server

Requested Web page

Access denied

Off-campus machine

No indexing

If you are considering adding access restriction to your Web site, you may want to take steps to ensure that your pages are not "crawled" by search engine spiders; your materials are not available and so should not be listed as accessible Web content. You can do this on your Web pages or on the server. Neither method guarantees protection because they are conventions, not barriers, which the spiders can heed or ignore. The only way to guarantee that your materials will not be indexed is to keep them off the Web.

HTML EXCLUSION

You can keep spiders from indexing pages by including the robots META tag in the <HEAD> section of your restricted pages: <META NAME="robots" CONTENT="noindex">. Unfortunately, as of this writing, at most a handful of the major search engines recognize and respect the tag.

SERVER EXCLUSION

A more reliable method for preventing indexing is to put a "robots.txt" file on the Web server. This simple text file has two parameters: "user-agent," which allows you to specify which search engines should be excluded, and "disallow," which allows you to specify which directories or file names you want to prevent spiders from indexing.

```
User-agent: *
Disallow: /courses/music101/essays/*
Disallow: /courses/music101/classlist.html
```

The criteria above would exclude all spiders from all files and folders in the essays directory and from the class list file.

The robots.txt file must reside at the top, or root, level of the Web server directory in order to be recognized. Chances are that your Web server account provides access only to your subdirectory on the server, which means that you cannot add or change files at the root level. You will need to ask your computing support staff about adding robots server exclusion for your restricted pages or directories.

Summary

You should now have a sense of what access restriction is, how it works, and why you might want to use it on your site. If you have determined that you want to restrict access to some or all of your course Web site, first check in with your computing support staff. As with most things Web, this feature can be implemented in many ways, so you should first determine what options your institution has available and supports.

Questions to ask at this stage include:

- Would your Web site be more successful if you allow site access only to class participants? Would your students be more or less active on the site if they knew that access was limited?
- If you decide to limit access, will you be able to realize your objectives? How important is a worldwide forum to your Web-teaching goals?
- What authentication methods are commonly used at your institution? Of those, which best suits your purposes?

REFERENCES

Boettcher, Judith, and Rita-Marie Conrad. 1999. *Faculty guide for moving teaching and learning to the Web.* Mission Viejo, Calif.: League for Innovation in the Community College.

Hunt, Craig. 1998. *TCP/IP Network Administration.* 2d ed. Sebastopol, Calif.: O'Reilly.

Lawrence, Steve, and C. Lee Giles. 1999. Accessibility of information on the Web. *Nature* July: 107–109. [See also http://www.wwwmetrics.com]

Sullivan, Danny. 1996. *Search engine watch.* http://www.searchenginewatch. com.

5   *Site assessment*

One never knows, do one.
– Thomas "Fats" Waller

ONCE YOU HAVE INVESTED valuable time and resources in setting up and maintaining a course Web site, it is well worth the effort to evaluate its effectiveness. Evaluation can reveal unexpected results: perhaps your students are using only specific areas of the site, or perhaps they're using the site in ways you had not anticipated, or perhaps they're not using the site at all. This knowledge, though potentially disheartening, can save you from misspending time and effort. Understanding the strengths and failings of your approach will allow you to adapt your strategy and to make best use of the medium.

Two main areas of your site warrant assessment: its usability and its effectiveness as a teaching tool. Usability testing is a method for evaluating the effectiveness of your site's information architecture, navigation, and design. It measures how successful users are in locating information on your site and how they felt about the experience: Were they lost or derailed at any point in the process? Learning assessment measures the effect your site has on the learning process: Did students learn the materials as presented?

And keep in mind that the purpose of the evaluation is not simply to measure the success of your project. The information and insights you gain through evaluation should be put to good use. The Web is not a fixed medium, and your site can be continually modified and improved. Use the evaluation process to refine your Web teaching method.

VEHICLES FOR ASSESSMENT

Your students' interactions with your course site are mediated by the technology used to deliver Web-based content. Because Web pages are "served" to users by computer, you can use its strengths of data collection, storage, and analysis to track requests for materials from your site.

Tracking how users interact with your Web site can yield data that will help you draw conclusions about the effectiveness of your site and your site content. For example, you may find by examining page-request statistics that your students are not requesting materials that are essential to the learning process. With this knowledge, you could provide a link to the materials in a more obvious location on the site and emphasize their importance in class. Or you might see that you are getting multiple requests for a specific page and discover a correlation between the number of hits and incorrect answers on a quiz question on the same topic. This may signify that students who are unsure about the topic as presented in class are turning to the Web site for clarity but remain uncertain at quiz time. As a result you may need to rethink your teaching approach for that topic.

Another means for assessment is to gather feedback from your students, either casually or through questionnaires.

Tracking software

Some courseware packages contain features that allow the instructor to view how students are using the Web site. The program logs information about each student's interaction with the Web site and gives the instructor reports. This information ranges from basic statistics, such as the number of times a page is requested, to more in-depth details, such as how much time students spend on each page or how many times each student has posted a comment to the class discussion or chat list. Courseware packages can provide usage information for individual students or summary information on overall class Web site usage.

Server logs

Most Web servers are configured to log information about how they are being used and by whom. For example, when a page request is made, the server knows the location, or IP address, of the machine that made the request. It can tell things about the machine, such as what operating system and browser it is running. It even knows the location, or URL, of the page the requestor arrived from (called the *referring page*). The server can store all this information in a log file.

Server logs are a wonderful tool for site assessment. They provide comprehensive information about how your site is being used. Analyzing the logs can reveal who is using your site and how they are using it.

Most servers provide software for easy viewing of the server logs. Because storing the data can be time-consuming and take up needed server space, you may find that usage data is discarded after a certain period of time – a week, perhaps. In that case, a good strategy would be to print the server statistics weekly and analyze them at the end of the term. See if you can identify usage patterns: Which pages are most popular on your site? Which pages are seldom or never requested? Eliminate site content that does not attract users and build on popular pages.

Feedback

Your students are the consumers of your Web site, and their reactions are the most critical measure of site effectiveness. Poll your students throughout the term: How are they using the Web site? What do they find most useful? What content do they wish was there? What content is there that they don't find useful? Distribute a formal questionnaire at the end of the term. Let their feedback guide your future course site efforts.

Sample questions

What areas of the site did you use the most?
What areas did you find the least useful?
What would you like to see more of on the site?
Did you encounter any technical difficulties using the site? If so, please describe.
Did you find the site well-organized? Were you able to find what you needed?
Do you think having a course Web site is a good idea?
Did you enjoy working with the site? Was the site fun?

Formal assessment

There is great demand for substantive evaluative studies on the effectiveness of the Web as a tool for teaching. Some institutions are investing heavily in such studies, particularly when the Web is used in place of regular classroom teaching. Formal assessment is complicated, costly, and time-consuming, however, and it must be done by professionals to ensure experimental rigor. You are probably not likely to have the resources to conduct a formal test for your course Web site, so outlining the parameters of formal assessment, with control groups and user tracking, is not covered here. For a project of significant consequence – an exclusively online course, for example – it is well worth exploring the possibility of formal assessment. If, for example, you are seeking funding for your project, include assessment as a budget item. Or check on the availability of on-campus resources for assessment – a curricular development program, perhaps, or an instructional technology center. If you find yourself without institutional resources for evaluating the effectiveness of your site, you will need to create your own assessment, or explore the commercial possibilities for course evaluation.

Frank Klucken: Landmark College

Frank Klucken faces more teaching challenges than most college educators. He teaches mathematics at Landmark College, a two-year college in Putney, Vermont, for students with learning disabilities. "They are at Landmark because they are not typical learners. Landmark students might have auditory problems, so they could miss concepts and ideas if you're only lecturing. Or, if dyslexic, students could interpret visual cues differently from the way you and I might see them. Or they have an attention disorder that doesn't keep them in the room, even though they're there physically." Frank found in teaching his freshman-level elementary statistics course that he needed a way to reach the students in his class that he wasn't reaching through other means. He wanted to find a way to "get the content of statistics across to students who weren't getting it through classroom discussion."

The opportunity came when, as a student in Teaching Using Internet Technologies at the Graduate Center of Vermont's Marlboro College, he was assigned the project of identifying and addressing a need using the Web. "I immediately thought of statistics." In working on this project, Frank created his course Web site, the Virtual Statistics Teacher, a carefully crafted integration of Web-based resources and online communication and collaboration.

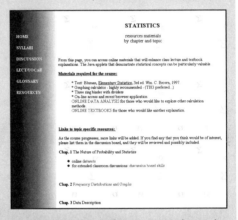

Frank began by searching the Web for resources he could use in his teaching. "Initially I thought, this will be great! I've got some visual learners here. Or students that just aren't getting it because of the way I'm saying it or the way the textbook is, so they can go look at another textbook, or they can go see it online." Frank found an abundance of materials, including sources for visual explanations and simulations, online textbooks, and data sources and online data manipulation tools. On his course Web site, he tied these resources into his syllabus and course topics, guiding his students' use of the Web by giving them direct access to resources that he has reviewed and integrated into his syllabus.

The Virtual Statistics Teacher also has a WebBoard: an online discussion area where students can post questions or discuss class topics. When teaching the course, Frank set the WebBoard as the home page in his Web browser, and he began and ended each day with a visit to the WebBoard to answer questions and sound out his students.

To create the site, Frank used a hodgepodge of tools – from visual Web authoring tools to conversion utilities to basic HTML coding using NotePad. But much of the work of creating the site was locating resources and linking his online syllabus to them. "The World Wide Web is a tremendous resource. There is no need to 'redo' because much of what you want to do in your teaching has already been done by others and is there to be used." Frank completed his program successfully and, in fact, now helps teach new students in the programs at the Graduate Center.

But back in the classroom at Landmark College, the Virtual Statistics Teacher had a limited impact. Frank presented the site to his students and assumed that they would use it without explicitly including use of the site in the course requirements. It turned out that his students needed an extra push to get online. "Why go online when assignments are due and Web site use is not required?" Frank faults his presentation, not the technology, for students' limited use of the site. "It was a very new thing having a Web site. I was one of two of a faculty of 130 that actually had a Web site for their class. Being new, it probably didn't reach as many students as it could have. And I couldn't take as much time out of class to really go over the features of the Web site and really bring them into it all of the time. So I didn't get the results that I wanted." He found that students' use of the site depended on their level of comfort with the Web and their willingness to spend additional time outside class.

For those students who did go online, some aspects of the site were particularly successful, especially online discussion. "Students who weren't active in the classroom because of their learning disability or shyness or whatever would log onto the discussion board and ask questions that they could not have asked in class." Frank thinks that students have preferences about how they want to ask questions, and under what conditions they will ask them. "There are some students – at Landmark particularly – that just have trouble speaking up in class. It's emotional, it's perhaps a speech impediment, or just the dominance of some other students in class, so they just sit there and you don't know if they're really there or not. Then they log onto the discussion board and ask a question, and you know where they are. I really like that."

The online simulations were also popular with the students. Frank explains that a common classroom exercise is to have students flip coins – heads, tails, heads, tails – as a demonstration of central tendencies. "Why flip coins in class, where you can do it only ten or twelve times, when you can do it online? Press a button and there it is, a hundred times. Press it again, and there it is another hundred times." Frank says that simulations do not replace having students do the calculations manually, but the use of visual explanations makes the concepts more accessible, particularly for his students. "For example, you can hold the attention of a student with attention deficit disorder if something dynamic is happening. It also gives them an opportunity to go back and work with the material when their focus is a little better."

The next time Frank teaches using the Virtual Statistics Teacher course site, he will do things differently from the start. "I will make sure there's time in the syllabus to demonstrate how to use the Web site. Maybe hold a class in the computer lab once every two weeks, so we can work with the site together." Frank feels that effective use of online

simulations is something best done in a computer lab. "And I would also require the students to go there: for example, tell them to go post something this week. Make part of their grade depend on interacting with the Web site instead of just leaving it as a stand-alone resource that they can explore when they feel like it, because that doesn't really work."

Although his course site was not heavily used, Frank remains enthusiastic about the Web as a tool for teaching statistics. "It's everything that statistics needs to be: it's visual, it's interactive, and all the different explanations and approaches are available. The fact is, I probably cheated my students by not requiring them to use the site." ■

Do-it-yourself assessment

For projects with limited resources, consider conducting an informal assessment study. You aren't likely to reach a scientific conclusion about the overall effectiveness of computer-based teaching, but you will gather useful information about the effectiveness of your course Web site. With this information you can structure your further development efforts.

In the summary sections that appear throughout the book, you have been encouraged to perform mini usability tests to evaluate the effectiveness of your site at each stage. In this section you will learn how to conduct a more thorough usability test on the finished Web site.

ESTABLISH A TESTING ENVIRONMENT

To test a Web site, all you really need is a quiet room with a couple of chairs and a computer. Make sure the computer is fully configured so that users won't encounter technical difficulties during the test. Choose your browser software, install all the necessary plug-ins, and make sure there is enough memory available on the system. A nonessential but highly valuable addition to the environment would be a video camera and tripod to record the testing sessions for review purposes.

DEFINE YOUR OBJECTIVES

You can achieve a number of objectives through informal testing. You can measure the success rate for participants using your site to perform a specific task, such as finding assignment information. You can measure the time participants take to complete the task and their overall satisfaction with the process. You can also test learning outcomes for certain tasks – whether the participant adequately understands the materials presented.

When defining test objectives, emphasize the tasks that you expect your students to perform most often. Use this opportunity to test areas of your site you are unsure about, for example, complex simulations or interactive features. Also focus your attention on aspects of your site that you feel are critical to your students' understanding of the course content.

Test objectives may include:

- Is the site navigation effective?
- Is it clear what materials are offered on the site?
- Does the media content take too long to download?
- Is the textual content read online or printed?

DEVELOP A TASK LIST

Next, design a set of tasks for the test participants to perform. These tasks should expose the participants indirectly to the areas in question. For example, one objective might be to test the effectiveness of your site navigation. Instead of pointing out the navigation and asking users to explain how they think it works, create a task that requires use of the navigation, such as, "What reading is assigned for week 7?" Then observe the participants' use of the site navigation to complete the task.

Write a task list, noting the task, how long participants have to work on it, and what you consider successful task completion to be.

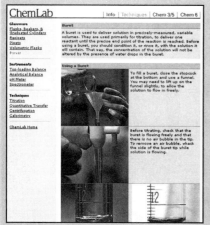

Sample task list	Time	Success
Fact retrieval		
How do you contact your TA?	2.5 minutes	Correct answer
When do you need to turn in your lab notebook?	2.5 minutes	Correct answer
What do you do if you get chemicals in your eyes?	2.5 minutes	Correct answer
Under what conditions would you use a buret?	2.5 minutes	Correct answer
Online activities		
What do you get if you mix barium chloride and baking soda?	5 minutes	Correct result
How do you make an ion exchange column?	5 minutes	Explanation of procedure

CREATE A TEST PLAN

Next you should establish a procedure for the test sessions. The nature of your test objectives will determine your method. If all you want is a general sense of how students work with the materials on your site, you can simply set participants down in front of the Web site and observe and record their interactions. If, however, you have specific objectives, such as determining whether students read the instructions before using an online quiz module, you will need to structure the test sessions more formally to ensure that your objectives are met.

Consider the following when constructing a test plan:

Participants. Because the purpose of this study is to gather insights, not statistics, you can use a small number of participants. One participant would yield useful information, four to five would expose most of the flaws in your site design. More is certainly better, but much of what you need to get accomplished can be done by testing a handful of users. Gather participants that have diverse profiles – different learning styles, familiarity with the Web, ages, and genders – but are representative of your typical users.

Test monitoring. A test monitor facilitates the test sessions by initiating and timing the tasks and logging data, such as how long each task takes, as well as any errors or other observations. The monitor can also be available to respond to or guide the participants. It is generally better to have an objective person handle the test monitoring. If you decide to monitor the test for your own course site, remain impartial and focused on the task at hand.

Test materials. Including such test materials as scripts and checklists can help with monitoring the test. For example, you might have the test monitor read an orientation script at the start of each session so that all participants hear the same explanation of the purpose of the test. You could also create lists that specify which data the test monitor should collect, such as "number of errors" or "time spent on task."

Sample test materials	
Orientation script	Read at the beginning of the test session to describe the purpose of the test and outline how the test session will proceed.
Questionnaires	Pre-test: Gather information about the participant's background and comfort with the Web. Mid-test: Measure the participant's feelings about the site, particularly any frustration or confusion. Post-test: Get feedback about the participant's overall impressions of the site.
Task list	List the tasks to be completed during the test session, with the amount of time allotted and a measure of successful completion.
Data log	Record such things as the amount of time spent on a task and the number of incorrect actions taken. Also use to record general observations during the test session.

Thinking aloud. When test participants "think aloud" they narrate their thought process as they perform the test tasks. With this technique you can monitor the less-observable aspects of the session, such as the participant's level of confusion or satisfaction. Keep in mind that some participants may be more comfortable speaking their thoughts than others. Also, the technique is tiring and cannot be sustained over long periods.

Videotaping. If test sessions are videotaped, the test monitor doesn't need to be as rigorous in taking notes, because the video is available for review. The monitor can also use the video in the debriefing session to review the test with the participant and collect additional feedback. If you use videotaping, make sure that participants know they are being taped before beginning the session. It may be wise to ask participants to sign a consent form.

Questionnaires. You can use questionnaires to gather information from participants at various stages in the test. Administer a pre-test questionnaire to determine each participant's experience with computers. Gather feedback during the test by issuing a questionnaire after each task. Administer a post-test questionnaire to gather the users' overall impressions about the site. The questionnaires should cover items that cannot be ascertained through observation, such as the participants' thoughts and feelings about the site.

Debriefing. A debriefing session allows the participant to communicate his or her feelings about the tasks. It also allows the test monitor to seek clarification about the participant's actions during the session. The test monitor can use the video or notes to review the session with the participant and ask such questions as, "Why did you pause before clicking 'Submit'?"

Write up a test plan outlining the structure of the session. Describe the tasks and the method in which they will be administered, and define the role of the test monitor. Prepare any test materials, such as questionnaires, scripts, and data collection lists.

Sample test plan	
1 Greet participant	2 minutes
2 Administer background questionnaire	5 minutes
3 Read orientation script	3 minutes
4 Have participant perform fact-retrieval tasks	10 minutes
5 Administer mid-test questionnaire	5 minutes
6 Have participant perform online activity tasks	10 minutes
7 Administer post-test questionnaire	5 minutes
8 Debrief participant	5 minutes
9 Transcribe notes and impressions	15 minutes

With participants selected and test plan in hand, you can administer the usability test. For the sake of simplicity, let's assume that you are the monitor for this test scenario.

Set up. Check the testing environment to make sure the computer is properly configured, that the video equipment is set up and functioning, and that you have assembled all written materials such as scripts, checklists, and questionnaires.

Pre-test. If you are videotaping the session, ask the participant to sign a consent form. Administer any pre-test questionnaire and read the orientation script. Explain how you would like the participant to behave during testing – whether they can ask questions or ask for assistance, for example. If you would like them to "think aloud" during the session, explain and demonstrate the technique.

Test. Describe the tasks to the participant either verbally or by providing a written task list. Record the start time and collect relevant information during the test. Where appropriate, interact with the participant, but remember to keep your statements impartial: for example, say, "Did that not take you where you expected to go?" when a participant shows frustration after following a link. Record any behaviors you want to have clarified at debriefing time. Time each task, and gently guide the participant through the session. Have the participant fill out any questionnaires developed for use during the test and the post-test questionnaire at the end of the test session.

Debrief. Review the questionnaires and video with the participant still present to gather additional feedback. For any unclear behaviors noted during the test session, ask the participant to explain his or her actions, for example, "Why did you click on the book titles on the course readings page?"

Summarize. After the participant leaves, spend a few minutes summarizing your thoughts about the session before starting with the next participant. If you are using videotape, you can record your impressions directly on tape.

ANALYZE THE DATA

What you do with the data you've collected depends on your objectives and your approach. You may through observation have already formulated a plan for developing or adapting your site based on the insights you gathered during the test sessions, in which case your assessment study is complete. You may, however, be looking for more concrete findings, in which case you should compile and summarize your data for analysis.

If you plan to pursue findings, transcribe all notes and quantitative data to the computer as soon after the test sessions as possible, while your impressions are fresh in your mind. For example, if you want to calculate statistics on the participants' timings – say, the mean time to complete each task – record and calculate those times using a spreadsheet application. If you collected data using questionnaires, collate the responses in your word processor for easy grouping and comparison.

Review the data in summary form to identify the problem areas on your site. Focus on tasks that most participants were unable to complete in the allotted time. Compare the different behaviors with the task to see if you can identify the cause of the difficulty. For example, if participants were asked to define a term using the site, but none clicked the "Resources" link that would lead them to a glossary, it may be that you need to include a "Glossary" link as one of your sitewide navigation links.

Refine and expand

A Web site author's work is never done. When publishing in a fixed format, such as a book or videotape, there comes a time when the author must release the project to the public, warts and all. Letting go of control is both terrifying and liberating at the same time. Before letting go there are hours, days, years of picking and tweaking and hair-pulling, but once the project is released, life resumes.

The good news about Web publishing is you do not have to relinquish control over your content: you can always remove warts, correct mistakes, repair inaccuracies. But the good news is also the bad news. The pace of other publishing fields is glacial in comparison with that of the Web. Web design styles change more often than skirt hems. New technologies are constantly introduced that promise to revolutionize the way we do things on the Web. Those that can keep pace change the design and methods they use on their sites about every year. Those sites that are not regularly updated quickly become long in the tooth.

Keeping current is more essential in commerce than in education, so the drive to stay with the pack is not as keen for most authors of course Web sites. That does not mean that you should let your course site lag entirely. Use insights gained through feedback and evaluation to refine and expand your site. Make simple modifications regularly, and plan for major over-hauls, perhaps every time you teach the course. Keep an eye on developments in technology, particularly as applied to educational endeavors. Talk with colleagues about your project, and observe how others use technology in teaching. Participate in conferences, seminars, and presentations and continue to develop your technology skills.

Summary

You should now have an idea of various methods for evaluating the effectiveness of your course Web site, ranging from simple tracking to full-scale usability testing. Whatever method you choose, you should also understand that your course Web site endeavor is a task without end: that revision is fundamental to authoring Web-based content. These inevitable refinements should be guided, at least in part, by insights gained through site evaluation.

Questions to ask about site assessment include:

- What is your opinion of the site? Does it meet your expectations?
- Do you get much feedback from your students about the site? Have you actively solicited their opinions, either through informal discussion or using a formal questionnaire?
- Do you plan to assess the site to gain a more objective measure of the project's success? Are you sufficiently committed to the project to use the insights you gain through assessment to improve the site?

REFERENCES

Boettcher, Judith, and Rita-Marie Conrad. 1999. *Faculty guide for moving teaching and learning to the Web.* Mission Viejo, Calif.: League for Innovation in the Community College.

Nielsen, Jakob. 1995. *The alertbox: Current issues in Web usability.* http://www.useit.com/alertbox.

Rubin, Jeffrey. 1994. *Handbook of usability testing: How to plan, design, and conduct effective tests.* New York: John Wiley & Sons.

Spool, Jared M., et al. 1999. *Web site usability: A designer's guide.* San Francisco: Morgan Kaufmann.

Bibliography

WEB SITE DESIGN

Information design

Norman, Donald A. 1988. *The psychology of everyday things.* New York: Basic Books. [Also sold as *The design of everyday things.*]

Rosenfeld, Louis, and Peter Morville. 1998. *Information architecture for the World Wide Web.* Sebastopol, Calif.: O'Reilly.

Shriver, Karen A. 1997. *Dynamics in document design.* New York: Wiley Computer.

Tufte, Edward R. 1990. *Envisioning information.* Cheshire, Conn.: Graphics Press.

Site design

Lynch, Patrick J., and Sarah Horton. 1999. *Web style guide: Basic design principles for creating Web sites.* New Haven and London: Yale University Press. [See also http://info.med.yale.edu/caim/manual]

Nielsen, Jakob. 2000. *Designing Web usability: The practice of simplicity.* Indianapolis, Ind.: New Riders. [See also http://www.useit.com]

How-to guides

Castro, Elizabeth. 1998. *HTML 4 for the World Wide Web.* Berkeley, Calif.: Peachpit.

Niederst, Jennifer. 1999. *Web design in a nutshell.* Sebastopol, Calif.: O'Reilly and Associates.

Williams, Robin. 1998. *The non-designer's Web book.* Berkeley, Calif.: Peachpit.

TEXT

Writing

Hale, Constance, and Jessie Scanlon. 1999. *Wired style: Principles of English usage in the digital age.* New York: Broadway Books.

Walker, Janice R., and Todd Taylor. 1998. *The Columbia guide to online style.* New York: Columbia University Press.

Zinsser, William. 1998. *On writing well: The classic guide to writing nonfiction.* 6th ed., rev. and updated. New York: HarperCollins.

Typography

Bringhurst, Robert. 1996. *The elements of typographic style.* 2d ed. Point
    Roberts, Wash.: Hartley and Marks.

Lie, Håkom Wium, and Bert Bos. 1997. *Cascading Style Sheets: Designing for
    the Web.* Reading, Mass.: Addison Wesley.

Microsoft Corporation. 2000. *Microsoft typography.* http://www.microsoft.
    com/typography/default.asp.

MULTIMEDIA

Images

Blatner, David, Glenn Fleishman, and Steve Roth. 1998. *Real world
    scanning and halftones: The definitive guide to scanning and halftones from the
    desktop.* 2d ed. Berkeley, Calif.: Peachpit.

Day, Rob. 1995. *Designer Photoshop.* 2d ed. New York: Random House.

Weinman, Lynda. 1997. *Designing Web graphics.* 2d ed. Indianapolis, Ind.:
    New Riders.

Williams, Robin, and John Tollett. 1998. *The non-designer's Web book: An
    easy guide to creating, designing, and posting your own Web site.* Berkeley,
    Calif.: Peachpit.

Audio and video

Kelsey, Logan, and Jim Feeley. 2000. Shooting video for the Web. *DV*
    (February). http://www.dv.com/magazine/2000/0200/
    videoforweb0200.html (18 February 2000).

Kitchens, Susan A. 1998. *The QuickTime VR book: Creating immersive imaging
    on your desktop.* Berkeley, Calif.: Peachpit.

Simpson, Ron. 1998. *Cutting edge Web audio.* Upper Saddle River, N.J.:
    Prentice Hall.

Stern, Judith, and Robert Lettieri. 1999. *QuickTime Pro for Macintosh and
    Windows.* Berkeley, Calif.: Peachpit.

Terran Interactive. 1995–99. *Media Cleaner Pro 4 User Manual.* San Jose,
    Calif.: Terran Interactive. [See also http://www.terran-int.com]

———. 1999. *How to produce high-quality QuickTime.* San Jose, Calif.:
    Terran Interactive. [See also http://www.terran-int.com/QuickTime/
    Article]

Waggoner, Ben. 1999. Making great Web video. *DV* (October).
    http://www.dv.com/magazine/1999/1099/webvideo1099.pdf (18
    February 2000).

USABILITY TESTING

Nielsen, Jakob. 1995. *The alertbox: Current issues in Web usability.*
http://www.useit.com/alertbox.

Rubin, Jeffrey. 1994. *Handbook of usability testing: How to plan, design, and
conduct effective tests.* New York: John Wiley & Sons.

Spool, Jared M., et al. 1999. *Web site usability: A designer's guide.* San
Francisco: Morgan Kaufmann.

COPYRIGHT AND INTELLECTUAL PROPERTY

Carter, Mary E. 1996. *Electronic highway robbery: An artist's guide to copyright
in the digital era.* Berkeley, Calif.: Peachpit Press.

Cavazos, Edward A., and Gavino Morin. 1994. *Cyberspace and the law: Your
rights and duties in the on-line world.* Cambridge, Mass.: MIT Press.

Gorman, Robert. 1998. Intellectual property: The rights of faculty as
creators and users. *ACADEME* May–June: 14–18.

Talab, R. S. 1999. *Commonsense copyright: A guide for educators and librarians.*
2d ed. Jefferson, N.C.: McFarland.

United States Copyright Office. 1999. *Copyright basics.* Washington, D.C.:
Library of Congress. [See also http://www.loc.gov/copyright]

USING THE WEB

Lawrence, Steve, and C. Lee Giles. 1999. Accessibility of information on
the Web. *Nature* July: 107–109. [See also http://www.wwwmetrics.com]

Maloy, Timothy K. 1999. *The Internet research guide.* 2d ed. New York:
Allworth.

Schlein, Alan M. 1999. *Find it online: The complete guide to online research.* 2d
ed. Edited by James R. Flowers, Jr., Shirley Kwan Kisaichi, and Peter
Weber. Tempe, Ariz.: Facts on Demand. [See also http://www.
deadlineonline.com]

Sullivan, Danny. 1996. *Search engine watch.* http://www.searchenginewatch.
com.

Tate, Marsha, and Jan Alexander. 1996. Teaching critical evaluation skills for
World Wide Web resources. *Computers in Libraries* December: 49–55.
[See also http://www2.widener.edu/Wolfgram-Memorial-Library/
webeval.htm]

Boettcher, Judith, and Rita-Marie Conrad. 1999. *Faculty guide for moving teaching and learning to the Web.* Mission Viejo, Calif.: League for Innovation in the Community College.

Brooks, David W. 1997. *Web-teaching: A guide to designing interactive teaching for the World Wide Web.* New York: Plenum.

Cárdenas, Karen. 1998. Technology in today's classroom: It slices and it dices, but does it serve us well? *ACADEME* May–June: 27–29.

Ehrmann, Stephen. 1995. Asking the right questions: What does research tell us about technology and higher learning? *Change* March–April: 20–27.

Fraser, Alistair. 1999. Colleges should tap the pedagogical potential of the World-Wide Web. *Chronicle of Higher Education* (6 August).

Frayer, Dorothy A. 1999. Creating a campus culture to support a teaching and learning revolution. *Cause/Effect* 22:2. http://www.educause.edu/ir/library/html/cem9923.html (5 April 2000).

Hall, Brandon. 1997. *Web-based training cookbook.* New York: John Wiley & Sons.

Horton, William. 2000. *Designing Web-based training: How to teach anyone anywhere anything anytime.* New York: John Wiley & Sons.

Keating, Anne B. 1999. *The wired professor: A guide to incorporating the World Wide Web in college instruction.* New York: New York University Press. [See also http://www.nyupress.nyu.edu/professor.html]

Kozma, Robert, and Jerome Johnson. 1991. The technological revolution comes to the classroom. *Change* January–February: 10–23.

McCormack, Colin, and David Jones. 1998. *Building a Web-based education system.* New York: Wiley Computer.

Schweizer, Heidi. 1999. *Designing and teaching an on-line course: Spinning your Web classroom.* Needham Heights, Mass.: Allyn and Bacon.

Index

Page references in *italics* indicate illustrations.

background graphics (*continued*)
  video 89
BBEdit (text editor software) 5
BeyondPress (conversion utility) 7
bias, Web site 54
Biology Project site *20*
Blue Web'n site *27*
boldface type 149
bookmarks 139
  Web-based classroom presentations
    and 198
brevity criterion, fair use test and 96
broken links 54–55
  checking for 139, 197
  classroom presentations and 198
broker, copyright 99
browsers
  classroom presentations preferences
    198
  history feature of 155
  inconsistencies in 115
browsing versus searching 26–27
buffering, streaming media and 177
bulletin boards. *See* discussions, online
button bars 131–132, *132*

cameras
  35mm 78
  digital 78–79
capitalization 148
card sorting 29
Cascading Style Sheets (CSS) 112–113,
    149–151
  consistency 141
  layout control with 117
  leading and 144, *144*, 151
  for paragraph marking 145
case sensitivity, file names 137
Celebration of Women Writers site *26*
Celtic Art & Cultures site *19*
centered text 141–142, *142*

Center for Academic Transformation,
    Rensselaer Polytechnic Institute
    12
Central Processing Unit. *See* CPU
    (Central Processing Unit)
CGIs (Common Gateway Interfaces)
    63, 68
change, planning for 14
channels, Web audio 84
Chat Blazer (software) 61
chat rooms 65. *See also* discussions,
    online
  versus MOO 82
  privacy and 201
  promoting participation 189–190
  software 61
  teaching use of 189
chemistry course site 24–25
  simulation *71*
Christensen, Paul 170–171
Chronicle of Higher Education site *46*
chunking, content 45–46, *47*
Circles of Light site *20*
class attendance 25
Classic Panos site *92*
class preparation, online discussions and
    61
class resource sites 18, *19*
class Web site usage 189, 196–199
  technology for 196–197
  Web-based presentation and
    197–198
clips preparation 178–180
clips processing 180–182
CMYK printing 156, *156*
codecs (compression algorithms) *174,*
    174–175
  audio processing 181
  video preprocessing and 179
  video quality and 182
collaboration, online 190

Illustration credits

The Web site illustrations are listed in order of appearance and are printed with express permission.

CHAPTER 1: PLANNING

Greek and Roman Studies 22: Greek Classical Archaeology. Copyright 1998–2000 Trustees of Dartmouth College. www.dartmouth.edu/~grs22

SALMON: Study And Learning Materials ON-line. Copyright 2000 Paul Kenyon, University of Plymouth. salmon.psy.plym.ac.uk/year1/bbb.htm

Linguistics 80: Niger-Congo. Copyright 2000 Trustees of Dartmouth College. dewey.dartmouth.edu/courses/LING80

Economics 309: The Economics of a Sustainable Society. Copyright 2000 Steven C. Hackett (www.humboldt.edu/~sh2). www.humboldt.edu/~envecon/e309.htm

Art 111: Celtic Art & Cultures. Copyright 2000 Gary Geisler and Dorothy Verkerk. www.unc.edu/courses/art111/celtic

The Biology Project. Copyright 2000 Arizona Board of Regents. www.biology.arizona.edu

Circles of Light: The Mathematics of Rainbows. Copyright 1997 The Geometry Center (www.geom.umn.edu). www.geom.umn.edu/education/calc-init/rainbow

Chemistry 5: Introduction to Principles of Chemistry. Copyright 2000 President and Fellows of Harvard College. www.courses.fas.harvard.edu/~chem5

A Celebration of Women Writers. Copyright 2000 Mary Mark Ockerbloom. digital.library.upenn.edu/women

Blue Web'n Learning Sites Library. Copyright 2000 Pacific Bell (retrieved 23 April 2000). www.kn.pacbell.com/wired/bluewebn

Dartmouth College: Academic Computing. Copyright 2000 Trustees of Dartmouth College. www.dartmouth.edu/~ac

Nietzsche Chronicle. Copyright 1999–2000 Malcolm Brown. www.dartmouth.edu/~fnchron

Looking at Student Work. Copyright 1999, 2000 Annenberg Institute for School Reform. www.aisr.brown.edu/LSW

Math 115: Calculus 1. Copyright 1999, 2000 University of Michigan Department of Mathematics. www.math.lsa.umich.edu/courses/115

Mr. William Shakespeare and the Internet. Copyright 1995–2000 Terry A. Gray. daphne.palomar.edu/shakespeare

Library of Congress. www.loc.gov/harvest

The Hero's Journey. Copyright 1999 Maricopa County Community College District (www.maricopa.edu). www.mcli.dist.maricopa.edu/smc/journey

F. Scott Fitzgerald Centenary. Copyright 1996 University of South Carolina. www.sc.edu/fitzgerald

Sources: Their Use and Acknowledgement. Copyright 1998–2000 Trustees of Dartmouth College. www.dartmouth.edu/~sources

The Particle Adventure. Copyright 2000 Particle Data Group, LBNL. ParticleAdventure.org

CHAPTER 2: DEVELOPING CONTENT

The Chronicle of Higher Education: Information Technology. Copyright 2000 The Chronicle of Higher Education. www.chronicle.com

Only a Matter of Opinion? Copyright 2000 Carol Lange, Xian Ke, et al. library.thinkquest.org/50084

American Verse Project. Copyright 1996 Regents of the University of Michigan. www.hti.umich.edu/english/amverse

Chemistry 4B: Principles of Chemistry with Quantitative Analysis. Copyright 2000 Regents of the University of California (www.chemistry.ucsc.edu). www.chemistry.ucsc.edu/teaching/Winter00/Chem4B

History 53: Europe in the Twentieth Century. Copyright 1997–2000 Trustees of Dartmouth College. www.dartmouth.edu/~hist53

Education 204: Computer Technology & Instructional Media. Copyright 1999, 2000 Joseph Winslow. www.coastal.edu/education/courses/ed204/ educ204.htm

LinguaMOO. Copyright 2000 Jan Rune Holmevik and Cynthia Haynes. lingua.utdallas.edu

Sociology 7: Poverty in America. Copyright 1998–2000 Trustees of Dartmouth College. www.dartmouth.edu/~socy7

History 12: The American Civil War. Copyright 1998–2000 Trustees of Dartmouth College. www.dartmouth.edu/~hist12

Italian 10: Lezioni de Chirico. Copyright 1998–2000 Trustees of Dartmouth College. www.dartmouth.edu/~ital10

WebPath: The Internet Pathology Laboratory. Copyright 1994–2000 Edward C. Klatt. medstat.med.utah.edu/WebPath/webpath.html

General Chemistry *Online!* Copyright 2000 Fred Senese (antoine.fsu.umd.edu/ chem/senese). antoine.fsu.umd.edu/chem/senese/101

ChemLab: Applets. Copyright 1999 B. P. Reed. www.dartmouth.edu/~chemlab/ info/resources/applets.html

The Computer and the Campus: An Interview with John Kemeny. Copyright 1998–2000 Trustees of Dartmouth College. Video Copyright 2000 EDUCAUSE (www.educause.edu). www.dartmouth.edu/~kemeny

ChemLab: The Chemistry 3/5 & 6 Laboratories. Copyright 1997–2000 Trustees of Dartmouth College. www.dartmouth.edu/~chemlab

Classic Panos: Panoramas from Greece and Turkey. Copyright 1999–2000 Trustees of Dartmouth College. www.dartmouth.edu/~cpano

A Teacher's Guide to the Holocaust. Copyright 2000 Florida Center for Instructional Technology, College of Education, University of South Florida. fcit.coedu.usf.edu/holocaust/resource/gallery/kollwitz.htm

The J. Paul Getty Museum. Copyright 1999 The J. Paul Getty Museum, Los Angeles. www.getty.edu/museum

CHAPTER 3: CREATING THE SITE

Dartmouth Faculty Web User Group. Copyright 1999–2000 Trustees of Dartmouth College. www.dartmouth.edu/~wug

Women's Studies 37: Jocks, Gender and Justice: Title IX and American Education. Copyright 2000 Trustees of Dartmouth College. www.dartmouth.edu/~ws37

Sources: Their Use and Acknowledgement. Copyright 1998–2000 Trustees of Dartmouth College. www.dartmouth.edu/~sources

Spanish 1 & 2: Modulos Culturales. Copyright 2000 Trustees of Dartmouth College. www.dartmouth.edu/~spanmod

History 6: Health Care in American Society: History and Current Issues. Copyright 1999–2000 Trustees of Dartmouth College. www.dartmouth.edu/~hist6

Dartmouth College: Academic Computing. Copyright 2000 Trustees of Dartmouth College. www.dartmouth.edu/~ac

Beyond Bio 101: The Transformation of Undergraduate Biology Education. Copyright 1996 Howard Hughes Medical Institute. Photo by Taro Yamasaki. www.hhmi.org/BeyondBio101

Kairos: A Journal for Teachers of Writing in Webbed Environments. Copyright 2000 Kairos. english.ttu.edu/kairos

Physics 1: Introductory Physics. Copyright 2000 Eric Mazur. physics1.harvard.edu

Voice of the Shuttle. Copyright 2000 Alan Liu. vos.ucsb.edu.

The WebQuest Page. Copyright 2000 Bernard J. Dodge. edweb.sdsu.edu/webquest

German 3: Rainer Maria Rilke: 3 Gedichte. Copyright 1997–2000 Trustees of Dartmouth College. www.dartmouth.edu/~germ3/rilke

ww2010. Copyright 1997 Univerity of Illinois, Department of Atmospheric Sciences. ww2010.atmos.uiuc.edu

Interaktiver Text im Web: Bernhard Schlinks *Der Vorleser.* Copyright 2000 Alex Chapin and Caroline Schaumann, Middlebury College. cweb.middlebury.edu/s00/gn480a

Film 46: The Industrial Roots of the Information Superhighway. Copyright 1997–2000 Trustees of Dartmouth College. www.dartmouth.edu/~film46

A Teacher's Guide to the Holocaust. Copyright 2000 Florida Center for
Instructional Technology, College of Education, University of South Florida.
fcit.coedu.usf.edu/holocaust

Spanish 1 & 2: Modulos Culturales. Copyright 2000 Trustees of Dartmouth
College. www.dartmouth.edu/~spanmod

Religion 212: Magic and Astrology in the Greek and Roman World. Copyright
2000 Megan Williams. www.mtholyoke.edu/courses/meganw/rel212

Greek and Roman Studies 80: Platonic Love and Its Cultural Context. Copyright
2000 Trustees of Dartmouth College. www.dartmouth.edu/~grs80

Africa Focus. Copyright 2000 University of Wisconsin System Board of Regents.
Photos by Robert Newton. africafocus.library.wisc.edu

Greek and Roman Studies 19: Theories and Methods in Ancient History.
Copyright 2000 Trustees of Dartmouth College. dewey.dartmouth.edu/
courses/GRS19

The Computer and the Campus: An Interview with John Kemeny. Copyright
1998–2000 Trustees of Dartmouth College. Video Copyright 2000 EDUCAUSE
(www.educause.edu). www.dartmouth.edu/~kemeny

NOVA Shackleton Online Adventure and Photos. Copyright 1999 WGBH
Educational Foundation. Photo Credits and Online Text: Kelly Tyler.
www.pbs.org/wgbh/nova/shackleton

CHAPTER 4: USING THE SITE

Spanish 1202: Intermediate Spanish II. Copyright 2000 Columbia University.
www.columbia.edu/~dlf26

CHAPTER 5: SITE ASSESSMENT

The Virtual Statistics Teacher. Copyright 1998 Frank Klucken. www.techteach.
org/classes/stats

ChemLab: The Chemistry 3/5 & 6 Laboratories. Copyright 1997–2000 Trustees
of Dartmouth College. www.dartmouth.edu/~chemlab